Madonnas That Maim

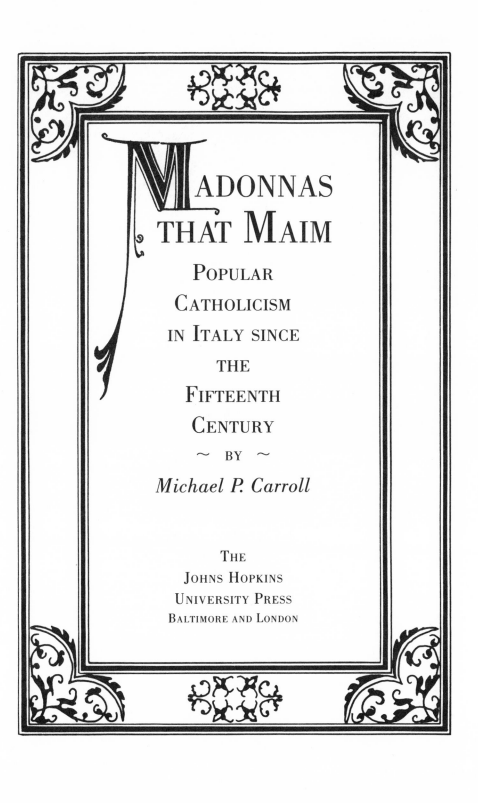

Madonnas that Maim

Popular Catholicism in Italy since the Fifteenth Century

~ BY ~

Michael P. Carroll

The
Johns Hopkins
University Press
Baltimore and London

The Johns Hopkins University Press
701 West 40th Street
Baltimore, Maryland 21211-2190
The Johns Hopkins Press Ltd., London

The paper used in this book meets the minimum requirements of American National Standard
for Information Sciences—Permanence of Paper for Printed Library Materials,
ANSI Z39.48-1984.

Library of Congress Cataloging-in-Publication Data

Carroll, Michael P., 1944–
Madonnas that maim : popular Catholicism in Italy since the
Fifteenth Century / Michael P. Carroll.
p. cm.
Includes bibliographical references and index.
ISBN 0-8018-4299-9 (alk. paper)
1. Catholicism—Italy—Religion. 2. Italy—Religious life and
customs. I. Title.
BX1543.C35 1992
282'.45'0903—dc20   91-36685

To GIORDANO BRUNO, who entered then left the Dominican order; who believed in an infinity of different peoples on an infinity of different planets circling an infinity of different suns; sometimes resident in England but forever proud of his roots in Nola, near Naples; burnt alive in Campo di Fiore at Rome in 1600, because he was, in the words of the Holy Office, "an obstinate heretic, who had capriciously formed various dogmas that were against our faith, and in particular against the Holy Virgin and the Saints."

CONTENTS

LIST OF TABLES

ACKNOWLEDGMENTS

This book owes its existence to more than just a scholarly interest in the study of popular Catholicism. That something more is associated with two hill towns in the Ligurian region of Italy and with two individuals whom I never met. The towns were Lorsica, in the Val Fontanabuona, and Castevoli, in the region called the Lunigiana. The individuals were Pasqualina Demartini, born in Lorsica in 1819, and Raffaele Ciarlanti, born in Castevoli in 1859.

Sometime in the latter half of the nineteenth century, these two individuals left their natal communities and found their way to San Francisco. As far as I can tell, each was the first in his or her family to emigrate to North America. This could not possibly have been an easy decision. Lorsica and Castevoli are isolated places even now. Simply walking down into the valley would have been an adventure. To walk down into the valley, then travel to the coast, then to Genoa, then take a boat to the United States, then move to California—all this required great courage.

Pasqualina worked as a domestic; she died in 1893. Raffaele did a bit better: he became a moderately successful small businessman who sold goods to the miners in northern California. Both are buried in the Italian cemetery in Colma, near San Francisco. Pasqualina's grave, one of the oldest in that cemetery, is marked by a nondescript stone that is already hard to read because it has sunk so far into the ground. Raffaele's is more elaborate. As was the custom among Italians in the early twentieth century, affixed to his tombstone is an enamel cartouche to which has been bonded his photograph.

Raffaele and Pasqualina never met, but their families became intertwined. Raffaele's son Pietro Ciarlanti was my maternal grandfather and Pasqualina's great-granddaughter Aurelia Demartini was my maternal grandmother. Because Raffaele and Pasqualina each made a decision in the nineteenth century to walk down from a mountain village in Italy and come to the United States, I came to be born and raised for the first part of my life in the Italian quarter of San Francisco. I came to know and love things Italian. At first, this meant only things like the language, my grandfather's Italian restaurant and the food it served, the ambience around Saints Peter and Paul, which is the Italian national church in San Francisco, and the saints and madonnas

Acknowledgments

from various regions of Italy that were (and still are) crowded into the back rooms of that church. Later, thanks to six months spent in Florence during my university years and to subsequent visits, I have come to know more about Italy and the nature of life there.

This book is the natural outcome of a professional interest in religion and a lifelong involvement with Italy and things Italian. But it all started with Raffaele Ciarlanti and Pasqualina Demartini, and so they must be acknowledged first of all.

I also want to thank my lovely wife, Susan, mainly for putting up with me in general. My children, Ian and Emily, must also be mentioned. They do not as yet have a clear sense of what I do, but they will enjoy seeing their names in print. Finally, there are my parents, William Carroll and Olga Ciarlanti, whose very real financial sacrifices and constant encouragement enabled me to enter academia.

Finally, I want to thank the Social Sciences and Humanities Research Council of Canada (SSHRC) for funds that were used to finance some of the research reported in this book.

Madonnas That Maim

INTRODUCTION

The years 1414–1418 mark the dawn of an important period in the history of popular Catholicism. These were the years during which the Council of Constance met to end the Great Schism, which had split the Western Church and had seen the emergence of three separate papacies, centered at Avignon, Rome, and Pisa. Unlike previous councils, in which the delegates had voted as individuals, the delegates at Constance were organized into national traditions. Initially there were four national groups: English, French, Italian, and German. A Spanish group was added later. Each national group met separately to decide upon its position, and each group had one collective vote in the deliberations of the council as a whole. The idea was to insure that no one national tradition predominate, and to a large extent the system worked. It was agreed, for example, that a new pope would be elected by an assembly composed of the twenty-three members of the College of Cardinals who were at Constance and by thirty delegates drawn equally from the five national traditions. The person elected pope at Constance was Cardinal Oddone Colonna, an Italian, and he took the name Martin V. One of this new pope's first acts was to make the necessary political alliances that would enable him to reestablish the papacy at Rome. This accomplished, he entered Rome in September 1420.

The emphasis upon national equality that had structured the experience at Constance evaporated very quickly, however, and Italians came to dominate the structure of the Catholic Church far more thoroughly than they had ever done before. By the middle of the fifteenth century, for example, Italians held virtually all the important curial posts, and by the end of that century the Italian language had replaced French and Latin as the working language of the Curia. The Italian hold on the College of Cardinals, always strong, became even stronger. In the first few papal conclaves after the Council of Constance, Italians constituted something like 50 percent of the voting cardinals. By the late 1500s, this figure had increased to 90 percent.[1] With both the Curia and the College of Cardinals firmly in Italian hands, it is hardly surprising that fifty-six of the fifty-nine popes who reigned between 1417 and 1978 were Italian.

But these men, these Italians who came to dominate the structure of the Catholic Church, had been raised in a particular cultural milieu and were used to a certain style of religion. It was only to be expected that the Italianate origins of the leaders of the Universal Church would influence the shape and texture of Catholicism generally. Indeed, in an earlier book I argue that this is just what happened and that several of the most important differences between Catholicism and Protestantism generally were reinforced and magnified by the Italianate influence on Catholicism (Carroll 1989: 154–75).

One difference between Catholicism and Protestantism, for example, concerns Mary. Quite apart from the greater devotional emphasis upon Mary in Catholic tradition, Catholics have tended to splinter the image of Mary into a range of personalities, each of which has become the object of an extensive cult. Thus Catholics venerate Mary as Our Lady of Mount Carmel, Our Lady of Lourdes, Our Lady of Fatima; they speak of The Immaculate Conception, The Immaculate Heart of Mary. Each of these Marys has her own iconography and her own set of prayers. But this Catholic tendency to splinter the image of Mary almost certainly was reinforced by the fact that the Italians, who came to control the Church, came from a society in which a tendency to splinter the image of Mary into separate madonnas was especially strong.

Or consider the matter of apparitions. Catholics over the centuries have routinely reported that they have seen and heard supernatural beings— Christ himself or the Virgin Mary. While such experiences are not unknown among Protestants, they are certainly much rarer and have generally not led to the establishment of sanctuaries like Lourdes, Fatima, and the Shrine of Our Lady of Guadalupe in Mexico City, which draw literally millions of Catholics each year. Here again the experience of the Italians who controlled the Church would have created a climate that favored this difference, since (as we shall see in chapter 3) Italian Catholics tend to experience apparitions more than Catholics in other areas.

But what I discovered when I began to explore the similarities and historical links between Catholicism generally and Italian Catholicism in particular was that the latter is not very well described in the English-language literature. Although I made use of what was available, the analysis in the closing chapter of Carroll (1989) would have been greatly improved if I had been able to consult works that gave a detailed overview of popular Catholicism in Italy. This current book springs from that experience, and one of my primary goals here is to provide an English language overview of popular Catholicism in Italy.

~

Many readers will likely be puzzled by my suggestion that Italian Catholicism is not well described in the English-language literature, since they will be able to think of several works that appear to do just that. Let me justify my negative judgment.

WHAT'S AVAILABLE AND WHAT'S NOT

Previously, anyone who wanted to learn about popular Catholicism in Italy by relying entirely upon English-language materials would have had to go to one of three sources. The first is the anthropological literature, which consists mainly of monographs that describe particular communities in Italy. Whatever the value of such monographs in general, their usefulness as regards popular Catholicism in Italy is limited, for several reasons. First, religion is usually treated only in passing. This is especially true for the more recent monographs, which are far more likely to be concerned with systems of land tenure than with processions, apparitions, and *festas*. Second, most of the communities studied by English-speaking anthropologists have been located in southern Italy and thus provide no basis for establishing which forms of Catholic devotion are common to Italy as a whole and which are specific to the South.[2] Third, these anthropological studies generally lack historical depth. Indeed, as I establish in chapter 5, this lack of concern with history has led anthropological investigators to overlook entirely a form of ecclesiastical organization, the *chiesa ricettizia*, that is central to an understanding of Italian Catholicism up until the nineteenth century.

A second source of information on Italian Catholicism comes from studies that describe the type of Catholicism that was (and often still is) practiced within the Italian immigrant communities of North America. There are hundreds of such studies (e.g., Tomasi and Stibili 1978), but they are useful only if we are willing to make the assumption that the Italian Catholicism that flourished within these immigrant communities was more or less the same as the Catholicism these immigrants practiced in their home villages. As regards some of the external forms, this is likely true. The festas in honor, say, of San Gennaro or the Madonna del Carmine held in New York earlier in this century probably looked very much like analogous festas held in Italy. But as regards function, there were almost certainly differences between Italian Catholicism in Italy and in North America.

In Italy, as we shall see, there was a specific relationship between the members of a village and the village's patron saint: the saint was charged with protecting the physical space of the village and was owed deference by all those living within that space. No such relationship could possibly exist in North America, where particular cities did not have particular patrons and where Italians were only one of several ethnic groups. Likewise, in Italy a Catholic could discharge a vow by making a pilgrimage to a nearby Marian shrine, often one that the Madonna herself had visited. This was just not possible in North America. In short, the link between Italian Catholicism in Italy and Italian Catholicism in the United States and Canada is not as straightforward as some might think. It would seem prudent to learn about Italian Catholicism in Italy by studying this form of Catholicism directly, without the distortions and changes that might have been introduced by the emigrant experience.

A final source of information on the practice of Catholicism in Italy is to be found in works by historians. Putting aside those works concerned with Church history rather than with popular religion, the literature here can be subdivided into two categories. The first includes those works that focus upon the religiosity of particular individuals. In recent years, for example, several books have been written on female mystics, and many of these mystics were Italian. Judith Brown's *Immodest Acts: The Life of a Lesbian Nun in Renaissance Italy* (1986), despite its lurid title, is far more an account of the religious experiences of one particular Italian mystic than about her sexual experiences. Other works in this vein include the well-known studies by Rudolph Bell (1985) and Caroline Bynum (1987). But most of the women studied in these works were living in convents, and the three authors cited agree that women who voluntarily entered convents did so to insulate themselves from the concerns and pressures of the larger society. That a convent was able to insulate its members from the outside should in itself make us cautious about seeing convent religiosity as a microcosm of religiosity in the larger society.

In any event, it is not difficult to establish that the religious experiences of these female mystics were atypical of their time. These women, for example, were quite often visionaries, but the being they saw in their visions was usually Christ. Visionaries living outside the convent walls were far more likely to see Mary. Similarly, female mystics were prone to undertake long fasts, which most modern commentators suggest was a way for the nuns to take control of their lives. Outside the convent, the concern of a religious ritual was far more likely to be about obtaining food through a good harvest. Finally, the religiosity of these female mystics was intensely individualistic. They were primarily concerned with establishing a one-to-one relationship with God or Jesus Christ. Outside the convent, the most important rituals were centered upon the relationship between a particular patron saint and a group of human beings. Although these studies might give valuable insight into female mysticism, they are not very useful in understanding the type of Catholicism practiced at large.

Far more useful are those works on popular religion by historians. Mary Rose O'Neil (1981) has sifted through the records of the Inquisition in three northern Italian cities and has uncovered many popular beliefs and practices.

Introduction

Richard Trexler (1980) has produced an excellent account of community ritual in Florence. There are now at least three good English-language works on confraternities in Italy. Brian Pullan (1971) and Ronald Weissman (1982), for instance, have written accounts of confraternity organizations in Venice and Florence, respectively, which are sufficiently definitive as to be regularly cited in the Italian-language literature. It seems likely that Christopher Black's (1989) study of Italian confraternities in the sixteenth century will likewise become widely cited. But these works, useful as they are, are relatively few in number and usually focus on only one aspect of popular Catholicism in only one area or in a relatively restricted time period.

THE MATTER OF TRANSLATIONS

In the end, anyone who wants to learn about popular Catholicism in Italy must rely upon works written by Italian authors. Unfortunately, the most important Italian-language works on popular Catholicism have never been translated. Ernesto De Martino (1908–65), for instance, wrote a series of books that are central to the study of all forms of popular religion in southern Italy. The value of De Martino's work lies less in his theoretical interpretations (which have generally fallen from favor) and more in his eye for the details of particular practices. These descriptions have come to provide a common frame of reference for those writing about popular religion in Italy. It is fairly routine in the Italian-language literature for an author to make a point by using an example taken from De Martino, simply because the author knows that it is an example that will be familiar to all his or her readers. Yet as far as I have been able to determine, none of De Martino's books on religion has been translated into English.

By contrast, those Italian-language works on religion which do get translated into English tend to be works concerned with the exotic and the atypical. A good example here is Carlo Ginzburg's *The Cheese and the Worms*, a translation of his *Il formaggio e i vermi* (1976). Ginzburg tells the story of a miller called Menocchio, who was examined several times by the Inquisition in Friuli and who was eventually executed for his beliefs. The records of the Inquisition allowed Ginzburg to reconstruct Menocchio's worldview, and there is no denying that that worldview is fascinating. Menocchio believed that life originated on earth by a rotting process, which gave rise to angelic beings—one of whom was God himself—in much the same way that (as people generally believed) rotting cheese generated worms.

Ginzburg argues that Menocchio's worldview was a deeply rooted popular tradition, which coexisted with the cultural views of the dominant classes in Friuli at the time. Yet Ginzburg presents no evidence that Menocchio's view was widely diffused among the common people of Friuli. In fact, what emerged during Menocchio's questioning suggests that he was very much outside local Catholic traditions. For instance, he seems to have been much concerned with denying Mary's virginity and with denouncing the excessive emphasis upon Marian devotion. He denied the authority of the clergy, from the pope down to the local parish priest, the existence of Purgatory, and the utility of masses for the dead. He also denounced the value of confession and the use of an incomprehensible language like Latin in Church ceremonies. Was this popular Catholicism? Of course not. Some of these elements (notably the deemphasis of Mary and the souls in Purgatory) were directly counter to popular Catholic tradition, while the rest dealt with abstract theoretical issues that would have been irrelevant to most of the Catholics living in Friuli.

I have dwelled on Ginzburg's work only because I have often seen it cited in the English-language literature as a source of information on popular religion in Friuli. It is no such thing. Menocchio was clearly what he was accused of being: a heretic. He may indeed have been, as Ginzburg seems to suggest, a highly intelligent and very creative individual who came to his beliefs mainly on his own, with only fleeting contacts with Lutheranism and other intellectual traditions. But whatever else he was, Menocchio clearly stood outside of and unconnected with the mainstream traditions of popular Catholicism in Friuli or in other regions of Italy.

~

I can do little about the general failure to translate the most important Italian-language works on popular Catholicism into English. What I can do, and what constitutes another of this book's major goals, is to provide summaries of some of these works. Perhaps these summaries will pique the interest of a sufficient number of readers to create a demand for their translations.

POPULAR RELIGION: WHAT IS IT?

So far, I have been talking about *popular religion* as if it were a term with a clear meaning. It is not. Moreover it is a term whose meaning has become increasingly less clear over the past two decades, and this is directly attributable to the rise of a new perspective in the study of popular religion in Europe. In retrospect, Natalie Zemon Davis's (1974) article on popular religion, still widely cited, epitomizes the themes that have become most associated with this new perspective.

Introduction

Davis argues that there were two suppositions implicit in most earlier attempts to study popular religion. First, they tend to take official religion as a given, and so studying popular religion meant studying the degree to which it conformed to or deviated from this official standard. Second, they tend to portray the peasants or common people mainly as passive recipients of what was handed down to them. If they were seen as being creative, it was a creativity attributed to the emotional and primitive nature of the peasant mind, which distorted the content of the official religion that had been passed to them. Davis and a number of other scholars reject both suppositions. Their studies suggest that popular religion arises mainly from creative processes originating from within the people themselves, rather than from the distortion of an official religion.

Unfortunately, this new perspective provides few guides for deciding what does and does not count as popular religion. The result is that definitions of popular religion have proliferated. Pierre Boglioni (1984) brings some order to the proliferation of definitions by suggesting that there are four approaches to the study of popular religion, two associated with the work of older theorists and two with the work of more modern theorists. One of the older approaches is the psychological perspective, which sees popular religion as reflecting psychological predispositions characteristic of the peasant mind. This mind is characterized by a diffuse emotionalism, by an emphasis upon the concrete, and by the absence of an articulated logical structure; these attributes are also a defining feature of popular religion. This tradition finds its roots ultimately in the romanticism of Rousseau and was especially popular in the nineteenth century.

The second approach of the older school is folkloric or anthropological, which sees popular religion as shaped by long-standing indigenous traditions. It is common in this approach to see popular religion as incorporating pagan or magical traditions established in a pre-Christian past. Although most readers will associate this approach with turn-of-the-century works like Sir James Frazer's *The Golden Bough* (1922), it is an approach that was regularly encountered in the Italian-language literature on popular religion right up until the late 1960s. Among recent works, Boglioni singles out those that see popular religion as resulting from a dialectical process in which official religion adapts to local circumstances. In Italy, this approach is associated with Gabriele De Rosa, whose work on popular religion is cited often in this book.

Finally, there is the sociological approach, which emphasizes the relation between popular religion and the lower socioeconomic classes. A typical example of this approach is Roberto Cipriani (1979), who suggests that the devotion of the lower classes to Sant' Antonio di Padua, and the correspond-

~ 7 ~

ing belief that this saint is especially effective in curing illness, indicate that the lower classes in Italy are effectively cut off from the medical care provided by official agencies (238).

Boglioni's four categories do not exhaust all possible approaches to popular religion. I would, for example, find it difficult to fit the studies of myth done by structural anthropologists into his scheme. Nevertheless, if we are limiting ourselves to studies of popular religion in Europe, then most authors, past or present, have probably used one of these four basic approaches.

My own position is that any attempt to focus upon a single definition of popular religion is fundamentally misdirected, for two reasons. First, such an attempt presupposes that popular religion is something produced by similar processes in all societies. This may be true, but it has not been established as yet, and so I see nothing to be gained by building it into the methodology here. Second, we must be careful not to reify definitions. Definitions are intellectual tools whose function is to sensitize us to particular aspects of the phenomena being investigated. They can thus be useful or not useful, but not true or false. All the definitions so far mentioned direct our attention to particular aspects of popular religion that are worth studying and so are probably all useful to some degree. The important issue is which definition—or which approach—is most useful in the particular context being investigated, which in this case is Italy. The definitions that follow, then, should be considered with these qualifications in mind.

POPULAR CATHOLICISM

As a start, I should make it clear that my concern is entirely with popular Catholicism in Italy, rather than with popular religion in general.[3] Furthermore, I think that De Rosa is quite right in suggesting that popular Catholicism in Italy derives from the interaction between official Catholicism and local circumstances. But whereas De Rosa sees official Catholicism as adapting to local conditions, I find it more useful to see official Catholicism as setting broad limits, which define what is allowable. *Popular Catholicism is the religion that develops within these allowable limits.*

In saying that official Catholicism sets limits, I mean something very specific. The core of popular religion in Italy (and most other areas of Catholic Europe) are beliefs about supernatural beings. In all cases, these beings are endowed with distinct personalities and are seen as having the power to intervene in the affairs of this world. For such beliefs to be considered "Catholic" (and remember that the only justification for my definitions is that I have found them to be useful), these beings have to be legitimized by a member of the Catholic clergy. If the supernatural being has been attested to by the hierarchy of the Church, it is legitimized. A saint not canonized by Rome but whose statue resides in a local church is also legitimized. Even the simple fact of a local priest taking part in the procession associated with the festa of a particular saint or madonna can legitimate that being as Catholic.

It is my contention that only those beliefs and rituals organized around supernatural beings legitimized by the Catholic clergy can be considered part of popular Catholicism. But whereas the presence of such a legitimized supernatural being might be a *necessary* condition for a belief or ritual to be part of popular Catholicism, it is not always *sufficient,* which is made clear by considering the issue of magic.

MAGIC AND RELIGION

To turn-of-the-century thinkers like Frazer, the distinction between magic and religion seemed clear. Magic, according to Frazer, is an essentially mechanical process and involves the belief that the use of particular objects, verbal formulas, or actions will invariably produce an associated effect. Religion, by contrast, involves an appeal to supernatural beings, whose acquiescence to the request being made is a matter of their volition, with the result that the appeal is not invariably successful. For Frazer, magic and religion were not simply different, they were mutually exclusive. He drove home this last point by seeing magic and religion as corresponding to different evolutionary stages, with the magical stage of human development preceding the religious stage.

There have always been problems with this neat distinction. Even Frazer (48–49) admits that there are cases of magic that seem to involve an appeal to spirits. Over the past century, any number of other scholars, most of them anthropologists like Frazer, have sought to refine, revise, or replace entirely the sharp Frazerian distinction between magic and religion.[4] I have no wish to take sides in this often acrimonious debate. What is important here is only that Frazer's distinction seems particularly ill-suited to the study of Catholicism (in any of its variants), since Catholicism has long contained elements that would seem magical according to the definition given above. Perhaps the most obvious such element concerns the doctrine of transubstantiation, which holds that when a Catholic priest says the words of consecration at a Catholic Mass, the bread and wine in front of him is changed in a real way into the Body and Blood of Christ. Although Catholic theologians have always balked at the term *magical,* it is difficult to see how it fails to meet the Frazerian definition given above. After all, although the power to transubstantiate might in theory derive from God, the effect is fairly mechanical as long as the priest is in good standing and observes the proper words and actions.

Part of the difficulty here likely arises because the Frazerian distinction is itself very much a product of a Protestant intellectual tradition. Keith Thomas (1973: 51–77), whose study of magic in medieval and Renaissance England is one of the most important studies of magic of the past few decades, makes the point that the sharp distinction between magic and religion, and the concomitant suggestion that they are two qualitatively different sorts of things, did not emerge until the Reformation and then was most of all associated with Protestant theology. It was the Protestant reformers, for instance, who most clearly suggested that the consecration at a Catholic Mass was a magical practice, and it was the Protestant reformers who were most concerned with purging Christianity of its magical elements. At one level, then, Frazer's suggestion that magic and religion are separate and mutually exclusive categories is seen as a Protestant thinker's attempt to give social scientific legitimacy to a distinction that had started life as a Protestant theological orientation (Tambiah 1990: 51–54).

Thomas's (1973) careful study of magic in England also demonstrates that, prior to the Reformation, the Church in England (and likely the Church in all areas of Europe) embraced and openly endorsed a range of practices that would be deemed magical by Frazer's definition (25–50). In the medieval Church, the important distinction was not between "magic" and "religion" but rather between "proper religious practice" (which might include what would later be called "magical elements") and "superstition," which were those magical practices (according to the Frazerian definition) that did not serve ends recognized as legitimate by Church authorities. In the specific case of Italy, I see little to be gained by viewing magic and religion as mutually exclusive, much less opposed to one another.

In Italy, the term *magical* seems reasonably applicable to any verbal formula or standardized ritual that is believed to affect the material well-being of human beings if performed properly. It is also very common in Italy to find physical objects associated with supernatural power. When it is believed that simple contact with or proximity to these objects will affect the material well-being of some individual, then it seems reasonable to characterize this belief and the associated actions as magical. The problem, at least as far as this book is concerned, is to decide when magical practices (defined in either of these ways) are a part of popular Catholicism and when they are not.

In some cases, this would seem to be a simple matter. For example, many magical practices in Italy contain no reference to any of the supernatural beings—the saints, the Madonna, Jesus Christ—who populate the Catholic pantheon, so this type of magical practice clearly lies outside the boundaries of popular Catholicism. Somewhat more problematic are those magical beliefs and rituals that make reference to legitimized—and thus quite Catholic—supernatural beings, but that are not legitimized by the clergy. As an example, consider the following two formulas, which were used in parts of southern Italy to cure someone affected by the evil eye:

> Santa Lucia came from Rome
> She carried a golden chalice in her hand
> Eye and counter-eye, *furtecille* against the eye
> She sent away the envy and so drove away the evil eye.

> Eye and the one who has been charmed
> Three eyes have set themselves upon you
> Three saints have helped you
> Three eyes three evil eyes
> Three evil wills.[5]

The first of these formulas makes reference to a popular Catholic saint (Santa Lucia), whose cult is endorsed by the Church, and the second makes references to three saints, who likely are saints recognized by the Church. Yet formulas such as these would typically be said in private and so would not form part of public ceremony in which a member of the clergy took part. For this reason, I do not consider magic like this to be part of popular Catholicism.

But there is a third category of magical practices—those practices associated with one of the supernatural beings in the Catholic pantheon and which form part of public ceremonies in which members of the clergy participate. Such practices include ceremonies whose purpose is to cause blood relics of saints to liquefy on a regular and predictable basis; processions in honor of a saint in which the amount of excrement deposited by a cow in the procession predicts the size of the next harvest; the bringing of dead infants to particular Marian sanctuaries so that these infants can be brought back to life just long enough to receive baptism; and so on.[6] However much these practices might have been condemned by the higher clergy in the centuries following the Council of Trent, they must in all reasonableness be considered a part of popular Catholicism in Italy.

Popular Catholicism: A Final Definition

In summary then, *popular Catholicism*, as I use that term in this book, refers to all those beliefs associated with supernatural beings that have been legitimated by the Church (at least at the local level), as long as the associated rituals are performed publicly and involve the participation of the clergy. It is important to emphasize that the term *clergy* in this context need only be the local clergy. In the history of popular Catholicism, it is commonplace to find cults or beliefs that are discouraged by the Church hierarchy being tolerated—if not actually encouraged—by the local clergy. Legitimation by the local clergy is sufficient, at least under the definition being offered here, to make a cult or belief Catholic in the eyes of the local population. Whether this definition helps us focus upon phenomena worth studying is an empirical question, and one that the reader will be in a position to answer at the end of this book.

HISTORICAL PERIOD

I have limited myself in this book to what is generally called the modern period. Roughly, this is the period that began in the fifteenth century. Indeed, it is conventional among Italian investigators studying religion to date the modern period from the close of the Council of Constance in 1418. In addition, a view that has increasingly come to win favor with historians concerned with Church history is that the Catholic Counter-Reformation of the sixteenth century was as much a continuation of concerns for reform that first developed in the fifteenth century as it was a response to the Protestant Reformation.[7] The *terminus ad quem* of my analysis will generally be World War II, though many of the beliefs and practices to be described are still in place.

Professional historians may blanch at my casual suggestion that I will limit myself to a five-hundred-year period that begins in the fifteenth century. After all, this was a period in which Italy underwent a number of very profound changes, many associated with religion. It was also a period in which the experiences of the countryside and the cities were in many ways quite different. It would seem unconscionably extravagant and superficial to suggest that I could capture the nature of those changes in a single book. In fact, that is not my goal. It is my contention that, in the midst of all the changes that have occurred in Italy since the fifteenth century, certain relatively constant patterns with respect to popular Catholicism have characterized both city and countryside. My goal is to convey to the reader a sense of what those constant patterns are.

THE ORGANIZATION OF THIS BOOK

Popular Catholicism is best seen as being concerned with supernatural beings, and the most important such beings in Italy are the ones associated with three terms: *Christ, Mary,* and *saint*. Chapter 1 is concerned with the three metacults that have formed around these three terms and with the relations that exist among these three metacults. The two most important of them, those centered on the saints and on Mary, respectively, are discussed in greater detail in chapters 2 and 3. Chapter 4 is concerned with some of the some darker elements associated with both saints and madonnas in Italy. Chapter 5 deals with the matter of regional differences between the north and south of Italy; my concern here is as much with historical change as with historical constancy. Chapters 6 and 7 discuss two emphases—magic and masochism, respectively—that have come to be associated with particular forms of popular Catholicism in southern Italy. Having laid out the most important of the patterns associated with Italian Catholicism, I offer in chapter 8 an explanation (really, several interrelated explanations) of these patterns. The book closes with an epilogue.

A NOTE ON TRANSLATION

For the sake of consistency and simplicity, I have generally left Italian place names untranslated. The only exceptions to this are in connection with those cities (like Firenze, Napoli, Roma, Milano, Genova, Venezia) that have English-language equivalents too entrenched for there to be any other option. In the case of the Italian word *festa*, most discussions use the word *festival*, but in my view there is a certain lightheartedness about *festival* that does not quite fit. As result I have quite arbitrarily anglicized *festa* and given it a plural (*festas*) that does not exist in Italian. The only warrant for this is that much the same thing happened to the Spanish *fiesta* quite some time ago, and *fiesta* now appears in most English-language dictionaries as a perfectly legitimate English word.

THE THREE METACULTS

In a national survey carried out in all regions of Italy in 1968, Italians were asked the following question: "When going to church, outside of Mass, to whom do you first direct your prayers?" The suggested answers were "to God or Jesus," "to the Madonna," and "to the saints" (Burgalassi 1970: 250).[1] What is most important about this question is not the data that it elicited (in fact, each category was chosen by about one-third of all respondents) but rather the way in which the question was constructed: it forced respondents to choose among three categories of supernatural being: Christ, Mary, and the saints. Building a forced choice into the survey gave implicit recognition to what everyone who studies popular Catholicism in Italy knows: it is a Catholicism resting upon three distinct metacults, centered respectively on the gods of the Tridentine Church (Christ, the Trinity), on Mary in her various guises, and on the saints. Establishing the relation among these three metacults is the necessary first step in coming to understand Italian Catholicism.

THE OFFICIAL RANK ORDERING

The official Church has long held a consistent position on what the relations among these three metacults is: Christ comes first, then Mary, then the saints. This theological rank ordering is clear and employs a specialized vocabulary: *latria* is the worship that is due to God and God alone (with the understanding that this includes Christ), *hyperdulia* refers to the veneration due to Mary, and *dulia* to the veneration due to the saints. Furthermore, Catholic theologians have always insisted that "the difference is one of kind and not merely of degree; dulia and latria being as far apart as are the creature and the Creator" (Pace 1913: 188). One manifestation of this difference lies in the doctrinal insistence that Mary and the saints have no power of their own but can only intercede with Christ (or God) on behalf of human beings.

Abstract theology aside, Christ lies at the center of those religious rituals most emphasized by the official Church. The central ritual of the Catholic Church is the Mass, and the Mass is the ritual commemoration of Christ's death and resurrection. Holy Communion, now a regular part of the Mass experience, is the ritual ingestion of a consecrated wafer of bread thought to be the literal Body of Christ.

There is no question but that this emphasis upon Christ, so prominent in official Catholicism, has also found expression in a great many popular devotions in Italy. Holy Week processions in honor of the Passion of Christ, for example, are among the most important religious events of the year in many Italian communities.[2] Italy is the birthplace of a number of Christocentric devotions that have spread to other parts of the Catholic world. The first Eucharistic confraternities to win the official approval of the Church, for example, were established in northern Italian cities like Parma, Perugia, Orvieto, Genoa, Bologna, Ravenna, and Milan during the late 1400s (Beringer 1925: 87). Similarly, the Forty Hours devotion, which would become the single most popular Eucharistic devotion of the Counter-Reformation period, originated in Milan about 1530.[3]

Nevertheless, despite the fact that some Christocentric devotions have always been widely popular in Italy, and despite the official emphasis upon Christ, almost every previous commentator who has studied popular Catholicism in Italy has concluded that the de facto rank ordering of the three metaculus in Italy is the reverse of what the official doctrine would suggest.

HIERARCHIES IN THE SOUTH

Emilio Sereni (1968: 195–96) assessed the relative importance of the three metaculus in southern Italy in this way:

> Among God, the Madonna and the saints, the peasant in Sicilia and many other parts of the Mezzogiorno has in his own way established a kind of hierarchy: Christ is more powerful than God the Father, Mary is more powerful than Christ; and Saint Joseph, the universal father, is more powerful than God the Father, Christ, and the Madonna together. But more powerful than God and all the saints is the one saint that—from as far back as the distant centuries of the Middle Ages—the inhabitants of a given place have selected as their

patron, often—as the old accounts tell us—by means of elections. The Patron Saint is a veritable *deus loci*, the god of the place, to whom the peasant turns in times of despair.

Sereni's book is primarily concerned with the ways in which the local economies of the Mezzogiorno became intertwined with national and international markets in the decades following the unification of Italy.[4] His discussion of religion takes up a scant two pages of text and is obviously based upon secondhand information. What makes his characterization of southern Italian religion important is only that it has so often been cited approvingly in Italian-language commentaries on popular religion in Italy (e.g., Di Nola 1976: 16; Stella 1976: 165). That in itself is some evidence that the characterization rings true. Even so, it would be useful to know if his characterization is supported by systematically collected data.

Where precisely did Sereni get his ideas about southern Italian religion? He cites no sources, but I think he borrowed them directly from Giuseppe Pitrè's (1899) *Feste patronali in Sicilia*. Compare for instance the Sereni passage given above with this passage from Pitrè:

> The Madonna—sometimes under the different titles sanctioned by the Church, sometimes under titles sanctioned by local tradition—surpasses all, even God himself. . . . The patron saint is without a doubt a type of local divinity, that [the peasant] prays to, entreats, as if he were God, and from whom everything is requested. . . . Of the saints, the most beloved is Saint Joseph. (xxix, xxxi)

The value of tracing Sereni's passage back to Pitrè is that Pitrè does give the data on which his conclusions are based: his statistical survey of the supernatural patrons associated with 150 communes in Sicilia. Pitrè, in other words, is talking very specifically about the saints chosen as community patrons (as we shall see, there are other sorts of patrons), and even then, he is talking specifically about Sicilia. Does his characterization hold true for most of the rest of the Mezzogiorno, as Sereni suggests?

Consider first what is probably the least important of Pitrè's conclusions: that the most popular single saint in the Mezzogiorno is San Giuseppe. If by "most beloved" he means the saint to whom individuals are most likely to devote their private prayers, then this is probably true, at least for the recent past. National surveys conducted in Italy in the post–World War II period suggest that the saints to whom people most often direct private prayers are, in order of popularity, Giuseppe, the Apostles, Francesco, Antonio abate, Antonio da Padua, Teresa, and Rita di Cascia (Burgalassi 1976: 411). But if he means by most beloved the saint most likely to be chosen as the community patron, then his conclusion is incorrect.

Pitrè's data does show that San Giuseppe was the single most popular community patron in Sicilia. But in his study of the supernatural patrons associated with 1,725 communities located in the continental Mezzogiorno,

TABLE 1.1

Supernatural beings chosen as community patrons, southern Italy

Place	Christ		Mary		Saint		
	No.	Percentage	No.	Percentage	No.	Percentage	Total (N)
150 communes in Sicily	17	11	45	30	88	59	150
1,725 communities in continental Mezzogiorno	18	1	290	17	1,417	82	1,725

Sources: Derived from Pitrè (1899); Galasso (1982).

Giuseppe Galasso (1982) found that the saints most likely to be chosen as community patrons were, in order of popularity, Nicola da Bari, Rocco, Michele, Giovanni Battista, and Antonio da Padua. San Giuseppe ran a distant nineteenth in the rank ordering. Even this masks regional variation. Galasso's data also indicate that in Basilicata the single most popular patron saint was not San Nicola da Bari but rather San Rocco; in Terra di Lavoro, it was San Michele; and in Terra di Oltranto, it was Sant'Antonio. The point to be made, in other words, is that there is no single saint—not even San Giuseppe—who is preeminent in all regions of southern Italy.

On the other hand, the suggestion that a saint is far more likely to be a community's supernatural patron than either Mary or Christ—and this is probably the most important of Pitrè's conclusions—does hold up beyond Sicilia. Table 1.1 shows the results of the Pitrè and Galasso studies. In both cases, saints are far more likely to be chosen as community patrons than either Mary or Christ. The data seem to suggest that the rank ordering among the three metacults is, after all, very much like that suggested by Sereni: the cult of the saints is more popular than the cult of Mary, which in turn is more popular than Christ or the Trinity.

It would be useful to complement the data in table 1.1 with analogous data on community patrons for northern Italian communities. Unfortunately, as far as I can tell, a statistical study of community patrons in northern Italy has not yet been published. But there are other sorts of data that can be used to assess the relative popularity of the three metacults in the North.

THE METACULTS IN NORTHERN ITALY

Gregory Martin (1542?–1582) is best known for his role in producing the Douai Bible, which was a translation of the Latin Vulgate into English. But

Martin also wrote one of the earliest English-language books on Italy, *Roma Sancta*, completed in the early 1580s but not published until 1969. The text of *Roma Sancta* was based partly upon Martin's experiences while living in Rome from late 1576 to July 1578 and partly upon earlier guidebooks written in Italian. Martin's book describes a range of things relating to the practice of Catholicism in Rome, including churches and their contents, religious processions, and charitable organizations.

Roma Sancta is valuable on another level as well. Although Martin was a Catholic thoroughly committed to the ideals of the Counter-Reformation, he was an Anglo-Saxon, and he recognized those aspects of Catholic practice in Italy that would seem unusual if not outrageous to non-Catholics, especially those unfamiliar with Latin cultures. Indeed, in some passages he explicitly acknowledges the culture shock the Anglo-Saxon would feel in Rome. Martin notes, for instance, that his "Gentle Reader and deere countrie man" might easily be troubled by the miracles associated with Rome's many relics (46). Speaking of flagellation, he admits that in "our cold countrie men will laugh at this perhaps, that any man should punish him selfe" (95). Martin legitimizes miraculous relics and flagellation by finding precedents for them in the Bible or in the writings of the Church Fathers.

One of the first practices Martin felt compelled to justify was the practice of naming churches after saints. This was a problem for Martin, as for many other Catholic intellectuals of the Counter-Reformation, since they were familiar with the Protestant charge that some saints in the Roman Catholic tradition had been elevated above Christ. Martin's defense of this practice begins by conceding that the naming of churches after saints does indeed bear a superficial resemblance to the pagan practice of erecting different temples to different gods. He then develops a typically Tridentine interpretation of what was really being done in the Catholic case:

> [Churches named after saints] are dedicated and consecrated principallie to God whose Saints they are, and in whom he is by these means glorified, by one more speciallie in this Churche, and by an other in that Churche . . . for they have neither Churche nor altar . . . dedicated principally to them . . . but only in this respect that they are his Apostles, his Martyrs, Confessours, Virgins, and so forth. (26)

In short, in honoring saints we are honoring God, from whom all sanctity derives, and such an argument undoubtedly provided an acceptable rationale for Tridentine reformers like Martin.

But the Protestant claim to which Martin was responding has a certain face validity: naming a local church after a supernatural being might seem a reflection of that being's perceived importance in the local community. There was, after all, no theological reason—before or during the Counter-

Reformation—why all Catholic churches could not have been dedicated to Christ (or the Trinity) directly, with saints being venerated at the side altars in these churches. This suggests that by looking at the names given to churches in a particular area we can assess the relative importance of the three metacults in that area.

Martin himself names 134 churches located in Rome. Table 1.2 provides a breakdown of the dedications associated with these 134 churches, by type of supernatural being. Rome, of course, is hardly a typical Italian city, and so it is useful to examine data on church dedications from other areas of the North. Table 1.2 also provides data on the dedications of parishes in Pavia (Lombardia) in 1460, parishes in the western part of the Diocese of Brescia (in Lombardia) in October 1540, parishes in Perugia (in Umbria) in 1782, and parishes in the Diocese of Siena (Toscana) in 1834. Each of the five data sets in table 1.2 suggests the same conclusion: the cult of the saints seems more important than either the Mary cult or the Christ/Trinity cult.

The dedication of entire churches aside, Pierantonio Gios (1976) suggests that the rough outlines of popular piety in earlier centuries can also be established by considering the altar dedications reported in pastoral visits.[5] In his study of the pastoral visits made by Pietro Barozzi, Bishop of Padua (in the Veneto) from 1487 to 1507, Gios notes that Barozzi is recorded as having dedicated 185 altars in various churches throughout his diocese. In each case, the name of the supernatural being or beings to whom the altar was dedicated was duly noted. Most of the altars dedicated were side altars, and Gios implies that side altar dedications are more indicative of popular piety than main altar dedications. The dedications made by Barozzi, by type of supernatural being, are given in table 1.3. For comparison, table 1.3 also includes the distribution of altar dedications associated with the side altars in the churches found in Chioggia (Venezia) in 1580. In both cases, the dominant pattern is the same as that which emerged from the study of church dedications: dedications to saints outnumber dedications to Mary, to Christ, or to the Trinity.[6]

Finally, the relative importance of the three metacults can be assessed by looking at confraternity titles. In centuries past, confraternities played a key role in organizing the activities associated with popular festas, and the most important festa for most confraternities was the one in honor of the patron after whom the confraternity was named. Indeed, the choice of a name was a very serious matter and could provoke serious conflict:

> The "title" of these confraternities certainly did not represent something arbitrary or conventional but rather was the historical justification for these associations. . . . Nothing was more significant than conflicts regarding namesakes: the use of the same images "confounds the indulgences and swindles the people." . . . The authorities forbade a company from assuming the title of

TABLE 1.2

Supernatural beings associated with parish dedications, northern Italy

Parish	Christ/Trinity		Mary		Saint		Mixed[a]		Other		Total (N)
	No.	Percentage	No.	Percentage	No.	Percentage	No.	Percentage	No.	Percentage	
Churches in Rome mentioned in Martin (1581)	10	8	27	20	93	69	0	0	4	3	134
Parishes in Pavia during the pastoral visit of 1460	2	4	11	20	41	76	0	0	0	0	54
Parishes in the diocese of Brescia during the pastoral visit of 1540	1	3	7	18	29	72	3	7	0	0	40
Parishes in Perugia in 1782	2	6	5	15	27	79	0	0	0	0	34
Parishes in the diocese of Siena in 1843	2	2	5	5	99	90	4	3	0	0	110

Sources: Derived from Martin (1969); Toscani (1969); Zannini (1974); Tittarelli (1979: 166); Repetti (1843: 388–93).

[a] Multiple dedications that cut across the three categories, e.g., a dedication to both Mary and a saint, to Christ and a saint, etc.

TABLE 1.3

Supernatural beings associated with altar dedications, northern Italy

| Altar | Christ/Trinity | | Mary | | Saint | | Mixed[a] | | Other | | Total (N) |
	No.	Percentage	No.	Percentage	No.	Percentage	No.	Percentage	No.	Percentage	
Altars in the diocese of Padua dedicated by Bishop Pietro Barozzi, 1487–1507	14	8	19	10	138	74	14	8	0	0	185
Side altars of nine churches in Chioggia, 1580	14	19	17	23	39	53	3	4	1	1	74

Sources: Derived from Gios (1976); De Antoni (1980: 884–86).
[a]Multiple dedications that cut across the three categories.

one already existing: nevertheless, the possibility remained, and the tendency to do just this [assume an already existing name] documents the success of a particular cult. (Grendi 1976: 125–26)

It must be stressed that these older confraternities were quite unlike the Catholic confraternities over the past century, which tend to be pious organizations, composed mainly of women and children with little or no property under their control, and firmly under the authority of local church officials. Older confraternities, by contrast, were composed mainly of males and were administered by lay officials. They usually had substantial economic resources of their own and far more control over the public processions and other religious events that they sponsored than their modern counterparts. The fact that members controlled their confraternities indicates that the choice of a title reflects popular preference.

On the other hand, this independence from church authorities had its limits. To be legitimized as a Catholic organization, every confraternity needed some visible sign of approval by the local church authorities. Sometimes this sign was conveyed by the confraternity having its seat in a local church, or at least in an oratory erected with the approval of local authorities. Sometimes approval was communicated by the willingness of local clerics to participate in processions organized by confraternities. All this gave a local bishop some control over the type of confraternity established. During the Counter-Reformation, in particular, bishops sought to use confraternities to promote the doctrines promulgated at Trent. This meant that bishops favored confraternities centered on Christ, like the Eucharistic confraternities. After these, bishops tended to favor confraternities that promoted universalistic Marian devotions—like the rosary—that could be used to bind together Catholics in all regions of Europe. For this reason, it is fairly routine to find that, in communities that could support only a single confraternity, that one confraternity was a Eucharistic confraternity; in communities that could support two confraternities, those two would be a Eucharistic confraternity and a Rosary confraternity.[7] More generally, we would expect that the smaller the number of confraternities in a community, the more likely their titles will show a Tridentine bias.

The methodological implication of all this is that confraternity titles can be used to assess popular attitudes toward the three metacults only in those areas that could support a fairly large number of confraternities. Fortunately, one of the best studies of confraternities in northern Italy (which is our area of concern at the moment) does deal with a community in which a fairly large number of confraternities flourished. Edoardo Grendi (1976) presents information on the confraternities active in the city of Genoa over the period 1480–1800. For our purposes, the most relevant data appear in the two lists at the end of his article. The first list gives the titles of all the confraternities (131) that existed in Genoa during the period 1480–1582; the second, the titles of those established (124) in Genoa during the period 1582–1800. Table 1.4 presents the distribution by type of dedication for each of these samples. In both samples, the rank ordering is the same and is consistent with what has emerged previously: the saints seem more popular than Mary, who seems more popular than Christ.

It might seem that I have somewhat laboriously established with a few bits and pieces of quantitative data what Sereni and all those who cite him have said all along: the popular rank ordering of the three metaculls is very much the reverse of the official rank ordering. But there is one more data set that is not at all fragmentary and that, in and of itself, prevents us from reaching this commonly held conclusion.

SANCTUARIES

There is no official definition of the term *sanctuary*, but it is generally agreed, both by Church officials and by scholarly commentators, that what distinguishes a sanctuary from other churches is that a sanctuary is the object of pilgrimage (e.g., Marcucci 1983: 8). Sanctuaries, in other words, draw people not just from the local area but also from areas beyond the particular place in which the sanctuary is situated.

Commentators also agree that pilgrimages occupy a central place in Italian Catholicism. Lello Mazzacane and Luigi Lombardi Satriani (1974) suggest that pilgrimages to sanctuaries, along with patronal festas and Holy Week processions, are the most important religious events in southern Italy. Giovanni Bronzini (1985: 422–23) has called attention to the unique nature of pilgrimages: they have a heroic quality, given that pilgrims have to overcome all sort of obstacles—the weather, the long distance to be traveled, their personal comfort—to reach their goal.

Some sanctuaries attract people from all of Italy; others from the region in which the sanctuary is located. Some attract Catholics from all social classes; others attract mainly those from the lower classes. Annabella Rossi (1969) in particular stresses the importance of pilgrimages to lower-class Catholics in Italy, and the opening paragraph of her *Le feste dei poveri* captures the spirit of what is involved:

Each year in the South of Italy hundreds of thousands of people leave their homes for one or two days and once again travel to the innumerable sanctuaries scattered throughout Lucania, Puglia, Calabria, and Campania. They are

TABLE 1.4
Confraternity dedications in Genoa, 1483–1800

Confraternity	Christ/Trinity		Mary		Saints		Mixed[a]		Other		Total (N)
	No.	Percentage	No.	Percentage	No.	Percentage	No.	Percentage	No.	Percentage	
Confraternities existing in 1480–1582	32	24	26	20	50	38	5	4	18	14	131
Confraternities established in 1583–1800	20	16	30	24	54	44	15	12	5	4	124

Source: Derived from Grendi (1976).
[a]Multiple dedications that cut across the three categories.

The Three Metacults

TABLE 1.5

Sanctuary dedications in Italy, by type and region

Region	Marian dedication		Non-Marian dedication		Total (N)
	No.	Percentage	No.	Percentage	
Northern Italy	1,106	88	145	12	1,251
Southern Italy	433	85	79	15	512
Total	1,539	87	224	13	1,763

Source: Derived from Marcucci (1983: 10).

pilgrims, people who have had little or no schooling, and who are from the lowest economic strata in Italy. The houses that they are temporarily leaving behind are shabby hovels, almost always lacking in proper sanitary facilities and barely containing furniture.

But what is it, or rather, *who* is it, that pulls so many people, both rich and poor, from their homes each year and that draws them to these distant sanctuaries? It is not usually a saint, and it is certainly not Christ. It is Mary.

Domenico Marcucci (1983: 10) lists 1,763 churches in Italy labeled *sanctuaries* in official Catholic publications. Of these, 1,539 (fully 87 percent) are dedicated to Mary under one of her various titles. Nor is this a phenomenon limited to southern Italy. As the data in table 1.5 make clear, sanctuaries are overwhelmingly Marian sanctuaries in both the North and South of Italy. This same Marian dominance is true also of the "supersanctuaries," those Italian sanctuaries that attract extraordinarily large numbers of pilgrims from all regions of Italy each year. The four most popular are at Pompei, Padua, Montevergine, and Loreto (De Lutiis 1973: 27). Of these, three (Pompei, Montevergine, and Loreto) are dedicated to Mary; only one is dedicated to a saint (Sant'Antonio da Padua). None are dedicated to Christ.

~

What then can we conclude about the relative popularity of the three metacults? Not too much. Certainly, all the data presented so far does suggest that the Christ cult is the least popular of the three, but there is no clear basis for deciding which of the remaining two metacults is the more popular. A comparison of table 1.5 with tables 1.1 through 1.4 shows that Mary dominates sanctuaries and that saints dominate patronal relationships, side-altar and parish dedications, and confraternity titles.

SEPARATION AND DISTANCE

The data presented so far suggest that the cult of the saints and the Mary cult are separate and incommensurable. If so, then attempts to decide which of these two metacults is more important are probably misguided. The concepts *saint* and *Mary* evoke quite different connotations in Italy. A saint is much more likely to be associated with the local community. A saint, for example, is likely the protector of that community. The local church will likely be dedicated to a saint. Most of the images that peer down from the altars in that church will be the images of saints. A saint, in other words, is someone close and accessible.

Madonnas, however, are distant. In part, distance is established by the fact already mentioned—that madonnas are more likely than saints to be associated with sanctuaries far away from population centers. This is not to deny that some madonna cults grow up in urban areas. On the contrary, it is quite common to hear about an outdoor image of Mary in some city that suddenly starts dispensing favors, becomes the object of popular devotion, and is then brought into a church. But these are not usually powerful madonnas; the most powerful madonnas in Italy are almost always those whose images are kept in distant rural sanctuaries.

Powerful madonnas are kept at a distance even when a strong devotional bond develops between a particular city and a particular sanctuary. The most well-known and well-documented example involves the Madonna dell'-Impruneta, whose sanctuary is located in a small village just south of Florence.[8] From the fourteenth century onward, Florentine devotion to the Madonna dell'Impruneta increased until she became one of the most popular madonnas in Florence. Florentines turned to this madonna in times of war, famine, drought, excessive rain, and plague. This devotion drew many Florentines to her sanctuary, to be sure, but often the image of the Madonna dell'Impruneta came to Florence. Between 1354 and 1540, the image of the Madonna dell'Impruneta was brought to Florence seventy-one times to be carried in procession (del Grosso 1983: 54). But the important point is that the Madonna was always brought back to her sanctuary, despite her large following in the city of Florence. As is true of all powerful madonnas in Italy, she was kept at a distance except on special occasions.

Keeping powerful madonnas at geographically distant sanctuaries is not the only way Italian Catholics distance themselves from these madonnas—they distance themselves from them by the way they address these beings.

TABLE 1.6

Terms of address used in Marian titles, by region of Italy

Term of address	Northern Italy		Southern Italy		All Italy	
	No.	Percentage	No.	Percentage	No.	Percentage
Madonna	240	51	76	34	316	45
Maria Santissima	21	4	64	28	85	12
Nostra Signora	46	10	8	4	54	8
Santa Maria	81	17	55	24	136	20
Vergine	60	13	13	6	73	11
Madre	6	1	3	1	9	1
Regina	7	2	0	0	7	1
Other	11	2	6	3	17	2
Total	472	100	225	100	697	100

Source: Derived from Medica (1965).

Madonnas are always identified by a title, which almost always has two parts. The first part is usually Madonna, Maria Santissima, Nostra Signora, Santa Maria, Maria Vergine, or Madre, while the second part associates the madonna with some location, object, or attribute. The relative frequency of the terms of address used in the first part of the title can be found in table 1.6, which shows the titles associated with 697 Marian sanctuaries in Italy.[9] Notice that Mary is not usually identified as Virgin or Mother; the titles that identify her in this way constitute only about 12 percent of the total.[10] The importance of this fact is that it is precisely Mary's position as the Virgin-Mother of Christ that makes her important in the official theology of the Catholic Church. The fact that these official connotations are so infrequently evoked in Marian titles suggests that they are not important in defining the popular image of Mary. Mary is most often called Madonna or Maria Santissima. *Madonna* is an archaic term of address, corresponding to the English *Milady* and used to connote respect. *Santissima* is a superlative form of *santa*. There is a regional pattern in the use of these titles, in that *Santissima* is more commonly used in southern Italy.[11] But the more basic pattern is that, in both northern and southern Italy, "respectful" terms of address (like Madonna, Maria Santissima, or Nostra Signora) are used far more often than either the more familiar Santa or the Church-derived Vergine or Madre.

Madonnas That Maim

The devout Catholic will likely see in the use of *Madonna* and *Santissima* a reflection of the great reverence in which Mary is held. But these terms can also be seen as reflecting social distance. Terms denoting social distance are never found associated with saints, who are always addressed simply as san, santo, or santa, which means *holy*. The use of terms denoting social distance in connection with madonnas is thus another indication, along with the association of madonnas with distant sanctuaries, of a tendency for Italian Catholics to establish greater psychological distance between themselves and their madonnas than between themselves and their saints. This pattern must be accounted for in explaining the distinctive features of Italian Catholicism; it is a pattern we will return to in chapter 8.

The fact that saints are local while madonnas are distant has social consequences. Precisely because madonnas transcend the local community, devotion to a madonna can pull different communities together; the local nature of a saint, by contrast, promotes religious factionalization. That this occurs has been noted by several previous investigators. After conceding that devotions to a madonna and a saint can flourish side by side, for example, Antonietta Lima (1984: 55) notes: "But what is important to point out is that the Madonna cult is common to many communities and for that very reason becomes a means of furthering cohesion. In the case of the saints, on the other hand, the intense veneration offered to them often divides the community, or even a given family, into factions." Giuseppe Pitrè (1899: xlviii–lvi) considers the competition between religious factions within the same community in some detail; in most of the cases, each faction is dedicated to a different saint.

The contrast being established here is one based on psychological associations, not ritual practice. A given community will generally celebrate a variety of festas, some dedicated to saints and some dedicated to Mary. But the madonna who is the object of the festa is likely to be associated with a distant sanctuary, whereas the saint is likely to be associated with the village itself. Moreover, although the churches and homes of a village may contain images of both saints and madonnas, the image that counts—that is, the one image endowed with miracle-working properties—is likely to be located in the village itself in the case of a saint, but at some distant sanctuary in the case of a madonna.

~

To treat Mary as just another saint, which often happens in English-language accounts, is fundamentally to distort Italian Catholicism. There are similarities between the cult of the saints and the cult of the Madonna in Italy, but we must start with the realization that the concepts *saint* and *madonna* evoke quite different associations in the mind of the Italian Catholic. For that reason alone, the two corresponding metacults must initially be considered separately.

THE CULT OF THE SAINTS

H ow does the cult of the saints in Italy differ, if in fact it does differ, from the cult of the saints in other European countries? There is no easy answer to this question, but the beginnings of an answer can be found in two statistical studies of Catholic sainthood. The one most likely to be familiar to readers of this book is Donald Weinstein and Rudolph Bell's *Saints and Society* (1982).

THE WEINSTEIN / BELL STUDY

Weinstein and Bell started with a sample of 864 saints who died between A.D. 1000 and 1700. They coded the life of each saint, as portrayed in the relevant hagiographical literature, on a range of variables. The resulting statistical data, as well as a detailed consideration of particular cases, were used to provide an overview of the cult of the saints in Europe. The end result is quite impressive, and the Bell and Weinstein work is required reading for anyone interested in the cult of the saints. Even so, in connection with the specific issue of concern here—the cult of the saints in Italy as compared to the rest of Europe—I think that Weinstein and Bell misread their own data.

In their chapter "Place," for instance, these authors conclude that there were two distinct types of saint (182). The Germanic category includes saints from the Holy Roman Empire. The typical Germanic saint, they suggest, is male, a high Church official, and likely to have been associated with miracle working during the course of his life. The so-called Mediterranean saint from Italy or Iberia, in contrast, is more likely to be of lower-class origin, to have been involved in emotional conflicts with family, and to have had problems with sexual temptation or chastity. Weinstein and Bell also conclude that, on most of these attributes, French saints tend to fall midway between the Mediterranean and Germanic types. It is important to keep in mind, as Weinstein and Bell themselves do, that the patterns being described here have less to do with objective features of the lives of the saints being considered than with the image of their lives that emerges from the hagiographical literature. Yet even with this caveat in mind, their Mediterranean/Germanic typology seems unsupported by the data they themselves present.

Consider the "struggle with chastity" attribute of the Mediterranean saint. Weinstein and Bell report (in their table 8) that 20 percent of Italian saints and 20 percent of Iberian saints were characterized by a "struggle to preserve chastity," while the corresponding figure for Holy Roman Empire saints (the most clearly Germanic of their categories) was 9 percent. Although these figures do justify the conclusion that Iberian/Italian saints were more likely to struggle with chastity than Germanic saints, one could just as easily argue that Germanic and Iberian/Italian saints were more similar than different in this regard, in that in both subsamples the overwhelming majority of saints did *not* "struggle with chastity." The problem here is even clearer in the case of Weinstein and Bell's "supernatural signs" attribute, supposedly characteristic of the Mediterranean type of saint.[1] We are told that supernatural signs were associated with 29 percent of the Iberian saints, 24 percent of the Italian saints, and 17 percent of the saints from the Holy Roman Empire. There is a difference, since 29 percent and 24 percent are greater than 17 percent—and the difference may even be statistically significant (though Weinstein and Bell do not report significance levels). But once again, one could just as easily stress the fact that the overwhelming majority of saints in all three subsamples were *not* associated with supernatural signs. Generally, Weinstein and Bell identify no attribute that characterizes a majority of Mediterranean saints but only a minority of Germanic saints (or vice versa). The idea that Latin Catholicism is different from northern European Catholicism has been around for a long time, and I am not suggesting that such a distinction does not exist. My point is simply that Weinstein and Bell's data do not justify the contrast they draw between Mediterranean and Germanic sanctity.

On the other hand, one national pattern does emerge from the Weinstein/Bell data, and it is fairly dramatic: in their sample, Italy accounts for more saints (38 percent of the total) than any other national group. Nor is this Italian predominance part of a general Latin predominance. If we rank the remaining national groupings in the Bell/Weinstein sample by relative frequency, we get, after Italy, the British Isles (17 percent), France (15 percent), the Holy Roman Empire (11 percent), Iberia (10 percent), the

Low Countries (4 percent), eastern Europe (3 percent), and Scandinavia (2 percent).

At first glance, the Italian predisposition to produce saints might be attributed to the disproportionate influence that Italians have historically exerted over the papacy and, thus, over the canonization process. Fortunately, this hypothesis can be evaluated by turning to a second statistical study of Catholic sainthood developed by Pierre Delooz (1969).

DELOOZ'S STUDY

Delooz starts with a somewhat larger sample: 2,610 saints (from both Europe and elsewhere) who were canonized or beatified between the years 993 and 1967. On the other hand, he coded his sample on a much smaller range of variables than Weinstein and Bell. The two samples are not independent, since Weinstein and Bell used Delooz's sample as their base. But the important point for our purposes is that Delooz provides information on "type" of canonization for each of the saints in his sample. Specifically, he divides his sample into four categories: (1) saints canonized by pontifical authority between 993 and 1634, (2) saints "canonized" by local tradition or local authority between 993 and 1634, (3) saints canonized by pontifical authority after 1634, using the new rules for canonization that had been introduced in that year, and (4) saints beatified by pontifical authority after 1634. Obviously, if we wish to gauge national predispositions to create saints while simultaneously controlling for the effects of Italian influence over the papacy, then the key category is category (2). With that in mind, table 2.1 presents the national origins of the saints in the Delooz sample, first for his whole sample, then for only those saints canonized as a result of local traditions or local authorities. Italy accounts for the largest proportion of saints in both the total sample and the subsample. More important, Italian predominance is more evident in the subsample, that is, among saints canonized by local traditions and local authorities.

This suggests that the Italian predominance among Catholic saints does not result from Italian influence over the papacy but, rather, from some aspect of the social milieu in Italy. In other words, there has long been something about life in Italy, in contrast to life in other cultures, including other Latin cultures, that predisposes Italians to create saints. Delooz reaches much the same conclusion:

> The conclusion is that Italians are more often regarded as saints than others. We are led to ask ourselves why? . . . In fact, we are in the presence of a phenomenon having to do with social perception. Italians are more often

The Cult of the Saints

TABLE 2.1
Canonized European saints, by country of birth, 993–1967 (%)

Country of birth	All European saints	Saints canonized by local tradition or authority
Italy	32	42
France	29	18
England, Ireland, Scotland	14	11
Spain, Portugal	11	9
Germany, Austria	6	8
Belgium	3	5
Poland	1	2
Other European countries	4	5
N	1,969	1,042

Source: Derived from Delooz (1969).

perceived as saints than [say] the French. But it is also necessary to ask ourselves by whom are they perceived as saints. [The answer is] by the Italians themselves. . . . Italians are "programed" more for perceiving sanctity than other populations. (179)

This greater propensity of Italian Catholics to create saints is one of the most distinctive features of the cult of the saints in Italy, and it must be explained by any account that purports to provide insight into Italian Catholicism. An explanation that does just that is offered in chapter 8. In the remainder of this chapter, I address two much simpler questions: What is the nature of a saint in Italy? And how do Italian Catholics go about creating a saint?

THE NATURE OF A SAINT

Popular saints in Italy are always, without exception, wonder-working saints. This does not necessarily mean that they worked miracles during their earthly lives nor does it refer to the two or three instances of miraculous intervention required by the Church before officially canonizing someone. Rather a saint is a supernatural being who has the power to heal and to protect and who is known to use that power on a fairly regular basis *now*—in the present.

This image differs considerably from the image of a saint offered by the official Church. True, the Church has long argued that saints can intercede with God on behalf of human beings. This belief in saintly intercession, in fact, has always provided a theological legitimation for the popular practice of asking a saint for favors. Asking for a favor from some saint looks much the same whether the supplicant thinks of the saint as a wonder-worker or as a simple intercessor, and local bishops can give their blessing to popular festas in honor of a saint without too much damage to their Tridentine consciences.

Nevertheless, saints as intercessors is *not* what the Church has emphasized in promulgating the cult of the saints. Rather, the Church has consistently presented the saints as exemplars of virtue. What exactly constitutes virtue, of course, is something the Church decides for itself, and being a political organization with a political agenda, it has often emphasized those virtues that serve that agenda.

Giuseppe Galasso (1982: 78), for example, points out that saints canonized in the post-Reformation period were increasingly individuals whose lives showed evidence of "control," in that they tended to practice bodily mortification to suppress earthly appetites, and to be resigned to their fate and obedient to the established hierarchy of the Church. It hardly seems coincidental, Galasso suggests, that this emphasis upon control in the daily life of saints occurred simultaneously with Counter-Reformation attempts to exert more control over the daily lives of individual Catholics by imposing on them a Tridentine orthodoxy.

Romeo De Maio (1973: 257–78) suggests that the Church's introduction of a "heroic virtue" criterion to determine sainthood is another example of how the cult of the saints has been used to achieve political ends. Up until 1602, De Maio notes, a saint was officially defined as someone who had lived a virtuous life. In that year, however, the College of Theology at Salamanca, Spain, petitioned Clement VIII for the canonization of Teresa d'Avila. As part of their petition, they introduced the idea of heroic virtue as a way of measuring the virtuousness of a saint's life. At one level, heroic virtue meant a relatively high level of virtue exhibited on a more or less continuous basis over the course of one's life.

As it came more and more to be used in the deliberations of the Sacred Rota at Rome, heroic virtue also came to mean the continual ability to overcome great *threats* to virtue. In particular, Roman investigators came increasingly to recognize that heroic virtue reached its zenith when a person was able to overcome attacks by the Devil himself. Indeed, struggles with the Devil, successfully overcome, became a standard feature of the hagiographies associated with the saints who were canonized by the Church in the 1600s. The parallel seems clear: during the period when the Church saw itself as being under sustained attack from Protestant heretics, it came to emphasize a type of saint whose heroic virtue enabled him or her to overcome sustained attacks from Satan. The analogy not only affirmed in the mind of the faithful the commonly made association between Protestants and Satan but also suggested that, with heroic virtue, the Church could overcome the former, just as saints had overcome the latter.

The distinction between the *santo edificante* (the exemplary saint) favored by Church authorities and the *santo miracolante* (the saint with miraculous powers) favored by the public, though well established in Italian-language commentaries on the cult of the saints in Italy, is often overlooked or at least applied incorrectly by foreign scholars.[2] Even investigators like Weinstein and Bell, sensitive as they are to the distinction between the official and the popular, miss the importance of this distinction. Consider, for example, their discussion of San Giuseppe di Cupertino.

TYPICALLY TRIDENTINE DESPITE THE LEVITATION

Weinstein and Bell (1982: 141–51) distinguish two distinct sets of criteria for defining saintliness. The first are the criteria used by the Church: doctrinal purity, heroic virtue, and some evidence of miraculous intercession after death. They then suggest that there is a second set of criteria, which was always more important when it came to establishing the saint's cult among the public. Foremost among these popular criteria, they argue, was some evidence of supernatural power. By supernatural power, they mean some event *from the saint's life*—or, at least, from that life as portrayed in popular hagiographies—that associated the saint with miracles. They give examples of how this supernatural power might manifest itself: the saint might cure the sick, send rain to end droughts, experience the stigmata, make dried flowers bloom, or foretell the future. In the case of the Italian saint Giuseppe di Cupertino (1603–63), his ability to levitate was the most important of the manifestations of supernatural power that gave rise to his being perceived as a saint by the general public. A reproduction of an early engraving showing this saint doing just that—levitating—accompanies their discussion.

There are several problems with all this. First, Weinstein and Bell present no evidence that the saints who fulfilled their popular criteria for sanctity really did become the object of cults widely popular with the laity. In the case of Giuseppe di Cupertino, nothing in the existing literature on Catholic devotions in Italy suggests that this saint was particularly popular. For example, he does not appear to have been chosen as a community patron to any significant degree, his feast day (18 September) does not appear to have become the occasion of any important festas or processions, few churches are dedicated to him, and so on.

It is also worth noting that the hagiographical traditions surrounding Giuseppe di Cupertino have a decidedly Tridentine feel about them.[3] Thus, we are told that Giuseppe was much admired by over a dozen cardinals; that his advice was sought by princes from all over Europe; that at his death his bier was guarded by twenty-four persons, including eight noblemen; and that his funeral was attended by religious from all over the city. Such associations with the upper clergy and the nobility make it difficult not to form the impression that Giuseppe di Cupertino was likely one of those exemplary saints, whose cult was promulgated in order to serve Tridentine goals. But what Tridentine goals? What was there in the life of this levitating saint that would have served the interests of the Tridentine reformers?

The key lies in Piero Stella's (1967: 171) observation that it was the experience of attending Mass and having a "sense of Christ's presence" in the Eucharist that most often provoked Giuseppe's mystical flights. San Giuseppe's levitations, in other words, were most often provoked by those two particular Christocentric events (the Mass and being in the presence of the Eucharist) most favored by the Tridentine Church. But a Christocentric emphasis was also present in those minority of levitations that occurred outside the context of the Mass. Thus on one occasion Giuseppe levitated in order to help plant a large cross onto a hill, on another he flew to the altar of a village church in order to verify the presence of the Blessed Sacrament. This pairing of Tridentine Christocentrism with something as miraculous as levitation is hardly coincidental. On the contrary, this is precisely the sort of psychological association that would be favored by an official Church anxious to promote Christocentrism in a culture whose members would be impressed by extravagant manifestations of the miraculous, like levitation.

Saints such as this are not the saints around whom popular cults in Italy form. The popular saints are the ones who possess miraculous power, that is, the power to intervene and modify natural processes. It is not important that they exhibited this power during their lives; what is important is that they can utilize this power in the here and now.

Two Important but Distinct Powers

Popular saints are in fact thought to have two sorts of supernatural power: (1) the power to heal (or, more generally, to improve some aspect of the present situation); and (2) the power to protect from future dangers. Although these two types of power are related, the relation—as we shall see—is not at all what most outsiders would probably expect.

The Cult of the Saints

With regard to the power to heal, there are a few saints who are useful for a variety of ailments and problems. Sant'Antonio di Padua, for instance, is probably an all-purpose saint, as is San Giuseppe in Sicilia. But the more common pattern of saints is characterized by a division of labor, with each saint being adept at granting particular favors. In Milocca, the Sicilian village studied by Charlotte Chapman (1971), Santa Lucia cured eye troubles, Santa Agata cured inflammations of the breast, San Calogero cured hernias, and Sant'Onofrio cured burns. Similarly, in his study of Pellestrina, a community near Venice, Angelo Gambasin (1980: 1053–54) points out that Santa Lucia (again) cured eye troubles, Santa Apollonia cured toothaches, Santa Monica brought back those who had strayed from the Catholic faith, and so on. In his study of the diocese of Treviso (Veneto) during the early fifteenth century, Luigi Pesce (1987: 78–79) reports that San Sebastiano or San Rocco cured the plague, Sant'Antonio abate cured fever, Santa Apollonia cured toothaches, San Pietro helped in the correct profession of faith, and so on.

But although some division of labor among the saints is found in virtually all Italian communities, the allocation of particular powers to particular saints is by no means standardized, even within a single region. This means that in different areas the same saint can be associated with quite different abilities, while the same ability can be associated with quite different saints. Thus Charlotte Gower's (1928) study of supernatural patrons in Sicilia, based mainly upon interviews with Italian emigrants to the United States, reports that the people of Chiaramonte invoke San Giovanni to cure convulsions in children, while those in Canicatti invoked him to learn the fate of dead relatives. Similarly, the people in Palermo ask San Nicola da Bari to help find husbands for their daughters, while in Isnello they ask him to cure epidemic diseases. To cure worms in Mazzara, people invoke San Cosimo and San Damiano, while in Milazzo, they invoke Sant'Elia for the same ailment; to cure convulsions in children in Chiaramonte, people invoke San Giovanni, while in Modica, they invoke Santa Margherita, and so on.

That Italian Catholics attribute to their saints the power to heal will come as no surprise to most North American readers. After all, Hollywood has given us a great many movies that patronize Latin Catholics by portraying them as having a naive recourse to the Madonna or to some saint in the midst of their troubles. What might come as a surprise to some readers is that Italian Catholics regard the power to correct a current misfortune of far less importance than the other power attributed to the saints—the power to protect from dangers yet to happen. This power to protect is usually what is being conveyed when a saint is called a patron. This supernatural patron lies at the core of Italian Catholicism.

Madonnas That Maim

SUPERNATURAL PATRONS

Italian Catholics have historically seen themselves as surrounded by malevolent forces, and they turn to their supernatural patrons for protection against these forces. Daniele Montanari (1987) expresses the essence of the patronal relationship thus: "in the worldview of the peasant ["la mentalità contadina"] the 'saint' must intervene continuously to hold in check and ward off the hostile forces of nature, to encourage good harvests, to keep epidemics at a distance" (202). It is primarily in their patronal roles—that is, in their roles as protectors from future dangers, not in their roles as beings able to solve a current problem, that saints are honored in Italy.

A patronal relationship can be established with quite literally any conceivable grouping of human beings. Most occupations, for instance, have particular patrons. In her study of supernatural patrons in Sicilia, Gower reports that, in Palermo, San Cosimo and San Damiano were the patrons of both barbers and bricklayers, San Crispino was patron of shoemakers, San Paolino was patron of gardeners, and San Pietro was patron of fishermen. Nor are patronal relationships limited only to morally respectable occupations. Gower also found that in the commune of Modica, Santa Caterina was the patron of prostitutes, while in Palermo, San Gerlando was the patron of thieves. Occupational categories aside, patronal relationships can also be established with groups that are distinguished only by common behaviors, and these need not be behaviors that carry the approval of the Church. Thus in Palermo, San Pantaleone was the patron of those who played the lottery, while in the commune of Casteltermini, San Paolo (Saint Paul) was the patron of those who practiced cunnilingus.

But easily the most important patronal relationship for any Italian Catholic is the one established between a saint and the community (a city, village, hamlet, etc.) in which he or she lives.[4] This is the patron that holds at bay the hostile forces that surround the individual, and it is this patron who is entrusted the task of establishing "an area secure against every possibility of harm, ranging from works of the devil to sorcery, from floods to wars, from fire to diseases" (Vecchi, 1968: 83). It must be emphasized that in this case the patronal relationship is not with the individual nor with the community as an abstract idea but with the community defined as a particular physical space, that is, as a geographical unit. Individuals have a claim on the protection of the patron only as long as they belong to a certain geographic community. This does not mean that the person must actually live in the community; it is sufficient that the person was born in the community and return to it on a regular basis. On the other hand, people who voluntarily move from one community to another and who do not make an effort to return to their natal communities quite often do change patron saints, placing themselves under the protection of the patron associated with their new home.

Furthermore, there is nothing in the logic of a patronal relationship that requires that any community have only a single patron. On the contrary, the more threatened the members of a community feel, the more they will seek additional patrons. This process is illustrated in a resolution passed by the municipal council of Montefalco (in Umbria) in 1649, a time of sickness and famine:

> The present calamities in which our country [*la nostra patria*] finds itself . . . lead us to ask for the intercession of the saints in paradise. Among these it appears that the glorious Sant'Antonio da Padua would be the intercessor most likely to obtain for us the favors demanded of His Divine Majesty. And although our country [still] clings to the glorious San Fortunato, San Severo, and the Beata Chiara as advocates and intercessors, we are adding the glorious Sant'Antonio da Padua to these our protectors so that we can more fervently ask the Lord God for help in the midst of our adversity. (Nessi, 1988: 225)

In fact, the accumulation of multiple patrons was quite common, especially in the larger urban areas. At the beginning of the modern era, for example, Florence had four important patrons: San Giovanni Battista, San Reparata, San Zanobi, and San Miniato (Cardini 1983: 80). Siena had four traditional patrons (Sant'Ansano Battista, San Crescenzio, San Vittore, and San Savino) and added two more (San Bernardino and Santa Caterina) sometime in the late seventeenth or early eighteenth centuries (Quinza 1722: 233). At the beginning of the nineteenth century, Padua had four patron saints: Sant'-Antonio, San Prosdocimo, San Daniele, and Santa Giustina (Bigoni 1816: 53). But the record for the largest number of copatrons must surely go to Naples. A guide to Italy published in 1692 reports that Naples had twenty-one primary patrons and that each of these had a statue and a reliquary in the Tesoro di San Gennaro (Sarnelli 1692: 72).[5] In 1741, a report prepared by Church authorities indicates that Naples had thirty-two copatrons, each of whom was represented in the Tesoro.[6]

Over time, the newer patrons often replace the older ones. In the plague year of 1633, for example, Florentines turned for deliverance and protection to four patron saints and held a special procession in honor of each. Three of these (San Zanobi, San Reparata, and San Giovanni Battista) were the same patrons who had protected Florence centuries earlier, but the fourth was San Sebastiano rather than San Miniato (Rondinelli 1634: 201–2). The net result of such additions and substitutions is that over the centuries the number of patrons associated with a single community, even a relatively small community, could be quite large.[7] An unpublished study by Luigi Randazzini indicates that the city of Caltagirone (located in Sicilia; it has a

Madonnas That Maim

modern population of 37,000) had thirty-four patrons and copatrons between 1090 and 1783 (Lima 1984: 330). Generally, as Alberto Vecchi (1968: 85) notes, the accumulation of multiple patrons is widespread and probably inevitable, since increasing the number of patrons can only increase a community's "sense of protection and security."

SAINTS IN THE STREETS

The fact that the patron saint of a community is so closely connected with the geographical space that defines the community explains what all commentators recognize as a feature of Italian Catholicism: the tendency for religion to spill out of the church and into the streets. If the patron is to prevent hostile forces from invading the space that defines a community, then he or she must be associated with that space. In the smaller villages, this often means literally carrying the patron's image (usually a statue or painting) past every home in the community. Often, an image will be paraded through a particular village and then through its neighboring hamlets.[8] The purpose of parading the patron's image through the streets is not simply to allow each person in the community to see the image. This could more easily be achieved by having every member of the community visit the image in the church. The patron's image is brought to each home to safeguard that place from danger in the coming year.

In the larger cities, the procession does not usually traverse the entire city. Instead, it passes along one or more of the major thoroughfares and by some of the more important buildings: these thoroughfares and buildings "stand for" the entire city. The entire community associated with a given patron is considered a single geographical unit, and during the procession this unit, in its entirety, is brought into contact with the patron's sacred image.[9] The importance of the procession is seen in the fact that in many communities families and groups bid at a public auction for the right to carry the patron's image through the town. The money raised in this auction, often a considerable amount, is used to defray the cost of maintaining the patron's cult.

One consequence of carrying religion into the streets is that church buildings in Italy are regarded in a different way from those in, say, English-speaking countries. To the Anglo-Saxon mind, churches are sacred places and, therefore, associated with reverence and respect. Indeed, Edmund Leach (1976: 81–82), the British social anthropologist, suggests that, as the result of "structuralist" processes inherent in the human mind, churches (lying as they do at the border between the natural and the supernatural) come to be associated with behavioral restrictions. Yet this is not what happens in Italy. As Richard Trexler (1987: 11–15) points out, churches in

Florence were essentially public places and not separate from other public places of the city. A church was simply a place to keep the sacred images and relics until such time as they would be carried in procession through the city. The procession was central, not the church, because the procession established the relationship between the patron and the space to be protected.

THE SPECTACULAR FESTA

In many cases, especially in the larger cities of southern Italy, the festa in honor of the patron saint evolved into a truly spectacular event. By the late eighteenth and early nineteenth centuries, several patronal processions regularly attracted outsiders. Some of these outsiders were from other regions of Italy, but a great many were from England, France, and Germany. Since these foreign visitors often wrote accounts of what they saw, these festas were once well known outside Italy. The festa in honor of Santa Rosalia at Palermo, in particular, was especially well known.[10]

According to legend, Rosalia was born in Palermo in the twelfth century. A woman of aristocratic birth and great beauty, she opted to live a life of penance in a grotto on nearby Mount Pellegrino. She died in 1160. When Palermo was struck by a plague in 1625, the people of Palermo naturally turned for aid to their "own" Rosalia. Her mortal remains were discovered on Mount Pellegrino and brought in procession into the city. The plague ended, and Palermo committed itself to celebrate an annual festa in July in honor of its patroness.

Initially, the procession associated with this festa involved a series of small floats, which were pulled along the two major thoroughfares of the city over a two-day period. In 1743, the festa was extended to five days. Around the same time, the many smaller floats were combined into one immense float that traveled only a little way along one of the main thoroughfares. The exact design of this immense float varied from year to year, but it was regularly two to three stories high and of such weight that it took fifty oxen to pull it. On the final day of the festa, there was another procession: several smaller but still elaborate floats, as well as someone carrying the silver urn containing the relics of the saint, went through the streets and alleyways of some of the older neighborhoods of the city.[11]

Another spectacular procession often described by foreigners took place on the festa of Maria Assunta at Messina, when the Vara was pulled through the streets of the city (e.g., Smythe 1824: 121–22). Basically, the Vara stood about three stories high and had three separate platforms, each of which rotated as the machine was pulled along. At the top stood a youth impersonating Christ and holding in the palm of his hand (with the aid of an iron platform) a young girl impersonating the Madonna. Children impersonating angels and apostles were positioned at the other levels. In addition to the lateral motion provided by the rotating platforms, these children were also attached to devices that could move them up and down, as well.

Other patronal festas involving spectacular processions occurred at Viterbo (near Rome) and at Nola (near Naples). In Viterbo, 62 men carried a large towerlike structure through the streets in honor of Santa Rosa (Bronzini 1974: 76–79). The procession at Nola, in honor of San Paolino, was even more impressive. It involved eight separate towers, each approximately three stories high and set upon a platform carried by 120 men. The Nola festa is one of the few spectacular festas still celebrated in Italy, though it has generally been ignored by English-speaking investigators.[12]

"A CHURCH IS NEVER ENOUGH"

But processions through the town—whether simple or elaborate—are not the only way in which the link between the patron and the space that he or she protects is established. This link is also established by virtue of the fact that every festa in honor of a patron saint always involves a range of activities dispersed over a fairly wide area within the community and a high degree of community participation. Such activities include fairs, contests, and markets:

> A church is never enough. Putting aside the usual ceremonies associated with all solemn religious events, like vespers, the High Mass . . . the vast majority of Sicilian festas always take place . . . in the open, in the middle of the streets where the Sicilian people live. [They are characterized by] markets, horse races, songs, processions, pilgrimages, music, fireworks, a sea of lights, many and various spectacular displays, and the inevitable drums, with their ear-splitting sounds that grate on the patience of even the most calm person. (G. Pitrè 1899: xxxii)

Saverio La Sorsa (1962) describes the patronal festas celebrated in Puglia in much the same terms:

> A special committee organizes a long list of activities for the occasion. Some of these activities are religious, but many have little to do with religion. Sunday morning the people may go to the cathedral, where they attend the High Mass, listen to the sermon . . . and raise up their prayers to the patron. But the focus of the festa is outside the church. The church may be more or less crowded in the morning, but in the afternoon, in the evening, and during the night, it will be the piazzas and the streets that will be jampacked with men and women, both young and the old, who all want to enjoy the various activities organized by the committee. Thousands crowd around the orchestra to listen to the music.

. . . They watch the fireworks . . . with its dazzling displays of color and fearful explosions. [There are also] bicycle races, soccer games, [and] foot races. (136–37)

Here too then, as in Sicilia, the activities associated with the festa of the patron overflow the bounds of the church and move into the space that defines the community. Similar accounts appear in connection with communities in all regions of Italy.

ESTABLISHING PATRONAL RELATIONSHIPS

How do saints become patrons? Italian Catholics usually justify a particular patronal relationship with a legend. Quite often these are widely diffused in the Catholic world and contain some element that legitimizes a particular power. Thus, San Biago cures sore throats because he cured a boy choking on a fishbone; Santa Agata cures diseases of the breast because her own breasts were cut off while she was being martyred; San Sebastiano cures wounds because his body was riddled with arrows; and so on.

But in many cases it is clear that the legends legitimating a particular power were developed after the patronal relationship had already become established. In Friuli, for instance, San Valentino is adept at curing epilepsy (Cantarutti 1966). This belief does not derive from official hagiographies for the simple reason that this particular San Valentino has never been officially recognized as a saint by the Roman authorities, even though his images appear in local churches. There are several local legends explaining why San Valentino cures epilepsy, but they are by no means consistent. Some Friulani say that San Valentino himself suffered from the disease, while others say that he once cured a youth of that disease. The presence of different legitimating myths is a sure sign that these myths were a response to, not a cause of, the association of San Valentino with epilepsy.

Another case in which the patronal relationship predates the legitimating myth concerns Santa Lucia, a saint who in many Italian communities is believed to heal diseases of the eye. The earliest hagiographical traditions about Santa Lucia describe her only as a martyr who died about 304, after she had been denounced to the authorities as a Christian by a rejected suitor. There is nothing in these early traditions that associate her in any way with eyes. Only much later did legends appear in Italy suggesting that Lucia plucked out her eyes when a suitor expressed admiration for them and that later her sight was restored by divine intervention. This myth legitimates Santa Lucia's power to cure eye disease. It hardly seems a coincidence that *Lucia* derives from *luce* (*light*, as in the light that strikes your eyes). The suggestion, in other words, is that the sound of the name *Lucia* suggested *luce,* that this phonetic similarity gave rise to the belief that this saint had the ability to cure eye diseases, and that this in turn led to a revision in the myth of Santa Lucia so as to legitimate her power.[13] An example of this pattern that is especially well documented involves a saint whose cult is particularly important in Italy—the desert hermit.

THE DESERT HERMIT WHO BECAME MASTER
OF THE STABLE

Sant'Antonio abate (the abbot) is without question one of the single most popular saints in the Italian Catholic pantheon, and his popularity extends the length of the Italian peninsula. Case studies document his popularity in areas of Lombardia (Tassoni 1966), Piemonte (Ramella and Torre 1981: 90–92), Romagna (Comandini 1966), and Abruzzo (Di Nola 1976: 181–294). Like all the saints in Italy, he is seen as having the power to heal and to protect. In Sant'Antonio's case, however, this ability to protect is not associated with human beings (he is hardly ever chosen as a community's patron saint) but rather with animals, domestic animals in particular—that is, animals raised by peasant farmers. What is most interesting about his association with domestic animals is that it makes no sense at all given the early accounts of his life in official hagiographies.[14]

According to these accounts, the historical Antonio was born in Egypt about the year 250 to a relatively well-to-do family. At the age of twenty he gave up his possessions and went to live in the desert. Although he attracted followers, who organized themselves into loosely knit monastic communities, he himself lived mostly alone. After his death, an account of Antonio's life was written by his friend Athanasius (who himself would become a saint), and this account became the primary source for all later hagiographies. Sant'Antonio is often credited with founding monasticism, but more important, he is regarded as the prototypical desert father. Desert Fathers were men who went off to the desert to seek God through contemplation, manual labor (they fed themselves, for instance, by maintaining their own gardens), and fairly extravagant self-mortifications.

There is nothing in Athanasius's account of Sant'Antonio's life that would justify an association with domestic animals. If anything, as Alfonso Di Nola (1976: 210) points out, the details suggest a disassociation with animals. We are told at one point that wild animals damage Antonio's garden. The saint sends them away and enjoins them in the name of Christ never to approach his garden again. In two other incidents in which Antonio confronts animals, these animals (a hyena and a monster with the foot of an ass) are the Devil in disguise. Add to all this the fact that Sant'Antonio never ate meat and it is hard to imagine anyone less suited to the task of protecting domestic animals. Yet he was given this task. Why?

A legend, which first appeared in 1534, traces Sant'Antonio's association with domestic animals to an event from his life, in which Antonio was miraculously transported to the city of Barcelona (ibid., 220). A sow had just given birth to a sickly piglet. Carrying it in her mouth, she brought it to the saint and deposited it at his feet. With her moans and grunts, she seemed to be asking Sant'Antonio for his help. Recognizing this, the saint quickly healed the piglet by making the sign of the cross, to the wonder and amazement of all present. But we know from other sources that Sant'Antonio's status as protector of domestic animals was established at least by the fourteenth century, a full two centuries before the appearance of this first legitimating myth. One such source, for example, is the *Decameron*, written by Giovanni Boccaccio (1313–75) circa 1350.

The *Decameron* tells the story of ten individuals who have moved into the country to escape the plague and who each tell a story each day. The tenth story on the ninth day is told by Fra Cipolla (Brother Onion), who belongs to an order (the Antonines) dedicated to Sant'Antonio abate. At one point early in this story, Fra Cipolla reminds his audience that once a year it has been the custom of his order to give offerings of grain and fodder to Sant'-Antonio "so that Sant'Antonio will look after their oxen, their donkeys, their pigs, and their sheep" (Boccaccio 1980: 548). Sant'Antonio, then, even more clearly than San Valentino and Santa Lucia, became a patron saint long before the appearance of a myth legitimating that status.

What, then, did establish him as patron of domestic animals? Most likely it was purely fortuitous circumstances involving the Hospital Brothers of Sant'Antonio, usually called the Antonines, which is the order mentioned in Boccaccio's story. Founded as a lay order in France about 1095, the Antonines became a monastic order in the late thirteenth century and quickly spread throughout France, Spain, and Italy. One of the special prerogatives that was granted to this order very early on, and later confirmed by the papacy, was the right to raise pigs, which were allowed to circulate freely throughout the communities in which the Antonines maintained houses. It was expected that these free-roaming pigs would be fed at the expense of the local communities as a way of subsidizing the order. Each pig wore a small bell around its neck; they were called "porci di Sant'Antonio" (Sant'Antonio's pigs), a term that turns up in a number of places. It appears, for instance, in *La Divina Commedia*, which Dante Alighieri (1265–1321) composed in the early 1300s. Thus in Canto XXIX (line 124) of *Paradiso*, Dante refers to the gullibility of the common people as something "on which Sant'Antonio [= the Antonines] fattens his [their] pigs."[15]

This Antonine privilege became so entrenched that it was eventually incorporated into a number of municipal statutes. The statutes for the city of Orvieto in 1581, for example, indicate

> that no hog or sow be allowed to wander through the city. If at any time during the day or night, a hog or sow does wander about the city or its environs, the owner . . . shall be punished with a fine of forty *soldi* for each pig or sow involved, and moreover the pigs or sows involved can be killed with impunity by anybody. The only exception is that two *porci di Sant'Antonio* are permitted to roam through the city. (Di Nola 1976: 226)

The fact that the Antonine order had a special right to raise free-roaming pigs who wore bells on their collars explains why Sant'Antonio's iconographical symbols are a pig and a bell, one or both of which usually appear in representations of the saint. Very likely, it also explains why the desert hermit Sant'Antonio abate came to be seen as the protector of pigs and, by extension, all domestic animals, even though the original hagiographical traditions surrounding this saint provided no rationale for this role (ibid., 217–31).

Had the Antonine order not diffused to Italy, had it been dedicated to some other saint, or had this order not received special rights relating to the raising of pigs—then likely some other saint, not Sant'Antonio, would have become the special patron of domestic animals. In several parts of Italy, in fact, the protector of domestic animals role is allocated to someone other than Sant'Antonio abate.

In the case of saints like Santa Lucia and Sant'Antonio, we are dealing with saints whose existence is attested to by traditions that date from the earliest centuries of the Church. These early traditions provided a core around which patronal relationships could crystalize. The Italian predilection for creating saints is sufficiently strong, however, that saints can be created *ex nihilio*.

SAN ZOPITO

By the eighteenth century, the town of Loreto Aprutino (in Abruzzo) had acquired three patron saints: San Pietro, San Michele arcangelo, and San Tommaso d'Aqino (Saint Thomas Aquinas). What it didn't have was a relic of these or any other saint. As a result, cathedral officials in Penne (which was the seat of the diocese in which Loreto Aprutino was located) sent a request to Rome in December 1710 asking that they be given the relics of a saint.[16] The request was approved immediately, and Pope Clement XI authorized the exhumation of the bones of a martyr from the catacombs of San Callisto.

The Cult of the Saints

The exhumation was carried out by an official from the cathedral at Penne. This official located a funeral tablet containing the name *Zopitus*, and also, in a corner, the term *Vicenne*. Since this latter term was somewhat similar to the name of an area near Loreto Aprutino, he felt that the relics of San Zopito would be ideally suited to his purpose. Consequently these relics— consisting of three teeth, a few small bones, and a glass vial containing what was thought to be dried blood—were transported with ceremony to Penne and later (in May 1711) from Penne to the church of San Pietro in Loreto Aprutino.

Although the initial importation of this saint's cult into Loreto Aprutino was due entirely to the efforts of the local clergy, San Zopito quickly became a very popular saint. Two festas were established in his honor. The first, on 12 October, commemorated the removal of the relics from the catacombs, while the second, held the Monday after Pentecost, commemorated the translation of his relics from Penne. As well, the saint came to be seen as having a special power to drive out demons, and a great number of individuals possessed by demons came to the church of San Pietro seeking release. But the most important of the powers associated with San Zopito was manifest in the ritual of the ox.

Forty days before the Monday after Pentecost, a pure white plough ox was released from all work and trained for the festa. This training consisted of teaching the ox to "genuflect" in response to pressure on his neck and accustoming him to bear the weight of a young child. On Pentecost Sunday, the ox—accompanied by a crowd—was brought into the church of San Pietro. It was made to genuflect at the threshold of the church and then taken on a tour of the community. The next day, which was the saint's feast day proper, the ox was again taken in procession to the church. On this occasion a boy about four or five years old was carried on the ox's back. This time the ox actually entered the church and was made to genuflect in front of San Zopito's statue.

After a Mass was said, there was yet another procession, this one far grander than the one the day before. Included in this procession was the ox (who was forced to genuflect whenever the procession passed one of the four other churches in the town); musical bands; various religious corporations; mounted horsemen; twenty or so wooden statues of various saints taken from a variety of churches in the area; and an effigy of San Zopito himself, in the form of a silver bust. At some point, of course, the ox would defecate. This usually happened during the procession but would sometimes occur while the ox was still in the church. It was commonly believed that the abundance of the next harvest would depend upon the amount of manure evacuated.

Despite the fact that the San Zopito cult was introduced by the local clergy, the ritual that coalesced around it—especially the ritual of the ox—

came increasingly to attract the disapproval of Church authorities. The cult's popular appeal, by contrast, only increased with time. The divergence between popular and official attitudes was perhaps most apparent in 1876, when a zealous cleric tried to block the entrance of the ox into the church. This provoked a "popular insurrection," which had to be suppressed by two companies of infantrymen, and the incident is said to have caused the heart attack of the cleric who tried to interfere with the ceremony (ibid., 274). It was only in the late 1940s that Church authorities succeeded in modifying the ceremony, by having the ox wait at the threshold of the church while Mass was being celebrated. Even then, most of the rest of the ceremony was left intact, and the festa was still being celebrated in the 1970s (ibid., 274–75).

Who was San Zopito that his cult should become so popular? What was there in the life of this saint that would lead his devotees to associate him with the ability to exorcise demons and to predict the amount of the next harvest? Neither question has an answer, because San Zopito never existed. It seems likely that what the cathedral official had actually found in the catacombs of San Callisto was the fragment of a tablet that had once said "sospitus in Domino," which would have meant something like "asleep in the arms of the Lord." The official mistook *sospitus* for a proper name.

The basis for the San Zopito cult, in other words, was originally just a *name*, though a name legitimized by high Church officials. But the fact that the original focus of the cult was just a name did not prevent the attribution to this saint of some very specific powers—namely, the ability to cast out demons and to determine the nature of the next harvest—nor did it impede the development of the elaborate cultic ceremonies described above. Over time, San Zopito was even given a "life." Devotees came to believe, for instance, that San Zopito had been martyred during the reign of the Emperor Diocletian while trying to protect the Eucharist from desecration. Since this sounds very much like San Tracisio, a saint already known in the area, Di Nola (ibid., 271) suggests that the traditions about Tracisio were "borrowed" in constructing the traditions about Zopito.

ANOTHER NAME, ANOTHER SAINT

Another instance of a cult crystallizing around a name legitimized by Church authorities involves Santa Filomena.[17] The bones of this saint and a vial thought to contain some of her dried blood were found in an urn uncovered during excavations in Rome in 1802. Found with the urn were three terracotta tablets, which were taken to be a funeral inscription. The tablets—in order—read LUMENA, PAXTE, CUMFI. It was thought that there had been some mistake in assembling (or reassembling) the tablets, and the proper order should have been PAXTE, CUMFI, LUMENA. This was taken to mean "Peace [be] with you, Filomena."

The bones of Santa Filomena were kept in storage in Rome until 1805. At that time, they were turned over to Bartolomeo Di Cesare, who was in Rome to be consecrated as bishop of Potenza. Di Cesare immediately turned them over to his friend and traveling companion, Francesco Di Lucia. Di Lucia was a parish priest from Mugnano, a village of about three thousand people just north of Naples. The relics were transported to Naples and later to Mugnano. Although there were supposed to have been a few miracles associated with the relics during this first year, these were witnessed only by members of the nobility or by clergy. Further, although a public cult organized around Santa Filomena existed at Mugnano from 1805 onward, there is no evidence that it was especially popular with the general public. All that changed in 1823.

In that year a number of healings in Mugnano were attributed to the miraculous intervention of Santa Filomena. From this point forward, the number of miracles attributed to the saint increased exponentially, as did the cult's popularity. Devotion to Santa Filomena developed first in Mugnano and the surrounding areas and then spread to the entire diocese and finally to the entire Mezzogiorno. By the 1830s, Filomena's cult had spread to northern Italy, France, and even the United States. Nevertheless, the vast majority of the miracles attributed to her took place in southern Italy (La Salvia 1984: 923–24).

In 1824, Di Lucia published a book purporting to give a historical account of Filomena's life as inferred from certain frescoes found near her urn. In Di Lucia's reconstruction, Filomena was a young Greek princess who had converted to Christianity and who had accompanied her father when he went to Rome to arrange a peace treaty. In Rome, her young beauty caught the eye of the Emperor Diocletian, and he became obsessed with a desire to possess her. When she resisted his advances, there began a series of tribulations, from which Filomena was rescued only by divine intervention. Filomena was whipped, but her wounds were miraculously healed by Mary herself; she was tied to an anchor and thrown into the Tevere, but angels came and liberated her before she touched the water; Roman archers shot arrows at her, but the Holy Spirit came down from Heaven and turned the arrows toward her attackers. At the sight of so many prodigies, many of the onlookers converted to Christianity. Trembling with fear at the sight of the forces opposing him, the emperor ordered Filomena to be decapitated.

A second edition of Di Lucia's book came out in 1827 and a third in 1829, each edition augmented by more accounts of the miracles of Filomena's life. Di Lucia's account of Filomena's life was "confirmed" in 1833 by a mystic living at Naples, Maria Luisa di Gesù, who reported having held conversations with the saint during visionary experiences.

Although the account of Filomena's life is pure fantasy, it is not folklore— that is, it did not develop through processes of oral transmission among the people. It was a literary fantasy created by one man, Francesco Di Lucia. Moreover, Di Lucia was a relatively educated man, well versed in the traditions of classical antiquity and in the hagiographical accounts associated with the saints approved by the Church. This enabled him to construct a story well suited to win the approval of the Church. Notice, for instance, that in Di Lucia's account Filomena herself is not given any miraculous powers. She is aided by supernatural beings like Mary, angels, and the Holy Spirit, all of whom figure in the sort of Catholicism favored by the post-Tridentine Church.

But here again, as in the case of Sant'Antonio abate and San Zopito, it is important to notice the timing: first came widespread attribution to the saint of the powers to heal and protect, then came the story giving a "life" to this saint or stories legitimizing those powers. Here again we reach the same conclusion: the only precondition that is absolutely necessary for the development and maintenance of a saint's cult in Italy is a name that has been legitimated by Church authorities. In Filomena's case, legitimacy was not bestowed as the result of official canonization; indeed, canonization proceedings were not begun until 1834. But the relics of this saint had been identified by Church authorities as likely being the bones of an early martyr, and a public cult dedicated to this saint had been allowed to function at Mugnano from 1805 onward. Furthermore, each edition of Di Lucia's account of Filomena's life carried the Church imprimatur, as did the account of Maria Luisa's visions published in 1833.[18] Further legitimacy was accorded this saint when Pope Leo XII sent the tablets containing the funeral inscription that had been found with Filomena's urn to Mugnano.

Santa Filomena's past, or more appropriately, her lack of a past, caught up to her in 1961, when the Congregation of Rites in Rome decided that she never existed and dropped her from the Church's liturgical calendar.[19] This decision produced some hostility at Mugnano, partly because Roman authorities did not bother to inform the rector of Santa Filomena's sanctuary of the decision (he first heard of it through news reports) and partly because they saw it as an arbitrary decision on Rome's part to damage "their" saint. In any event, a decision by far-off bureaucrats in Rome was not sufficient to end Filomena's cult. One of this saint's devotees, for example, who had been miraculously cured of a debilitating back pain, shrugged it off this way:

> I believe in Santa Filomena, and when one day I heard from the priest of my local church that Filomena had never existed, I came here to Mugnano to find out how things stood on this matter. Then the priest, the one here at Santa Filomena's sanctuary, told us that nothing would come of it if we stayed calm

and behaved ourselves. So I returned home. Since then I have continued to come here every year to thank the saint for the favor that she granted me. (Rossi 1969: 37)

Although Filomena was dropped by the Congregation of Rites, Church authorities—in one of those compromises that has always characterized popular Catholicism in Italy—continued to tolerate a sanctuary to this saint even after they had decided that she never existed. The church at Mugnano, in other words, staffed by Catholic priests, continued to display her statue and continued to receive pilgrims, who made votive offerings to Santa Filomena. True, the local clergy were instructed to diminish the popular appeal of this cult by educating the public, and this did have an effect, in that the number of pilgrims coming to the church did decline. Even so, in 1968, seven years after Santa Filomena had been declared nonexistent by the Roman authorities, two-hundred-thousand pilgrims came to worship her at her sanctuary.

CREATING SAINTS: THE GENERAL PROCESS

The mind of the Italian Catholic needs only one thing to create a saint: a name, a name that in some vague way is seen to have the approval of the Church. The official list of saints endorsed by the Church is one, but only one, source for such names. A saint can also be created *ex nihilio* from a name associated with a saint by members of the local clergy (as in the case of San Valentino, San Zopito, and Santa Filomena).

Once a Church-approved name has given existence to a saint, the saint will come to be attributed with special powers. If the saint is an official saint, and if the legends surrounding that saint suggest some special power, so much the better. But these particular powers can also result from purely idiosyncratic associations (like the happenstance of the Antonine order being associated with pigs) or even from purely phonetic associations (as in the case of Santa Lucia). In these cases, myths about the saint's life will be modified or created to legitimate these attributions.

The fact that a Church-approved name, and nothing else, is all that is needed to create a saint means that creating saints in Italy is relatively easy. It is this easiness that enables Italians to create so many saints, far more than other national traditions. But of course we still need to explain why Italians are driven to create so many saints. This question is addressed in the final chapter.

3

THE MARY CULT

The suggestion that human beings should strive for direct contact with
the sacred, that is, for a contact with the sacred that is not mediated by
institutional structures, will strike many readers as a prototypically Protestant position. By contrast, the reverse suggestion, namely, that the official
Church was formally established by Jesus Christ in order to provide divinely
inspired guidance, will seem to many a prototypically Catholic position.
While such views may indeed differentiate Protestants and Catholics at the
level of formal doctrine, this should not blind us to the fact that popular
Catholicism in general—and Italian Catholicism in particular—has long
been characterized by a type of direct contact with the sacred that has little
or no counterpart among Protestants, namely, the experience of apparitions.

An apparition occurs when a human being experiences face-to-face contact
with a supernatural being. Over the centuries, hundreds and possibly thousands of Catholics have reported this sort of experience. While apparitions
involving Christ or the saints are not uncommon, the vast majority of all
apparitions involve the Virgin Mary. Since the Marian apparitions most
familiar to the readers of this book are likely to be those associated with the
great Marian sanctuaries at Lourdes, Fatima, and Mexico City, all of which
are located outside of Italy, it may come as a surprise to learn that Italian
Catholics are, and have always been, more prone to the experience of Marian
apparitions than any other national group. This is evident in table 3.1, which
presents data on national origins for two samples of Marian apparitions.

The sample of 50 Marian apparitions are all relatively well known and all
received some degree of approval from the Church. The sample of 210
Marian apparitions were experienced between 1928 and 1971 and did not

The Mary Cult

TABLE 3.1

Marian apparitions by country of origin, two samples

Country	Approved apparitions, 1100–1900 (N 50)		Unapproved apparitions, 1928–1971 (N 210)	
	No.	Percentage	No.	Percentage
Italy	15	30	76	36
France	11	22	27	13
Germany, Austria	5	10	21	10
Spain, Portugal	4	8	11	5
England	4	8	2	1
Belgium	0	0	17	8
Poland	1	2	4	2
All other European locations	3	6	26	12
All non-European locations	7	14	26	13

Source: Derived from Carroll (1986: 131); Billet (1973).

receive Church approval. Despite the differences between the two samples, there is one common pattern: Italy accounts for the lion's share of all apparitions.

The greater propensity of Italians to experience apparitions of Mary has insured that such apparitions would play a central role in the Mary cult in Italy. A great many of the Marian sanctuaries in Italy, for instance, are supposed to have been erected on the site of a Marian apparition. Of the 697 sanctuaries in Giacomo Medica's (1965) sample, 112 are in fact apparition-site sanctuaries of this sort (and these do not include those sanctuaries dedicated to a Mary—like Our Lady of Lourdes, Our Lady of Fatima—who is believed to have appeared at another location). In the vast majority of these 112 cases, the apparition gave rise to the sanctuary because the Mary who appeared during the apparition explicitly asked for a sanctuary to be built in her honor. Indeed, "I am Mary, build a church here in my honor" is the most common message that these Italian Marys transmit when they come to earth. Nothing about sin, nothing about love, just "build a church in my honor." Such a message, of course, tells us far more about the Italian Catholics who are experiencing the apparition than anything else. In particular, it tells us something about how Italian Catholics conceptualize Mary: they see her as a goddess who craves veneration.

The sheer number of Marian apparitions in Italy necessitates considering such apparitions in a study like this one. But apparitions also provide an especially good context for studying the interaction between the limits set by the official Church and the folk religious beliefs that arise among the population. Apparitions, in other words, provide an especially good context for studying the processes that give rise to popular Catholicism, as that term is being used in this book.

THE CHURCH CONFRONTS APPARITIONS,
APPARITIONS CONFRONT
THE CHURCH

By its very nature, an apparition, because it involves direct contact between the sacred and a human seer, threatens the raison d'être of the institutional Catholic Church.[1] Nevertheless, under certain conditions, apparitions can be useful to the Church, and so the Church has evolved a series of guidelines, some explicit and some implicit, for deciding which apparitions to legitimate. One guideline, clearly, is that the apparition experience must have ceased, or at least become something more in the nature of a private inspiration. That this constitutes organizational good sense seems obvious. After all, if we rule out true supernatural causation (and not to do so would remove this book from the realm of social science), then these apparitions are almost certainly hallucinations or illusions that derive from the seer's personal experience.[2] Given this, the apparition experience will always involve an element of unpredictability. Endorsing a seer who is still transmitting public statements supposedly "directly from Mary" would raise the very real risk of endorsing someone likely to (eventually) say something inconsistent with Catholic doctrine.[3]

In the case of Italy, the importance of cessation as a determinant of the Church's attitude toward apparitions can be seen in the Church's differing reactions to apparition experiences of two pugliése seers, Marietta D'Agostino and Domenico Masselli, both of whom attracted a wide following in the post–World War II period and both of whose cults have been well studied by Italian investigators.

The Mary Cult
A Tale of Two Seers

Marietta D'Agostino was an illiterate peasant woman; she was born in 1899 and died at Orta Nova, in the province of Foggia, in 1977.[4] Marietta began to experience apparitions of the Madonna sometime around World War I. Although Marietta's husband reacted with hostility to his wife's first reports of her experiences, he too received a visit from the Madonna, and from that point forward he worked to promote a greater awareness of his wife's gifts. But Marietta was not only a seer; she was also a wonder-worker who could foresee the future, provide information unavailable from other sources, and cure illnesses. Her activities eventually brought her into conflict with Church authorities, and she was arrested in 1945. But the arrest provoked a public demonstration on her behalf, and she was released after spending only a single night in custody.

Marietta's popularity increased greatly over the next few decades, so that by the mid-1960s something like 300,000 pilgrims a year were visiting her in her home (Rossi 1969: 157). Furthermore, despite her initial conflict with the Church, Marietta and her cult did come to receive approval and legitimation from Church authorities. This was possible because Marietta willingly deemphasized her role as a seer, even though she continued in her role as a wonder-worker.

By the 1960s, for instance, Marietta and her followers were making a conscious effort to insure that the discourse that passed between them be kept private. Annabella Rossi (ibid., 71), an Italian scholar who studied Marietta's cult, notes that, although she was given permission to attend meetings between Marietta and her devotees, she was not allowed to get close enough to hear the conversation that passed between Marietta and each of her followers. Nor were any of those who consulted Marietta willing to talk with Rossi later on.

In addition, Marietta was no longer claiming to directly experience Marian apparitions. True, Marietta's statements about having seen Mary in the past were accepted at face value by her followers, and this added to her popularity. It also seems obvious that Marietta and her followers felt that her advice was being guided by Mary. Nevertheless, all this is a long way away from the claim that Mary was present in the room. The risk to the Church's role as mediator between the natural and the divine was thus minimized.

The key events occurred in the early 1970s. Church authorities constructed a church near Marietta's home dedicated to the Madonna di Altomare.[5] It became a parish church in 1974. Since the Madonna di Altomare was the madonna whom Marietta had claimed to have seen, the net effect of this was to establish what Miriam Castiglione (1981: 135) calls an "official seat" for Marietta's cult. Marietta, in her turn, regularly collected donations

Madonnas That Maim

for this church from the crowds who continued to meet with her in her home. This official recognition was extended to Marietta, even though she still remained a wonder-worker, often healing supplicants by anointing them with a special oil. In other words, the association of Marietta with elements that to most outside observers would smack of magic was not a bar to her legitimation. What was important, apparently, was only that she no longer claimed to be transmitting messages directly from Mary.

Marietta D'Agostino's experience contrasts with that of another pugliése seer who attracted a large following, Domenico Masselli of Stornarella.[6] Masselli (born about 1922) first saw Mary in 1959, when she appeared to him and told him of the need to urge repentance upon the world. From that day forward, he spoke directly with Mary on the first three Fridays of every month. With offerings collected from his followers, Masselli was able to construct an oratory (consisting of one large room) dedicated to San Gerardo Maiella, who is one of the most popular saints in the region, and it was in this oratory that these dialogues with Mary took place.[7]

Supplicants would write letters to Mary outlining their concerns; they would then place these letters, properly sealed in envelopes carrying the normal postage, at the base of the Madonna's altar. The service would start with a recitation of the rosary and the singing of hymns. Masselli would then enter a type of cell, described as a "roofless confessional." After a bit, he would levitate until he appeared above the cell. Simultaneous with his levitation, the bleeding wounds of the stigmata would be evident in his hands.[8] Eventually, the levitation ceased, and Masselli exited the cell in order to begin the second part of the ceremony. Kneeling near the Madonna's altar, he would "see" the Madonna and begin to speak to her. He would then open each of the letters and begin writing on a blank sheet (which each supplicant had enclosed in their letter) the response dictated by the Madonna. Subsequently, he would read the message aloud.

As outlandish as all this may seem to outsiders, it was taken seriously by a great many people, including a number of priests and nuns who attended the ceremonies conducted by Domenico Masselli (Cipriani 1976: 69). Furthermore, remember that Stornarella is not very distant from San Giovanni Rotundo on the Gargano peninsula (still in Puglia), where Padre Pio (1887–1968) had lived. Padre Pio was a Capuchin monk and probably the most well-known stigmatic of the twentieth century. He became (and still is) the focus of a devoted following. Although the Church has never endorsed the supernatural origin of Padre Pio's stigmata, it gave legitimacy to his cult by allowing him to remain in a Capuchin monastery and to continue performing his priestly functions (like saying Mass and hearing confession). Books describing Padre Pio's stigmatic experiences have also been published with a Church imprimatur, which means that a bishop has decided that they contain nothing counter to Catholic faith or morals (e.g., Carty 1953). In a region where Padre Pio had until recently been exhibiting the bleeding wounds of the stigmata on a regular basis, someone like Domenico Masselli—who both levitated and experienced the stigmata—was not as unusual as he would have been elsewhere in the world.

In any event, Domenico and his group were not at first condemned by the Church. The local bishop, though not favorably disposed toward the cult, made no public statements against it, nor did any of the local clergy (Cipriani 1976: 68; Castiglione 1981: 128). It was only in 1977, around the time that Domenico and his cult were constructing a new oratory—and several years after the cult had been functioning—that Church authorities admonished Catholics not to participate in the services at the oratory, under pain of being excluded from the religious activities of the local parish church (Barbati, Mingozzi, and Rossi 1978: 97).

Faced with this condemnation, Masselli—who, clearly, saw himself as very much a part of the Catholic tradition—toned down some of his cult's exhibitionistic elements to make the cult more acceptable. The "roofless confessional," for instance, was eliminated in the new oratory, and along with it the experience of levitation and stigmatization (Castiglione 1981: 128). Furthermore, Masselli's demeanor during his dialogue with the Madonna became less intense. This change in Domenico's personal behavior was mirrored in a change in the dedication of his oratory. The old oratory was dedicated to San Gerardo Maiella (1726–55). Maiella was (and is) strongly associated in the popular mind with some fairly flamboyant mortifications, not the least of which was violent and bloody self-flagellation. Domenico's new oratory, by contrast, was dedicated to only the Madonna del Rosario, one of the most universalistic and benign of the popular madonnas in Italy (Barbati, Mingozzi, and Rossi 1978: 82).

Nevertheless, despite all his toning down, Masselli still claimed to be seeing Mary and to be transmitting messages that came directly from her. While the Church might tolerate a cult organized around a Marietta D'Agostino, with her miraculous oil and her discreet "divine guidance," it simply could not endorse someone whose experience of a Marian apparition had not ceased. As a result, the relationship between Masselli and the Church became more, not less, conflictual, and his cult never was legitimized.

DOCTRINAL PURITY

While the cessation of an apparition may be a necessary condition for securing the approval of the Church, it is not sufficient. It seems obvious that the Church is unlikely to endorse apparitions whose content is inconsis-

Madonnas That Maim

tent with formal Church doctrine. The Church, in other words, is perfectly willing to grant that supernatural beings like Mary might come down and talk with ordinary mortals but not that Mary or Jesus have views outside the doctrines of the Church. Such a position flows logically from the presupposition that the Church, in establishing its doctrines, has always acted under divine guidance.

The Church's concern for doctrinal purity has quite often led it to overlook elements in an apparition that would strike non-Catholics, and even a great many Catholics, as bizarre. A good illustration of this can be found in Adriano Prosperi's (1984) account of a sixteenth-century apparition investigated by the Inquisition. On 25 May 1560, during a time of famine, a poor woman— identified only by the pseudonym Margherita in the records of the Inquisition—left the city of Piacenza (in Emilia-Romagna) to check on her nearby bean field. While in the field, Margherita began to express her worries aloud, complaining of having to raise children without the means to provide for them. She then heard herself being called, and saw a woman dressed in white. The woman consoled Margherita, who came to realize that the woman was none other than "the blessed Mother of God, Queen of Heaven, the Virgin Mary." Mary then said that her son, Jesus Christ, was very angry with Piacenza on account of its blasphemies.

At this point, Mary was joined by a male figure, whom Mary identified as Christ. Margherita was then told that Christ wanted to devastate Piacenza by causing the Po to overflow but that Mary herself had prayed to her son, asking him to pardon the city. As evidence of this, Mary then raised her gown to reveal that above her knees there was neither skin nor flesh, but simply bone. This, Mary said, had happened as a result of her having prayed too much on her knees. Margherita was then told that the people of Piacenza had to do three things to avoid divine punishment: (1) abstain from blasphemy, (2) fast for three Saturdays on bread and water, and (3) celebrate a festa each Saturday. Mary then vanished.

A few days later, Mary appeared again to Margherita in the field and asked if her commands had been carried out. Margherita replied that they had not, because people did not believe her. Mary then gave a sign that would engender belief: she caused Margherita's legs to become paralyzed. At that, Mary vanished once more. Terrified, Margherita screamed for help. Her screams were heard by some people nearby. She was carried home and recovered a few days later.

Margherita's report spread quickly. The bean field attracted a large number of people, a rough sanctuary was erected, and the popularity of the cult increased. Eventually, however, the Inquisition investigated. After some initial hesitation, the apparitions were declared false, and the cult was suppressed.

The Inquisitors were not particularly bothered by the suggestion that

Christ could cause a flood or that Mary would paralyze someone's legs as a sign of the apparition's authenticity. As we will see in the next chapter, this sort of thing is quite common in apparition accounts, including those approved by the Church. Nor did the Inquisitors devote much attention to the somewhat unusual image of a Mary reduced to bone above the knees. Certainly they weren't bothered by the requests to refrain from blasphemy and to fast or by the intercessory role assigned to Mary.

Right from the beginning, the Inquisitors focused on one and only one thing: the request to celebrate a festa every Saturday. This was seen as running directly counter to the traditional emphasis upon Sunday services. Under questioning, Margherita revised the message, saying that the Madonna had asked that the festa begin only late on Saturday. This did move the requested festa closer to Sunday, but it was still a Saturday festa. This one relatively narrow doctrinal consideration ultimately led the Inquisition to suppress this particular apparition.

MANY MADONNAS

So far in this book I have been talking of Mary and the Mary cult as if there is one Mary, just as there is one Sant'Antonio abate or one San Giuseppe. This has been a useful simplification, but it is a simplification that must now be set aside. The Mary cult in Italy, like the cult of the saints, is really a metacult that involves the worship of several different supernatural beings. While the Church's view may be that the term Mary refers to the single individual who was the Virgin-Mother of Jesus Christ, Italian Catholics clearly worship a range of madonnas.[9] While these different madonnas may indeed be vaguely associated with the official Mary, each madonna nevertheless has a separate identity, and each is the object of distinct cultic devotions. Like the saints, the madonnas of Italy are powerful supernatural beings, and each has the power to heal and to protect. Unlike what characterizes the cult of the saints, however, there is very little division of labor among the madonnas. Most madonnas are seen to have the power to protect and to aid in all situations.

The contrast between the official Mary cult and the Mary cult as it actually functions at the local level was summed up perfectly in a conversation reported in Edward Banfield's (1958) study of a village in Basilicata. It seems that a young man who had studied for the priesthood was explaining to an older woman of the village that there was only one Madonna. To which she replied, "You studied with the priests for eight years, and you haven't even learned the differences between the madonnas?" (131). Understanding these differences is a prerequisite for understanding the Mary cult in Italy.

Madonnas That Maim

SPLINTERING

Since Italy has long been characterized by a highly decentralized social and political system, it would be easy to conclude that the panorama of madonnas in Italy results from the fact that each community in Italy has created its own madonna as a way of distinguishing itself from other communities. In such a view, the proliferation of madonnas reflects only the fragmentation of Italian society. But here again, we must avoid stereotypical thinking.

It is true that in any given region or community, certain madonnas are more popular than others. But it is also important to realize that a multiplicity of madonnas is usually venerated in a single locale. In the village studied by Banfield, for example, five separate madonnas were venerated: the Madonna di Pompei, the Madonna del Carmine, the Madonna Assunta, the Madonna Addolorata, and the Madonna della Pace. In her study of Montecastello di Vibio, a small town near Rome, Sydel Silverman (1975: 150–53) found that there were communitywide festas in honor of both the Madonna Addolorata and the Madonna dei Portenti. Charlotte Chapman (1971: 172–73) reports that in Milocca (Sicilia) there were devotions in honor of the Madonna Immacolata, the Madonna Addolorata, the Madonna del Carmine, the Madonna Assunta, the Madonna del Monte Racalmuto, and the Madonna di Trapani. Similarly, the records associated with a pastoral visit made in the Diocese of Asti (in Piemonte) in 1742 indicate that the community of Priocca, with a population of 296 families, had devotions to four different madonnas; that the community of Monticello, with a population of 322 families, had devotions to seven different madonnas; that the community of Canale, with a population of 506 families, had devotions to thirteen different madonnas; and so on (Barbero, Ramella, and Torre 1981).

Daniela Ferrari and Gioia Lanzi (1985) surveyed 173 *edicole* dedicated to madonnas within the historic core of Bologna.[10] The largest number of these (33) are dedicated to the Beata Vergine di San Luca, long popular in Bologna. The precise titles of most of the rest of the madonnas are no longer known. Even so, based upon inscriptions or iconographical clues, it was possible to identify sixteen distinct madonnas, each associated with one or more *edicole*. Apart from the Beata Vergine di San Luca, these titles include the Madonna dell'Olmo, Madonna della Ghiara, Madonna della Seggiola, Madonna del Buon Consiglio, Madonna di Loreto, Madonna del Carmine, Madonna delle Lacrime, Madonna di Fatima, Madonna del Rosario, Immacolata Concezione, Beata Vergine della Cintura, Annunciazione, Assunta, Apparizione della Madonne a San Nicola da Tolentino, and Adorazione.

Such evidence suggests that the tendency to splinter the image of Mary into distinct goddesses, each with its own personality, is more than a reflection of the political and social fragmentation of Italian society. Even within a

The Mary Cult

community, Italian Catholics have a psychological predisposition to create and worship many madonnas, just as they have a predisposition to create and worship many saints.

MARIAN TITLES

In connection with the cult of the saints, we saw that the only thing needed to create a saint was a name that had been legitimized by the Church. Since Mary is a supernatural being that always enjoys legitimacy, the first step toward creating a distinct madonna is to create an association with Mary. The next step is to create a title that distinguishes a given madonna from most other madonnas. Marian titles are generated by combining one of the standard terms of address (see table 1.6) with some particular thing—and there are absolutely no restrictions on what that thing might be. The list below, of madonnas in the Diocese of Verona, gives some idea of the range of madonnas that can coexist even within a relatively restricted area (Borelli 1981).

— Annunciazione di Maria Vergine
— Concezione di Maria
— Madonna del Frascino
— Madonna del Pilar
— Madonna del Popolo
— Madonna del Rosario
— Madonna del Soccorso
— Madonna della Cintura
— Madonna della Corona
— Madonna della Fontana
— Madonna della Neve
— Madonna della Pergolana
— Madonna della Salute
— Madonna della Strà
— Madonna delle Grazie

— Madonna delle Salette
— Madonna dello Staffalo
— Madonna di Compagnamagra
— Madonna di Fatima
— Madonna di Lourdes
— Madonna di Monte
— Madonna di Monte Solane
— Madonna di San Tommaso
— Maternità di Maria
— Santa Maria di Monte Santo

— Natività di Maria
— Nostra Signora della Pellegrina
— Presentazione di Maria Vergine
— Purificazione di Maria Vergine
— Santa Maria

— Santa Maria Addolorata
— Santa Maria Annunziata
— Santa Maria Assunta
— Santa Maria Ausiliatrice
— Santa Maria degli Angeli
— Santa Maria del Carmine
— Santa Maria del Consiglio
— Santa Maria del Degnano
— Santa Maria dell'Alzana
— Santa Maria della Disciplina
— Santa Maria della Mercede
— Santa Maria della Misericordia
— Santa Maria della Pace
— Santa Maria delle Vallene
— Santa Maria di Fossa Dragone

— Santa Maria di Mezzacompagna
— Santa Maria di Minerbio
— Santa Maria di Monte Baldo
— Santa Maria Novella

Madonnas That Maim

- Santa Maria Immacolata
- Santa Maria in Bosco
- Santa Maria Janua Coeli
- Santa Maria Maggiore
- Santa Maria Mater Virgo

- Santa Maria Regina
- Santa Maria Valverde
- Santo Cuore di Maria
- Santo Nome di Maria
- Visitazione di Maria Vergine

Giacomo Medica's (1965) sample of the 697 most important Marian sanctuaries in Italy gives us some idea of the number of Italian madonnas in Italy as a whole. If we ignore the first part of the titles (Madonna, Maria Santissima, Nostra Signora, etc.) and focus only on the second part, we still end up with 397 unique titles. The range in this part of a Marian title is extremely broad. Table 3.2, for example, groups the titles associated with the sanctuaries in Medica's sample into general categories. The most common category includes those terms, like *delle Grazie* or *dei Miracoli*, that denote a madonna's willingness to dispense favors. The next most common category are place-names that predate the title. After these, however, no identifiable category accounts for more than 10 percent of the sample.[11] Since virtually anything can be used in the second part of a Marian title, creating a madonna in Italy is made simpler.

While a distinct title can give existence to a distinct madonna, the reverse is not necessarily true—that is, having the same title does not mean the madonnas are the same. The single most common Marian title in Italy (focusing only on the second part of the title) is delle Grazie. Indeed, fully 12 percent of the 697 sanctuaries in Medica's sample are dedicated to delle Grazie madonnas. But the historical circumstances surrounding these delle Grazie sanctuaries (and the value of Medica's work is that it does provide a brief sketch of each sanctuary listed) make it clear that most of these madonnas bear no relationship to one another. *Grazie* simply means *favors*, and the title *delle Grazie* means only that the madonna associated with that sanctuary dispenses favors. This means that a term like *Madonna delle Grazie* is fundamentally different from a title like, say, *Madonna di Fatima*. All the madonnas called Madonna di Fatima are in some sense the same madonna, since their identity in every case is defined by the apparitions at Fatima (Portugal) in 1917 (see Carroll 1986: 173–81).

Titles are not all that creates a madonna's identity. She is likely to have her own sanctuary, her own festa, her own processions, her own cult places where she alone is venerated, and so on. A sense of uniqueness can also be created by giving her a distinctive look. When Banfield's informant scolded the exseminarian for not knowing the "differences between the madonnas" she was probably referring to iconographical differences between the madonnas. Sometimes iconographical elements associated with a particular madonna are sufficiently obvious as to be recognizable even to outsiders. The Madonna del Carmine, for instance, always carries a scapular in her hand;

The Mary Cult

TABLE 3.2

Meanings of terms in the second part of Marian titles in Italy

Meaning of term	Percentage (N 697)
The madonna's willingness to dispense favors, e.g., delle Grazie (favors), dei Miracoli (miracles), del Soccorso (help)	25
A place-name predating the title	17
A landform, e.g., del Monte (mountain), delle Grotte (grottos), della Valle (valley)	7
A building or other structure, e.g., del Castello (castle), della Strada (street), dell'Arco (arch)	7
An event experienced by the "official" Mary, e.g., Addolorata (usually referring to Mary's sorrows at the crucifixion), Assunta (Assumption), Annunciazione (Annunciation)	6
A form of water, e.g., della Neve (snow), della Fontana (fountain), del Ruscello (brook)	6
A tree, flower, or other wild plant, e.g., dell'Olmo (elm), del Pino (pine tree), del Fiore (flower)	6
A human being or category of human being, e.g., dei Cappuccini (Capuchin friar), del Popolo (people), del Clero (clergy)	4
The "official" Mary's spiritual perfection, e.g., Cuore Immacolato (Immaculate Heart), Immacolata (Immaculate Conception)	3
A saint, e.g., di Santa Valeria, de Santa Luca	2
Christ, e.g., della Croce (cross), di Buon Gesù (Good Jesus)	2
Other	15

Source: Derived from Medica (1965).

not to represent her in this way would negate her identity. The Madonna del Rosario always has a rosary in her hand and appears with San Domenico. The Madonna di Monte Berico is always more matronly and pudgier than other madonnas.

But in many cases a more subtle logic underlies the iconographies associated with different madonnas. Unfortunately, while the iconographies associated with Mary and the saints in Italian high art have been well studied, the iconographies associated with the popular images of these madonnas have generally been ignored.[12] This lacunae in the study of popular Catholicism in Italy needs to be filled by future research. To illustrate what might be done in this area, I consider below three madonnas whose iconographies are clearly interrelated.

THREE MADONNAS, THREE SEERS

The sanctuary of the Madonna della Guardia, is located on Monte Figogna, just outside Genoa. According to tradition, this sanctuary was established following the apparition of a madonna to an adult male seer named Benedetto Pareto in 1490.[13] As with the images of all popular madonnas in Italy, images of the Madonna della Guardia are available on a variety of items: holy cards; ceramic wall plaques; small plastic statuettes; even small shot glasses, on which her image has been painted by the sisters who maintain her sanctuary. In addition, many side altars in churches in and around Genoa are dedicated to this madonna, and these side altars invariably contain either a commercially produced plaster statue madonna or a professionally done oil painting of her. Finally, the Madonna della Guardia appears in the painted *ex voto* that adorn the walls of her sanctuary.[14] The incidental features of these portrayals of the Madonna della Guardia vary greatly, but one iconographical element is invariably present: the seer, Benedetto Pareto, is always included in the portrayal and is always depicted kneeling in front and to the left of the madonna.

To anyone familiar with Catholic traditions in Liguria, this establishes a strong visual similarity between the iconography of the Madonna della Guardia and at least two other important Ligurian madonnas. The first of these is the Madonna di Montallegro, whose sanctuary is just outside Rapallo, a city that lies along the coast about thirty kilometers to the southeast of Genoa. This sanctuary was established following an apparition to an adult male seer named Giovanni Chichizola in 1557.[15] The second of these other madonnas is the Madonna delle Misericordia, whose sanctuary is in Savona, another Ligurian coastal city, which lies just to the southwest of Genoa. This sanctuary was established following an apparition to an adult male seer named Antonio Botta in 1536.

The iconographical similarity between these three madonnas is established first of all by the fact that all their popular portrayals include a portrayal of the associated male seer, and in all cases the seer is shown in the same position, that is, kneeling in front of and to the left of the madonna. In addition, these three seers bear a strong resemblance to one another; they are always portrayed with balding heads and closely cropped beards.

It seems highly unlikely that these three iconographical traditions developed independently of one another. On the contrary, the strong similarity among these traditions, plus the fact that the three sanctuaries are located near one another and were established in about the same historical period, make it highly likely that the earliest of these traditions (likely the one associated with the Madonna della Guardia) served as a model for the other two.

Now to the more interesting question: How do Ligurian Catholics distinguish among these three madonnas? The key lies with two iconographical contrasts: (1) the Madonna della Guardia is always portrayed holding the infant Jesus, while the other two madonnas hold nothing; (2) the cloak on the Madonna della Misericordia always covers both of her shoulders, while the cloaks of the other two madonnas cover only one shoulder, allowing the part of the madonna's tunic covering the other shoulder to be seen.[16] As long as these visual contrasts are maintained, individual artists are free to vary other elements. Thus, sometimes the seer associated with the Madonna della Misericordia is portrayed holding a hat in his folded hands, sometimes not; sometimes sheep appear in the scene associated with the Madonna della Guardia, sometimes not; sometimes the Madonna di Montallegro's hair is long and flowing, sometimes it is hidden under the cap of her cloak; sometimes the seer associated with the Madonna di Montallegro has his hands in front, sometimes one hand is in front while the other is on his chest; and so on.

The most important consequence of using the two contrasts above to define the iconography associated with these three madonnas—and the consequence that justifies considering this case in such detail—is that the iconographical tradition associated with the Madonna di Montallegro is defined not by the presence of some particular elements but rather by the absence of particular elements. Thus, faced with a madonna paired with an adult male who (1) is kneeling to the front and left of the madonna, (2) is bald, and (3) has a beard, most Ligurian Catholics would know immediately that it was one of the three madonnas being considered here. If the infant Jesus is present, then it is the Madonna della Guardia. If the madonna's cloak covers both shoulders, then it is the Madonna della Misericordia. Only if the infant Jesus is absent and the madonna's cloak does not cover both shoulders will it be the Madonna di Montallegro.

I assume that there are other madonnas in Italy whose identity is defined by similar iconographical subtleties. Possibly someone reading this book and concerned with popular art will pursue the matter further.

IMPARENTAMENTO DELLE MADONNE

Although madonnas have different identities and are venerated as unique individuals, they are not unrelated. At one level, the madonnas are related by virtue of the fact that they are all associated with the Mary of the official Church. But the metaphor that Italian Catholics use most often to express the relationship among the madonnas is based on kinship terminology. In interviews conducted in various regions of the Mezzogiorno during the early 1970s, for instance, respondents regularly described the various madonnas as "sisters" (Provitera 1978: 343).

The use of such a kin metaphor is by no means a recent phenomenon. In 1635 a statue of a madonna in the Cathedral at Melfi (Basilicata) was routinely carried in processions through the city in order to secure good weather or rain. Those sponsoring the procession, however, felt obliged to stop at two churches along the way, since one of these contained a madonna considered to be a sister of the madonna in the procession and the other a madonna considered to be a relative of the first two.[17] This tendency toward the *imparentamento delle madonne* (literally, "causing the madonnas to become relatives of one another") has been detected in other historical accounts, in both the South and the North (Corrain and Zampini 1970: 150n).

CONCLUSION

Although the concepts *madonna* and *saint* have different connotations, there is a strong similarity. Each metacult is organized around a multiplicity of beings. The tendency of the Italian Catholic mind to generate a multiplicity of saints and a multiplicity of madonnas distinguishes Italian Catholicism from other variants.

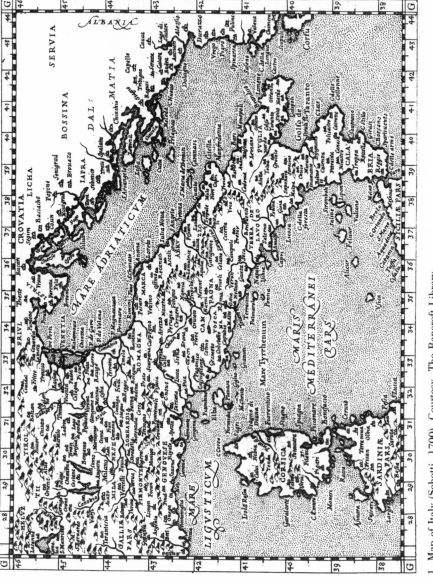

1. Map of Italy (Schotti, 1700). Courtesy, The Bancroft Library.

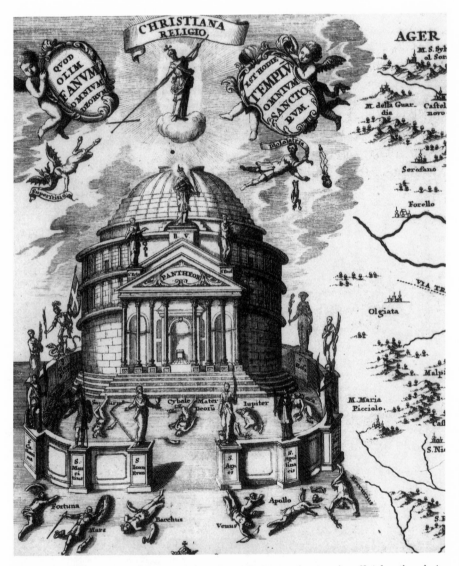

2. A detail from a map of Rome and the surrounding area, showing the official rank-ordering of the three metacults. Standing on the wall, above the broken statues of the pagan gods, are the bulk of the saints, then comes Mary at the summit of the church, flanked by the two most important saints, Peter and Paul, with Christ—the most important being in the Catholic pantheon—standing above them all (Scherer, 1703). Courtesy, The Bancroft Library.

LORETO

3. An early view of Loreto, now one of Italy's four "super-sanctuaries" (Schotti, 1700). Courtesy, The Bancroft Library.

4. The sanctuary of the Madonna dell'Impruneta near Florence (Casotti, 1714). Courtesy, The Bancroft Library.

5. The *Vara* used at Messina on the festa in honor of Maria Assunta (Smythe, 1824).

LA RAPPRESENTAZIONE

DI SANTO ANTONIO ABATE, IL QVALE CON-
VERTI VNA SVA SORELLA, E FECELA MONACA. E
come non volendo tre ladroni accettare el suo consiglio s'am-
mazzorno l'vn l'altro e furno portati a casa Satanasso, &
egli fu terribilmente baltonato da i diauoli.
Nuouamente Riltampata.

6. Title page of a pamphlet printed at Florence in 1589 by G. Baleni. The text gives the script for a sacred drama about Sant'Antonio abate. This saint's iconographic symbols in the popular imagination were a pig and a bell; in this case the bell is found on his staff. Courtesy, The Bancroft Library.

7. The image of the Madonna at the Loreto sanctuary (Mission, 1739). Courtesy, The Bancroft Library.

8. View of Santa Maria de'Miracoli at Rome (Rossi, 1689). Like so many of the churches dedicated to "dei Miracoli" or "delle Grazie" madonnas in Italy, this one was built to house an outdoor picture of the madonna that suddenly starting "dispensing favors." Courtesy, The Bancroft Library.

Plate 15. Vol. 2. P. 396

Tarantula

9. A representation of the tarantula thought to be responsible for *Tarantismo* (Mission, 1739). Courtesy, The Bancroft Library.

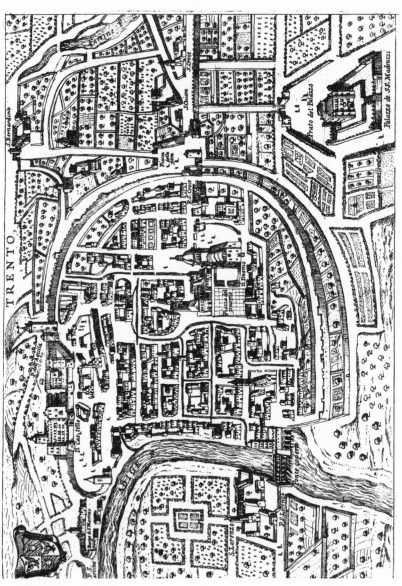

10. A view of the city of Trent (Schotti, 1700). It was here that the Council of Trent opened in 1545 and closed in 1563. Much of the distinctiveness of popular Catholicism in southern Italy derives from the fact that the South was insulated from the Tridentine reforms. Courtesy, The Bancroft Library.

ANTIDOTARIO
CONTRO LI DEMONII.
DEL M. R. THEOLOGO M. ALESSIO PORRI
della Congregatione Carmelitana d'Osseruanza, Consultore del
Santissimo Vfficio, & Publico Essorcista nella Città di Venetia.

NEL QVALE SI TRATTA, COME ENTRANO
ne'corpi humani , oue in quelli stiano , come da quelli si
scacciano, & altre cose degne di sapersi.

ALL'ILLVSTRIS. ET REVEREN.
Signor, & Patron Collendissimo.
IL SIGNOR CINTIO ALDOBRANDINI
CARDINALE S. GIORGIO,

Nipote del Sommo Pontefice Clemente Ottauo.

Con Priuilegio , & Licenza de' Superiori.

NON COMEDETIS
FRVGES MENDACII

IN VENETIA, Appresso Roberto Meglietti. 1601.

---

11. Title page from a handbook for exorcists published at Venice in 1601 (Porri, 1601).
Courtesy, The Bancroft Library.

TESORO DI S. GENNARO

12. View of the main altar in the *Tesoro di San Gennaro* at Naples (Sarnelli, 1692). It is here that the liquefying blood relic of San Gennaro is kept while not on public display. The statues in the niches along the walls are images of some of Naples's patron saints. Courtesy, The Bancroft Library.

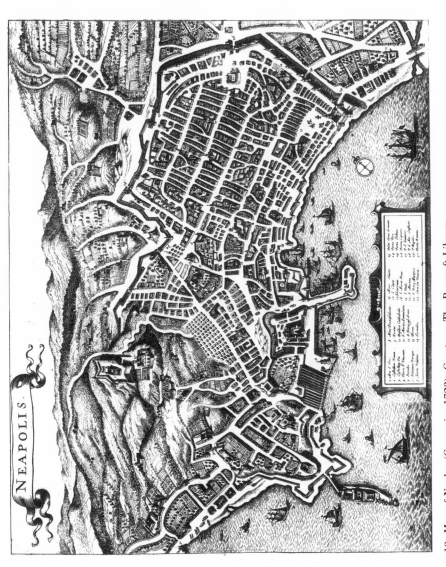

13. Map of Naples (Capaccio, 1723). Courtesy, The Bancroft Library.

14. The region of Campania where most of the blood-relics listed in Table 6.2 are found (Pellegrini, 1771). Courtesy, The Bancroft Library.

LE COSE
MARAVIGLIOSE
DELL'ALMA CITTÀ DI ROMA,
doue si tratta delle chiese, stationi, &
Reliquie de' corpi santi, che
ui sono.

Con vn trattato d'acquistar l'Indulgentie.

La Guida Romana che insegna facilmente a i fora-
stieri a ritrouare le piu notabil
cose di Roma.

Li nomi de i sommi Pontefici, Imperadori, & altri
Principi Christiani.

L'antichita di Roma breuemente raccolta.
Et vn discorso sopra i fuochi
degli antichi.

Tutti nouamente purgati, & corretti.

Et vna Epistola del Cardinale Borromeo, del Giu-
bileo dell'anno Santo.

CON LICENTIA DE' SVPERIORI.

IN ROMA,
Appresso Gioseppe degl'Angeli, alla Minerua.
M. D. LXXV.

15. Title page from a guidebook published for visitors to Rome in the Jubilee
year 1575. Some idea of the importance of relics in the Roman Catholic tradition generally can be seen in the title, which promises to tell pilgrims
where to find "marvelous things" and then singles out three types of such
marvelous things in particular: churches, stations (churches to be visited on
particular dates), and saintly relics. Courtesy, The Bancroft Library.

16. Sicilians praying at a freestanding *edicola* in the country (Smythe, 1824).

THE DARK SIDE OF HOLINESS

D uring the 1930s and 1940s a number of Italian intellectuals vented their opposition to Mussolini by writing novels with an anti-Fascist orientation. Quite apart from their political content, several of these novels contained sympathetic portrayals of the harsh realities of life in the rural South. One of the most famous of these was Ignazio Silone's (1900–78) *Pane e vino* (*Bread and Wine*), published in 1937 during the author's exile in Zurich.

Pane e vino tells the story of Pietro Spina, a political activist who returns to Italy after years of exile in order to foment revolution. Spina learns almost immediately that his presence is known to the police, and so for his own safety he breaks off contact with his socialist comrades. Survival, not revolution, becomes his primary goal. Since Spina's deteriorating health precludes flight, he contacts an old friend from his school days. The friend concocts a bold plan: Pietro Spina, the revolutionary, will become Dom Paolo Spada, a priest. Disguised as a priest, he will live for a few months in the country.[1] Making his central character a socialist agitator who assumes the role of a priest in a rural village allows Silone to explore the worldview that prevails in such a village from the perspective of an urban intellectual.

Early in the novel, Spina finds himself in a donkey cart taking him toward the village where he will reside. The driver, a local, associates each feature of the landscape with some terrible event in the past: here is where a usurer was murdered, here is where a husband lay in wait to murder his wife's lover, there is where the Devil appeared to the driver's own brother, frightening his mule and causing it to plunge over the cliff, killing the brother.

They also pass a chapel dedicated to Mary, under the title Our Lady of the Roses. The chapel commemorates an ancient miracle: roses had blossomed in

January. But the miracle had not been welcomed by the local population. On the contrary, it had caused panic, since the people believed the miracle presaged disaster. Sure enough, that summer the cholera struck. And why, Spina asks, did the people build the chapel? The driver responds that it was done to calm the Madonna down. The implication, in other words, is that Mary herself was responsible for the cholera and that she had stopped the epidemic only because she had been mollified by the building of the chapel. This implication is reinforced by the fact that the chapel dedication associates Mary with the very event (roses blooming in January) that presaged the epidemic. Silone has thus created a fictional incident that suggests that Italian Catholics see the Madonna herself to be a source of danger and that, in asking for the Madonna's protection, they are asking only that the Madonna *not* sent calamities.

Silone is not the only author to suggest that Mezzogiorno madonnas were seen in this way. Carlo Levi (1902–75) would later make the same point in *Cristo si è fermato a Eboli (Christ Stopped at Eboli)*. The novel was based upon Levi's experiences during his exile to an isolated village in Basilicata in 1935–36. In describing the festa of the Black Madonna of Viggiano as it was practiced in that village, Levi (1963) writes: "Homage was paid to her in abundance, but it was rather the homage due to power than that offered to charity. The Black Madonna was like the earth; it was in her power to raise up and destroy. . . . To the peasants the Black Madonna was beyond good and evil. She dried up the crops and let them wither away, but at the same time she dispensed food and protection and demanded worship" (121).

This Mary, like the one who appears in Silone's work, is hardly the Mary so favored by the Universal Church, the Virgin-Mother to whom saints and sinners turn for warmth and nurturance. Nor is she a representation of the feminine side of a loving God, which is how many liberal Catholic commentators now interpret Mary. Rather, the Mary who appears in these works is a powerful goddess, who demands worship and who is willing to use her immense power over nature to coerce human beings into honoring her.

Silone and Levi were novelists, and it is possible that their portrayal of Mary reflects their own biases more than folk beliefs. Yet it is not difficult to turn up evidence in the literature on folk Catholicism in Italy that suggests that Silone and Levi were right on the mark in their characterization of Mary.

"I AM MARY. BUILD A CHURCH IN MY HONOR . . . OR ELSE"

Marian apparitions have always been common among Italian Catholics and are best regarded as hallucinations or illusions (for the distinction between these two terms, see chapter 3, n. 2). But this suggests that their content—like that of all hallucinations and illusions—has been shaped by psychological associations in the mind of the seer. It is precisely this fact that makes apparition reports a valuable source of data. In other words, by analyzing such reports we can uncover the psychological associations that define Mary in the mind of the Italian Catholic.

Quite often the first written account of an apparition appears several decades after the apparition is alleged to have occurred. In these cases, we are almost certainly not dealing with a direct report from the seer but rather with folklore—that is, a report transmitted by word of mouth. From a methodological point of view, such accounts are probably more valuable than accounts directly from a seer. Oral transmission allows the original account to be changed and modified, and I take it as axiomatic that it would be changed and modified to reflect the values and psychological associations common to the group in which it is circulating. With this in mind, what do we find when we examine accounts describing Marian apparitions in Italy?

THE MADONNA DELLA GUARDIA

The sanctuary dedicated to the Madonna della Guardia is located on Monte Figogna, just outside of Genoa. For centuries, this has been the single most popular sanctuary in Liguria. Tradition suggests that it was established as the result of an apparition. The earliest account of that apparition appears in a document dated 1530. The following is my condensation of the account, which appears in Domenico Cambiaso (1933):

> In the year 1490, a humble peasant named Benedetto Pareto was cutting hay for his flocks on Monte Figogna. Suddenly he looked up and saw a majestic lady standing before him. The woman said "Don't be afraid, Benedetto; I am Mary, the Mother of Jesus Christ." Mary told Benedetto that she wanted him to build a chapel in her honor on top of Monte Figogna. When he complained that he was only a poor peasant, she told him not to worry, that with her help he would find everything easy. She then rose to the sky and vanished. Benedetto returned home and told his wife about the event. But his wife did not believe him and ridiculed him for telling such a story. Humiliated, Benedetto no longer dared talk of the apparition and put aside the thought of carrying out Mary's order. The next day, while on his way to work, he climbed a tree to get some figs for breakfast. The branch his foot rested on broke and he tumbled to the ground. He was hurt so badly that he had to be carried home by other men. Benedetto prepared himself for death. He was sad for not having obeyed the Queen of Heaven, and he recognized that his fall was punishment for his disobedience. But Mary appeared to him again, at his bedside, and after gently reproaching him for his disobedience, she renewed the order to build a chapel. When she left, Benedetto was perfectly healed. (17–20)

Here the original legend breaks off, but later traditions suggest that the fact of his instantaneous healing convinced everybody (including Benedetto's wife) of the reality of the apparitions, and the chapel was built. Certainly, a chapel dedicated to Mary under the Madonna della Guardia title did exist on Monte Figogna by 1530. This small chapel developed into a sanctuary, which became the most popular Marian sanctuary in Liguria. It seems unlikely that it would have achieved such popularity unless the image of Mary conveyed in the apparition report was congruent with the image of Mary that prevailed in the general population. What is that image? Quite simply, the Mary in this legend is a Mary who punished poor Benedetto Pareto for failing to build a chapel in her honor.

It is not the fact that Mary punished somebody that is unusual. In their study of Marian apparitions in the nineteenth century, Victor and Edith Turner (1982) point out that the best-known of these apparitions fall into two categories. On the one hand are apparitions whose tone is gentle and whose content reinforces traditional Catholic doctrine. The Turners point to the apparitions at Lourdes as the paradigm of this type. On the other hand are apparitions whose tone is apocalyptic; that is, Mary says that the world will be punished by the hand of her divine son if it does not turn from its sinful ways. Here the paradigm is the apparition at LaSalette, France, in 1846. The Mary who appeared at LaSalette warned of failed harvests, famine, and the consequent death of young children unless people fulfilled their religious obligations (like attending church and not eating meat during Lent).

This apocalyptic tradition has continued. The message associated with the apparitions at Fatima, Portugal, in 1917 was clearly apocalyptic: Mary asked the world to pray the rosary for the conversion of Russia and added that, if this was not done, Russia would spread its errors throughout the world, provoking "war, famine [and] persecution of the Church" (McGrath 1961: 194). William Christian (1984) pointed out that this emphasis upon an apocalypse provoked by the success of communism was part of a number of the Marian apparitions occurring in post–World War II Europe.

But the apparition associated with the Madonna della Guardia does not fall easily into either of the two categories identified by the Turners. A madonna who causes the body of Benedetto Pareto to be mangled can hardly be compared to the gentle lady who appeared at Lourdes. At first sight, there might appear to be a superficial similarity with the Marys of LaSalette and Fatima, but this similarity breaks down upon closer inspection. The Marys who appeared at LaSalette and Fatima threatened punishment because there was too much sin in the world, and their concern was to get people to abandon their sinful ways. These madonnas, in other words, were solidly Tridentine beings, working hard to promote the moral and religious codes endorsed by the Universal Church. The Madonna della Guardia, on the other hand, punished for a different reason, one that had nothing to do with sin, as the term is usually understood in the official Church. Poor Benedetto was hurled to the ground and mangled because he had not helped Mary erect the chapel she had requested. The punishment in this story is a personal matter between a goddess who wishes to be worshipped and a devotee who isn't quite ready to help her carry out that wish.

WITHERED ROSES AND DEAD PRIESTS

The particular castigation meted out to Benedetto Pareto was designed only to provoke compliance with this madonna's wishes and did not produce (as far as the story is concerned) any lasting damage. In other traditions, however, a madonna sends castigations that seem purely vindictive; certainly the consequences are more serious. For example, one of the more important Marian sanctuaries in Emilia is the one dedicated to the Beata Vergine della Sassola at Campogalliano. Legend has it that an image of the Virgin attached to an outdoor pillar had been venerated in the area for some time as a result of its association with prodigies (Bisi 1966: 65–67). On 25 May 1745, while a young girl named Domenica was praying before this image, the image came alive and said, "Domenica, Domenica, I am tired of being exposed to the inclement weather! It is my will that a church dedicated to me be constructed in this place. Communicate this order of mine to the parish priest at Campogalliano" (ibid., 66).

As often happens in such accounts, the initial report of the apparition was not accepted by Church authorities, represented in this case by the local parish priest. Two months later, on 31 July, the Madonna appeared a second time to Domenica and repeated her command; she also told the girl to bring to the unbelieving priest a rose that had been left at the base of the pillar and that was now withered. In the presence of the priest, just as he was once again about to scoff at Domenica's report, the rose became fresh and flooded the air with a heavenly fragrance. This was followed by other prodigies associated with the image, and eventually a church was built.

Most devotional guides to Marian sanctuaries in Italy stop at this point in the story. Nevertheless, there arose a folk tradition in the region that suggests that the premature death of the parish priest who at first blocked the madonna's request (this priest did in fact die in 1746) was "attributed to a just castigation from heaven for having so tenaciously opposed devotion to the sacred image" (ibid., 67). The people of Campogalliano, in other words, were quite at ease in seeing Mary as a vengeful goddess willing to shorten the life of someone who had opposed her cult, even though that person had relented and even though the sanctuary had been built.

Madonnas That Maim

THE MADONNA DELL'ARCO

One of the most important sanctuaries in Campania is the sanctuary dedicated to the Madonna dell'Arco, located in a small town near Naples. The devotees of this particular madonna are called *fujenti* (those who flee), and associations of *fujenti* exist in towns and villages throughout Campania. On the first Monday after Easter, the members of these organizations converge on the sanctuary to take part in a massive parade and to make votive offerings to the Madonna dell'Arco for favors received. As recently as the early 1970s, the number of *fujenti* attending the festa each year reached 25,000.[2]

The origin legend[3] associated with this sanctuary suggests that on 6 April 1450, some men were playing *palla e maglio* in the open space in front of an *edicola*, whose madonna was called the Madonna dell'Arco.[4] One of the players bungled his shot, and his ball struck a lime tree that shaded the *edicola*. Enraged, the player took the ball and threw it against the image of the Madonna. The ball hit her on the cheek and the cheek began to bleed. Frightened by what he had done, the young man wanted to flee, but found himself moving around and around the *edicola*, like a fool, without being able to leave the spot. After a summary proceeding headed by the count of Sarno, who had been passing by with his men, the man was hanged. Here again, someone is killed for not showing Mary the proper respect. True, in this case the punishment was meted out by a human court, not by Mary, but that detail was changed in the next punishment tradition to develop around the Madonna dell'Arco.

This tradition suggests that on the Monday after Easter in 1589, Aurelia del Prete, of the village of Sant'Anastasia (the village where the Madonna dell'Arco sanctuary is located) went with her husband Marco to the *edicola* of the Madonna dell'Arco. Marco had just been cured of a severe eye disease and went to make a votive offering. Aurelia had a small pig with her, and somewhere near the *edicola* the pig got away.[5] Aurelia's husband continued to move forward devoutly with the wax candle he had brought as an *ex voto*. His apparent indifference to her plight enraged Aurelia, and she exploded with a string of blasphemies against the Virgin. Marco reproached her, saying that her sacrilege was all the more serious given the favor he had received. But Aurelia was beside herself. She grabbed the *ex voto* from his hands, threw it to the ground, and trampled it. She continued to curse the Madonna, her festa, and everybody that participated in it. Exactly one year later, during the night before the festa, Aurelia's feet detached from her legs.

That the detachment of Aurelia's feet was seen by cult members as a punishment for her impiety (something only implicit in the 1608 text of the legend) is clear from a line on the cornerstone of the sanctuary erected in 1593: "To the Madonna dell'Arco [in reparation] for the blasphemer Aurelia who was punished in her feet [*castigati nei piedi*] on the 20th day of April in the year 1590." Indeed, the fact that this legend is the one mentioned on the cornerstone, not the one about the ballplayer who was hung, suggests that the legend of Aurelia del Prete was the more popular.[6]

This theme of an impious person severely punished by the Madonna appears in connection with a wide range of sanctuaries in Italy. Elisabetta Grigioni (1975) has surveyed stories of this sort; her examples include the following:

1. The Madonna del Popolo, Bologna: A soldier urinates against a wall on which had been painted an image of this madonna. He is struck blind and suffers strong pain "in the parts that offended the Madonna." He repents and is healed.
2. The Madonna del Sasso, Lucca: Losing a game, a soldier throws a stone against an image of the madonna. The earth opens up and swallows him.
3. The Madonna dei Miracoli, Lucca: A soldier who loses at dice hurls the dice against an image of the Virgin, but in doing so breaks his arm.
4. The Madonna Capreolana, Puglia: A Turk tries to hack an image of the Virgin to pieces with his scimitar, but falls dead.
5. The Madonna della Vendeta, Naples: During a siege of Naples, Pietro Aragonese hurls a cannonball against a sanctuary of the Virgin. The ball bounces back and kills him.
6. The Madonna di Baracano, Bologna: Two soldiers play at dice, and the loser strikes an image of the Virgin with a stone. The impious soldier is struck by lightning, and the surviving soldier is hanged, along with the corpse of his companion.
7. The Madonna della Villa, Palermo: A game player wounds an image of the Madonna and is condemned to death. A stone springs out miraculously from a wall so that it can be used for his hanging.

These stories may seem to modern readers like folktales, since only in folktales do we now normally encounter people struck by lightning, swallowed by the earth, and so on. Yet Grigioni culled them from the *Atlas marianus* (*Marian Atlas*). This work was originally published in 1652 by the German Jesuit Wilhelm Gumpennberg, and it made use of previous works on Marian sanctuaries as well as reports that Gumpennberg collected from contemporaries. It was subsequently updated by a later editor and republished in 1839–46. Silvano Cavazza (1981: 91) notes that Gumpennberg's work was not devotional literature aimed at the general public but a serious work meant to be included in the libraries of seminaries and convents. It was, in short, a reference work. The reports in the *Atlas marianus* (like those cited above) should be seen for what they represented themselves to be:

matter-of-fact accounts of miraculous events that in the eyes of a great many people had really occurred.

Accounts of vengeful madonnas who punish the impious were still being collected by investigators even in the early twentieth century. In Sardegna, for example, the people of Gúspini believed that a local statue of Nostra Signora dell'Assunta was flesh and blood and that the statue had once killed a man who pricked it with a pin in order to demonstrate (as he thought) that it was made of wood (Bottiglioni 1922: 119–20). At Cagliari (also in Sardegna) people believed that a soldier who in his anger stabbed a statue of the Madonna della Mercede was similarly killed (ibid., 15). Simply violating the prescribed rules surrounding the celebration of a madonna's festa can bring retribution. Another legend in Sardegna, for instance, relates how some peasants decided to do their threshing on the festa of the Madonna del Carmine (thus violating the taboo against working during the festa); as punishment, the threshing floor collapsed, killing the peasants and their horses (ibid., 132).

In all the cases considered so far, the people punished by the Madonna had undermined her cult by impiety or, at least, were reluctant to actively promote her cult. But other traditions make it clear that even those who are willing to promote her cult can be harmed.

THE TOUCH THAT DAMAGES

The sanctuary on Monte Berico near the city of Vicenza is one of the more important Marian sanctuaries in the Veneto region. The origin legend in most modern accounts (Medica 1965: 187–90; Marcucci 1983: 114) goes like this:

In the early decades of the fifteenth century, a poor peasant woman named Vincenza Pasini would leave the city of Vicenza each day and climb nearby Monte Berico in order to take a meal to her husband, who worked there in a small vineyard. It was Vincenza's custom on these occasions to pray before a wooden cross on the mountain. On the morning of 7 March 1426, while praying before this cross, the Virgin Mary appeared to Vincenza and told her that the plague currently raging in the area would stop if a sanctuary was erected to her (Mary) on this spot. Mary took the cross and traced the outlines of the desired sanctuary in the ground, and then plunged it onto the exact spot where she wanted the main altar to be placed. Vincenza reported her experience to those in the town, but no one believed her, and the plague continued. On 2 August 1428, on the same spot as before, Vincenza had a second apparition, and this time she was believed. Within three months, the sanctuary had been constructed.

There is a detail missing from this modern account that was routinely included in older accounts of this apparition. The account in Sebastiano Rumor (1911: 43), for instance, speaking of the first apparition to Vincenza, says,

> she [Mary] appeared in the form of a royal lady, adorned in bright golden vestments, filling the air with the fragrance of a heavenly perfume. Confronted with this wondrous sight, the poor woman fell to the ground in bewilderment; but the Virgin, putting her hand on Vincenza's shoulder and, comforting her with a celestial smile, said to her: Do not fear, Vincenza, I am Mary, the Mother of God, who died on the cross for the well-being of the human race.

The key detail here is that Mary touched Vincenza as she was lifting her from the ground. The text suggests that this touch was a source of comfort and reassurance for Vincenza. But other traditions surrounding this apparition suggest that Mary's touching of Vincenza was not always seen in so benign a light by the public.

During the ecclesiastical investigation held in 1430, it was established that this touch had left five marks (corresponding to Mary's five fingers) on Vincenza's body. The marks were "bright" and were in the shape of "roses." The Latin word used in the original report, however, was *stigmata*, which Rumor (1911: 48) translates into Italian as *stimmate*. In most religious contexts, but especially in Italy, *stigmata* and *stimmate* refer to wounds that bleed, the connotation that would certainly be evoked in the mind of the average Italian Catholic who heard this story. That Mary's touch had caused some physical damage to Vincenza was reinforced by a tradition that arose in the mid-seventeenth century. In a cemetery near the sanctuary, bones thought to be those of Vincenza Pasini were found; the "right shoulder bone . . . was found soft and reddish, similar in appearance to meat, made that way by the miraculous impression put there by the hand of Mary" (ibid.).

What we catch sight of in these official reports is a popular tradition of Mary as a mother whose very touch caused bleeding and internal damage. This is all implicit, I grant, but remember that we are dealing with official reports, and the image of Mary as a mother who harms even those trying to help her has no place within the logic of official Catholicism. Even so, the references to bright red *stimmate* and to a shoulder bone made soft by Mary's touch shows us a Mary who is a source of danger and harm, even to her devotees.

So far, we have considered evidence of madonnas in Italy as sources of danger to human beings. Saints too have their darker side.

"EVERY SAINT SENDS HIS ILLNESS"

On 6 and 7 August the villagers of Montesano, on the Salentine peninsula (the "heel" of the Italian boot) in Puglia, celebrate the festa of San Donato.

Madonnas That Maim

They come to implore the saint to cure those afflicted with *il male di San Donato*, really a collection of maladies, including epilepsy, severe anxiety, and other nervous disturbances. Annabella Rossi (1969) interviewed many of those attending this festival in 1965 and found that they had no doubts about where these maladies, and indeed, all maladies, came from. One of those interviewed, the husband of a woman afflicted by the *male di S. Donato*, said, "The sickness of San Donato—our saint sends it, he sends it, and he takes it away. He wants it that way; he selects someone and sends him the malady. He sends it to the poor like us to make us suffer on this earth" (ibid., 25).

Another man, echoing the same sentiment, was more precise as to why the saint would do such a thing:

> The sickness of San Donato—he sends it, the saint sends it. They [those afflicted] scream night and day . . . the blessed San Donato sends all nervous diseases, all of them. Those [diseases caused by] the *taranta* [are sent by] San Paolo of Galatina, those of the ear [by] San Marco. . . . Every saint sends his illness and [so] holds onto his devotion: Santa Marina [afflicts] the head; San Pantaleo [sends] boils; San Rocco is patron of the plague. (ibid.)

San Donato, in other words, harms human beings for the same reason madonnas harm human beings: to maintain his cult. Nor is San Donato unique among saints. We have already encountered Sant'Antonio abate, the protector of domestic animals and one of the most popular saints in Italy. But like San Donato (and in fact all popular saints), Sant'Antonio abate is both loved and feared—loved for the protection he can bring and feared for the harm he can send:

> He [Sant'Antonio abate] is seen to possess an ambiguous power. Thus on the one hand there are beliefs about him that provoke terror . . . and other beliefs, by contrast, that portray him as the good-natured protector of the peasants and the humble, [someone] rough-hewn and cheerful. Certainly it is the second aspect that prevails [but the fact remains] that in the Abruzzo, Sant'Antonio, San Sebastiano, and San Biagio are saints that are very much feared. (Di Nola 1976: 208)

Alfonso Di Nola's informants had no difficulty in remembering stories illustrating the dark side of Sant'Antonio. In one such story, an older woman regrets having made too large an offering to the saint; that evening as she slept, she was burned in a mysterious fire. In another story, a butcher is chastised by his friends for working on the day of Sant'Antonio's feast. "What's so important about Sant'Antonio? I have to earn a living," he replies. Just afterward, while riding past the cemetery, the impious butcher's horse drops dead. In a third story, three young men confront the statue of Sant'Antonio as it is being carried in procession, and one of them jokingly offers the saint a cigarette. The man is immediately struck mute and blind.

Further evidence of the danger that was seen to emanate from Sant'Antonio can be found in Gregory Martin's *Roma Sancta* (1969: 42). In discussing some of the better-known churches and chapels of Rome, Martin calls particular attention to "the famous Aultar of S. Anthonie the holie Eremite, where such experience of Gods justice against false and blasphemous swearers hath been so manifestly declared that no Italian dare take an othe at that Aultar, which he knoweth false, for feare lest S. Anthonies fyre consume him, as there is at this day example thereof, a burnt carcasse under the Chappel doore." It is not at all important, at least in the discussion here, to decide if these stories about Sant'Antonio (or other saints) are based upon some "real" experience or if they are pure fabrications. What is important is that these stories reflect the same attitude found in connection with madonnas: a saint is both a source of danger and a source of protection from that danger.

THE SAINT AND THE SPIDER

A study of local religion in Italy frequently cited by Italian authors is Ernesto De Martino's *La Terra di Rimorso* (1968). While De Martino's theoretical framework has been heavily criticized, his work has had an enormous influence on the study of popular religion in Italy. The particular phenomenon studied by De Martino in this work is *tarantismo*, a cluster of beliefs and practices he encountered on the Salentine peninsula in Puglia (the phenomenon has also been reported in other areas of southern Italy). Central to *tarantismo* is the belief that certain individuals are bitten by a *taranta* (a type of spider), are afflicted with a malady, and can be cured only through ritual dancing. The *taranta* is usually identified, both by believers and by many outside observers, with the tarantula *(Lycosa Tarantula)*. De Martino (ibid., 59–60) notes, however, that in the popular imagination the *taranta* often acquires characteristics associated with other spiders and with scorpions.

Tarantismo has been described by any number of commentators over the centuries, including many non-Italians. The English traveler George Sandys (1615: 249), for instance, encountered *tarantismo* in Calabria and described the phenomenon like this:[7]

They [tarantulas] lurk in sinks and privies, and abroad in the slimy filth between furrowes. . . . The sting is deadly, and the contrary operations thereof most miraculous. For some so stung are still oppressed with a leaden sleepe:

others are vexed with continued waking, some fling up and down, and others are extremely lazy. He sweats, a second vomits, a third runnes mad. Some weepe continually, and some laugh continually, and that is the most usual. . . . The merry, the mad, and otherwise actively disposed are cured by musicke; at least it is the cause, in that it incites them to dance indefatigably.

A particularly good first-hand account of the disease appears in Dino Provenzal (1912: 12–13), who gives the testimony of a woman who had suffered the bite of a *taranta*:

I was gathering grain with the other women. . . . The sun came down in waves of fire and made breathing difficult for all of us, so much so that we left our work before noon and lay down in the shade of a small wall. After eating a bit of bread, I tried to close my eyes to keep out the sun. Suddenly, something startled me and at the same time I felt a strong pain in my hand. I stood up and looked for the cause of the pain but saw nothing. Then suddenly I understood: I had been bitten by a *tarantola*. I started to cry: how unfortunate I was. For the poor this is a great misfortune, since it is a condition that lasts a long time and keeps them away from their work. When I returned home, I tried to cure the problem with various medicines and concoctions, but nothing worked. The problem pressed upon me for some time. . . . I understood that there was only one thing I could do: I had to dance. From that point on I almost never slept. Continual pain gripped my entire person. This however was nothing: the main problem was a profound melancholy that assaulted my soul. Everything appeared dark, dark; people [seemed] dressed in black, things [seemed] painted black. The thought of death weighed down my spirit. I thought that if I died I would be leaving a poor man with four children, the youngest of which was only two years old! During the two or three days of preparation before the dancing, I could not touch food. The night before I was on my feet the entire time, wandering continuously through the house. I felt short of breath, as if a "hand of iron" were gripping my chest and my heart.

The suggestion that the disease is caused by the bite of a real spider (either a tarantula or some other type) is the first hypothesis that De Martino (1968) considered. There are poisonous spiders in the region of Puglia where *tarantismo* is found. That real spider bites might be the cause of these maladies seems consistent with the fact that cases of *tarantismo* do increase during harvest, when those harvesting the crops (like the unfortunate woman in the passage cited above) are most likely to come into contact with poisonous spiders. Nevertheless, some social patterns associated with *tarantismo* suggested to De Martino that something else was going on.

First, reports by medical doctors who treated cases of spider bite in the hospital indicate that the vast majority of those bitten are male. However, the majority of the victims of *tarantismo* are female. In De Martino's sample, women account for thirty-two (86 percent) of the thirty-seven *tarantate* that he identifies (ibid., 48). Historical sources describing *tarantismo* also suggest that the majority of victims are female.

Then there is the cyclical nature of the disease: once having been bitten by a spider, a *tarantata* usually experiences the disease over and over again, year after year. The centrality of this observation is seen in the title of De Martino's book, *La Terra del Rimorso*, which is really a pun that does not translate into English. One of the meanings of *rimorso* in Italian is close to the English *remorse*, and so at one level *Terra del Rimorso* refers to the remorse generated by life in Puglia (and the Mezzogiorno generally). But *morso* also means *bite*. Since the suffix *ri-* in Italian functions in much the same as *re-* in English, it implies "to do again." Thus *rimorso* connotes being bitten again. In this sense *La Terra del Rimorso* refers to a land where certain unfortunates, once bitten, are condemned to suffer the effects of spider bite again and again.

These social patterns suggested to De Martino that *tarantismo* has a psychological origin. But if so, why do cases increase around harvesttime? For De Martino, the association is spurious and is produced by the fact that harvesttime coincides with the approach of the feast of San Pietro and San Paolo and the fact that San Paolo is associated with *tarantismo*. Only San Paolo can release the *tarantata* from the malady caused by the spider bite, and it is to San Paolo that a victim appeals for release during her ritual dancing.

There are in fact two forms of ritual dancing associated with *tarantismo*. One is associated specifically with the festa of San Pietro and San Paolo on 28 June, when *tarantate* from all over the Salento region, along with their friends and families, gather at the chapel dedicated to San Paolo in the town of Galatina. Galatina is believed to be under the protection of San Paolo, which is why (so the belief goes) people from the town of Galatina are never bitten by a *taranta*. At this chapel (either inside or out in front), the *tarantate* engage in ritual dancing. When finished, each dancer takes a drink from a miraculous spring at the chapel.

Ritualized dancing also takes place in a private home in or near the *tarantata*'s home village, usually before the visit to Galatina. Local musicians are hired and a sheet is laid on the floor to define the area in which the *tarantata* must dance. Onlookers sit in chairs around the edge.

The dance is not at all standardized. On the contrary, the purpose of the dance is to imitate the motion of the particular spider that bit you, and these spiders have individual personalities. They are given names (Rosina, Peppina, Maria Antonietta, etc.), and they are assumed to have different temperaments (ibid., 62f.). Some are tiny "ballerina" or "singer" spiders and so react forcefully to the music; some are "sad and silent" so hardly react at all.[8] The home dancing continues until San Paolo gives release, which might not occur for hours. Often nothing at all happens the first day, and the group must gather again the next day, or even for the next few days, to continue the ritual.

Tarantismo is fascinating in itself, and De Martino's extensive photographs of the dancing make his study even more fascinating. When one looks at female *tarantate* lying prostrate from exhaustion on the pavement outside the chapel at Galatina or on a white sheet in the middle of a room, surrounded by people, it is difficult not to feel the presence of an authentic religious experience, which springs from within the people themselves.

De Martino is concerned with explaining the psychological functions of *tarantismo* and identifying its roots in the classical world. He argues that *tarantismo* allows for the systematic and regular discharge of tension produced by irresolvable psychic conflicts. One of the *tarantata*, for instance, was a woman who loved one man but had been forced to marry another. The resulting conflict could not be resolved, but it could be discharged periodically through ritual dancing. De Martino claims that *tarantismo* derives from various mystery cults originally found in ancient Greece. Although the basis for this derivation seems tenuous, there is no doubt that in its original form *tarantismo* was not associated with San Paolo. The first clear association of *tarantismo* and San Paolo appears only in the late 1700s, whereas the belief that music could cure the bite of a *tarantula* seems to have been widespread at least by the 1300s (ibid., 228–41).

How did San Paolo come to be linked with *tarantismo*? On the one hand, San Paolo is seen to have the power to protect people from spider bite. This association is established by a legend that has been circulating in the Galatina area since at least the eighteenth century (ibid., 107). According to this legend, the historical San Paolo came to Galatina to avoid his persecutors and was warmly greeted at the home of a religious (that is, someone who had received Holy Orders). To repay this religious for his piety, San Paolo established a miraculous spring at this person's house that cures those bitten by poisonous animals. Some version of this story is also used to justify the immunity from spider bite enjoyed by the people of Galatina.

Apart from his role as protector, San Paolo is seen to have the power to release the *tarantata* from her illness, at least temporarily. This release occurs when the saint talks to the victim during the course of her dance. For this reason, it is routine for bystanders to inquire if the *tarantata* has yet heard San Paolo: "Often [the *tarantata*] responds in a low and dreary voice to the questions directed at her by her family: "How do you feel" [they ask]— "Better"—"Has the saint talked to you?"—"Not yet"—"Will he talk to you tonight?"—"I don't know" (ibid., 71). The *tarantata* also talks with the *taranta*, the spider, and the saint and the spider are not entirely separate. As De Martino notes, "The great majority of *tarantate* carry on a dialogue with a [hallucinated] voice assumed to be that of the *taranta* or of San Paolo—or of San Paolo/*taranta*—or the *taranta*/San Paolo: the distinction was not always clear" (ibid., 93).

The fact that the two personalities are interweaved suggests that, within the logic of *tarantismo*, San Paolo *is* the spider who bit the *tarantate*—or at least, he is the one who sent the spider to bite the *tarantate*. De Martino concludes: "The relationship between the *taranta* and San Paolo . . . is extremely confused and contradictory. It involves the coexistence of several things: a San Paolo who protects the *tarantate* and from whom she asks for release, a San Paolo who sends the *tarante* in order to punish some offense, and a San Paolo/*taranta* or a *taranta*/San Paolo who is to be exorcised with music and dance" (ibid., 106). Later investigations suggest that this merging of San Paolo and the spider is one of the central features of *tarantismo*.

In a study of *tarantismo* in 1976, almost twenty years after De Martino and his team began their fieldwork, Miriam Castiglione and Luciana Stocchi (1978) found that certain aspects of the practice had been lost. They were not able, for example, to locate any instances of the home dancing studied by De Martino.[9] Dancing still took place, however, at the chapel at Galatina, and the identification of the saint and the spider was still strong. Castiglione and Stocchi conclude that the two symbols, San Paolo and the *taranta*, are "used interchangeably" (ibid., 162). These same investigators suggest that what we are confronting here is "the theme that the saint has the dual role of 'the one who punishes' and 'the one who heals.' " This of course is the same attitude Silone's fictional peasant had toward Mary, the same attitude that comes through the apparition accounts associated with various popular madonnas, and the same attitude we have encountered in connection with saints like Donato and Antonio abate.

But why San Paolo? That is, why is he in particular associated with *tarantismo*? One obvious basis for the association is the incident reported in the Acts of the Apostles (28:1–6), in which San Paolo is bitten by a poisonous snake while on the island of Malta and suffers no ill effect. But most likely the association of San Paolo with poisonous bites is not central to the phenomenon being studied here; it could just as easily have been another saint who was associated with such bites. In fact, De Martino (ibid., 46–47) notes that, in other parts of the Salentine peninsula in other times, both San Foca and San Francesco (Saint Francis of Assisi) have been accorded the ability to protect from poisonous bites. There is even a tradition that suggests it was Mary who established *tarantismo*:

Madonnas That Maim

Satan incites an evil woman to play a trick on the Virgin Mary by having her [the woman] hide some spiders in the collection box, so that those devoted to Mary might stay away from the Church. The Madonna then gets revenge by causing the spiders to become poisonous. Throughout eternity, these spiders will transmit their poison through continuous rebites, preferring especially women. (Castiglione and Stocchi 1978:179)

The particular association of the *taranta* with San Paolo, then, likely results from some chance set of circumstances, which could easily have been modified. What matters, given our theoretical concerns, is that the danger from the *taranta* always comes by way of a saint or a madonna.

Ex Voto

Myths and legends aside, the association of madonnas and saints with danger can be detected in connection with at least one other practice central to Italian Catholicism: the use of *ex voto*. An *ex voto* is an object that has been brought to a church, usually a sanctuary, as the result of a vow. In the usual case, a person brings an *ex voto* to a sanctuary after having been saved from some danger by a saint or a madonna. An *ex voto*, in other words, is not meant to solicit a favor but rather to testify to the largesse and power of the saint or madonna in question. As such, it must be publicly displayed. Sometimes this is done by affixing the *ex voto* to an interior wall of the church; it might be displayed in a special room adjacent to the main body of the church.

Virtually anything can serve as an *ex voto*. In her survey of the *ex voto* that appear in various Mezzogiorno sanctuaries, Annabella Rossi (1969: 166–70) found that clothing, coffins, jewelry, orthopedic devices, weapons, locks of hair, living animals, and cigarettes have been offered. But by far the most common are those that fall into one of four categories: (1) a body part made of pressed metal or wax, (2) a heart made of pressed metal, (3) wax candles, and (4) painted tablets *(tavolette dipinti)*.

A body part *ex voto* is usually a stylized representation of some particular part of the human body—an arm, a leg, eyes, a breast or breasts, a stomach, a chest. They are either two-dimensional or three-dimensional; today, the two-dimensional sort are the most common. Usually a person offers an *ex voto* corresponding to the part of his or her body that was cured or saved by the saint or madonna. In the special case where the recipient of the favor is a very young child, the *ex voto* will typically be a stylized representation of the entire body of the child. It is not uncommon, especially in the South, to find all the walls in a side chapel of a church or sanctuary plastered with *ex voto* of this type.

The Dark Side of Holiness

A heart *ex voto* is usually enclosed in an oval frame. Unlike a body part *ex voto*, the heart is not meant to be taken as a literal representation of the supplicant's own heart. Elisabetta Grigioni (1976, 1983) shows that in the eighteenth and nineteenth centuries the practice of "giving a heart" was a way of expressing a desire for mythical union with a supernatural being; it derived in large part from traditions surrounding the cult of the Sacred Heart of Jesus.[10]

The wax candles that serve as *ex voto* fall into two categories. Some candles are relatively short, two to eight inches in height, and of varying widths. Sometimes they are lit and placed in front of a side altar dedicated to the supernatural being that is being honored; sometimes—especially in large sanctuaries—there are special rooms off the main body of the church where metal stands are set up to hold them. Other candles are substantially larger, since their weight is proportional to the favor obtained (Castiglione 1981:158). These candles can easily be as tall as the human beings carrying them. Reporting on the festa in honor of San Rocco at Potenza (Basilicata), for example, F. Pulci (1894) reports that several of the *ex voto* candles carried in this saint's procession were over six feet high and two or three inches in diameter.

Most of the research on *ex voto* in Italy, however, focuses upon painted *ex voto*, the type of *ex voto* I consider here in detail. A painted *ex voto* is usually a painting on wood or canvas, measuring about one foot in height, and one to two feet in width, though they can be much bigger or smaller. These paintings are typically not done by the person discharging the vow but are commissioned from artisans specializing in these paintings. The paintings portray a scene involving the supplicant, and somewhere in the painting there is a representation of the supernatural being who has granted the favor. Since painted *ex voto* are usually associated with sanctuaries, and since most sanctuaries are Marian, this figure is usually a madonna. The overall structure of a painted *ex voto*, however, is much the same regardless of whether it is being offered to a saint or a madonna.

Occasionally, the person discharging the vow is represented in the painting in the act of prayer. In the vast majority of cases, however, what is portrayed is a scene associated with the danger from which the person discharging the vow was delivered. Many *ex voto* are bedroom scenes, for example, in which we see the devotee lying in bed, obviously afflicted with some illness. But easily the most dramatic *ex voto* are those that portray an outdoor scene, where we catch sight of the protagonist at the very moment of the calamity from which he or she will eventually recover. We see the protagonist being crushed by the wheels of a horse-drawn cart; falling from a building or into a well; being set upon by bandits; being tortured by the authorities; or being threatened with earthquakes, storms, floods, or other natural calamities.

Madonnas That Maim

Since the use of these *ex voto* has continued right into the twentieth century, some of the dangers depicted are quite modern. It is not uncommon at some sanctuaries to find *ex voto* depicting houses being bombed from the air, ships being hit by submarines, automobiles crashing into ravines, people falling from trains, and modern operating rooms with surgeons cutting into patients.[11]

The majority of *ex voto* carry an inscription, almost always a stereotypical formula. The most common are G. R. or R. G., for Grazia Ricevuta (grace received), P. G. R. for Per Grazia Ricevuta (for grace received), V. F. G. R. for Voto Fatto Grazia Ricevuta (Vow completed for grace received), and Ex Voto, or more simply, E. V.[12] These formulas are often accompanied by a text giving the name of the person who contributed the *ex voto*, the date, and some commentary on the incident that gave rise to the *ex voto*.

Although painted *ex voto* are found in shrines in all areas of Catholic Europe, they play a special role in Italian Catholicism.[13] First, the popular practice of bringing them to sanctuaries seems to have originated in Italy. Up until the late fifteenth and early sixteenth centuries, there were two distinct traditions with regard to *ex voto* in Italy: members of the upper class would commission paintings by professional artists, while the lower classes would usually contribute body part *ex voto*. During the sixteenth century, these two traditions fused, and painted *ex voto* came increasingly to be used by the lower classes as well as the upper classes. From Italy, the practice spread to other areas of Europe. By the seventeenth century, the use of painted *ex voto* was widely diffused throughout all levels of Italian society— upper and lower classes, rural and urban classes—and this pattern maintained itself for the next three centuries.

Historical origins aside, the use of these *ex voto* seems more common in Italy than in other Catholic countries. This is the conclusion reached by Mary Lee Nolan and Sidney Nolan (1989: 352), who visited 852 sanctuaries across western Europe as part of their statistical survey of over 6,000 sanctuaries. Certainly the sheer number of painted *ex voto* on display in Italian sanctuaries is impressive. Arnoldo Ciarrocchi and Ermanno Mori (1960) identify 175 Italian sanctuaries that still had collections of painted *ex voto* in the 1950s. (Table 4.1 gives the name and locations of the ten sanctuaries in the Ciarrocchi and Mori list with the largest collections of *ex voto*.) I have visited several sanctuaries with *ex voto* whose names do not appear on their list, and so the number of sanctuaries with *ex voto* must be even larger.

In considering these numbers, remember that they represent only a fraction of the *ex voto* that have been brought to these sanctuaries. In the past, older *ex voto* were routinely discarded to make room for new *ex voto*. In other cases, *ex voto* deteriorated or were lost because they were not cared for. In

The Dark Side of Holiness

TABLE 4.1

Italian sanctuaries with the largest collections of painted *ex voto*

Location of sanctuary	Person the sanctuary is dedicated to	Approximate number of painted *ex voto*
Naples (Campania)	Madonna dell'Arco	5,000
San Giacomo Filippo (Lombardia)	Assunzione del Gallivaggio	5,000
Foggia (Puglia)	Maria SS. Incoronata	2,000
Serralunga di Crea (Piemonte)	Santa Maria di Crea	2,000
Turin (Piemonte)	Madonna della Consolata	1,500
Bra (Piemonte)	Madonna dei Fiori	1,000
Crescentino (Piemonte)	Madonna del Palazzo	1,000
Millesimo (Piemonte)	Madonna del Deserto	1,000
Nova Ponente (Alto-Adige)	N. Signora di Pietralba	1,000
Pompei (Campania)	B.V. del Rosario	1,000

Source: Derived from Ciarrocchi and Mori (1960: 36–40).

the modern era, *ex voto* have been "discovered" by middle-class elites who see them as quaint examples of primitive art. Many have been stolen over the past century, which was not difficult given the poor security at most of the sanctuaries. Some idea of the losses of *ex voto* can be imagined by comparing older inventories of holdings with modern inventories. In 1851, for example, there were 240 painted *ex voto* at the sanctuary of the Madonna del Pozzo at Capurso (Puglia) (Triputti 1978: 184). In 1972, only 85 paintings were there (ibid., 185). This dramatic decrease occurred despite the fact that additional *ex voto* had been brought to the sanctuary over the intervening 120 years.

Now consider a question whose answer seems so obvious that the question has been ignored by the many scholars who have turned their attention to these paintings: Why do most painted *ex voto* portray the moment of danger? There are other possibilities. I have already mentioned that a minority of *ex voto* portray the donor in the act of prayer. Another option is to show the donor in good health, that is, as having been delivered from danger. In fact, *ex voto* showing the donor hale and hearty after having been delivered from danger have become increasingly popular in the post–World War II period. It is not uncommon now at some sanctuaries to see framed *ex voto* containing only a photograph of the now-healthy person discharging the vow and an identifying inscription. So the question remains: Why did traditional painted *ex voto* so consistently portray the moment of danger? At this point it will be useful to look more carefully at the iconography of these tablets.

SEPARATE SPACES

A point made by every investigator who has studied the iconography of these tablets is that they are all divided into two spaces, one occupied by the human protagonist and the other occupied by the madonna or saint who granted the favor. Some commentators make the point that "every votive tablet, precisely because it portrays the happy encounter between two worlds that are profoundly different, is composed of two registers: the upper register, which is the space reserved for the divine and the supernatural, and the lower register, which is the space reserved for the human, for the historic universe, for biographical fact" (Beffa, Gaggioni, and Snider 1980: 144). This contrast between the human and the divine portions of the *ex voto* is accentuated by a number of visual techniques.

Not only is the madonna (or the saint) typically placed in the upper part of the picture and the protagonist in the lower part, but these two figures are typically placed in opposite corners as well. Angelo Turchini's (1980) statistical analysis of 1,226 *ex voto* from the province of Brescia shows that the most common arrangement was to put the madonna in the upper left-hand corner of the picture and the protagonist in the lower right-hand corner. This seems to be the usual arrangement in most collections. Dramatic contrast is also conveyed by enclosing the madonna or saint in a large halo of light, often with clouds along the bottom edge of the halo, while portraying the rest of the scene, containing the protagonist, in more somber tones.

An *ex voto*, therefore, is a merging of two distinct scenes, one containing human actors and one containing a divinity. In other words, the saint or madonna does not appear in these pictures as a statue or other image that can be seen by the protagonist in the picture. Rather, two separate pictures are shown: a picture of the saint or madonna in Heaven and a picture of the protagonist confronting his or her particular danger. In any other context, the merging of two disparate elements within the context of a single picture would be taken to reflect a psychological association, and I see no reason not to draw the same conclusion here. This means that the thousands of painted *ex voto* on the walls of Italian sanctuaries are evidence of a psychological association *between some madonna or saint and the danger that threatened the protagonist*.

This association is not conscious. The conscious rationale offered by the devout always refers to the role played by the saint or madonna in saving them from danger. Nevertheless, putting conscious rationales aside and looking only at the evidence of the paintings, we see a visual association of the concepts *madonna* or *saint* with the concept *danger*.

CONCLUSION

The notion that supernatural power can be both benevolent and malevolent has long been part of the Judeo-Christian tradition; the biblical account of Job is proof enough. Even so, the God of the early Old Testament notwithstanding, most official Christian theologies tend to associate these two sorts of power with different supernatural beings. Thus the Christian pantheon is presided over by a benevolent God, who punishes only to support human morality. In specifically Catholic theologies, this God is surrounded by the saints and Mary, who can intercede with God in order to obtain benefits for humankind. Malevolence, if present, is usually associated with the Devil or other demons.

In this chapter, I have gathered evidence—from literary works, from apparition accounts and other items of folklore, from interviews conducted at festas, and from the iconography of painted *ex voto*—that points to the conclusion that, while the madonnas and saints worshipped by Italian Catholics are seen to have the power to cure and to protect, they are also seen as a source of danger. This danger has nothing to do with the punishment of sin as defined by the Church. It derives from something much simpler: the saints and madonnas of Italy want to be worshipped, and it is toward this end, the maintenance of their own cults, that they use their great power. This merger of nurturance and danger within the character of a saint or a madonna is a distinctive feature of Italian Catholicism.

I am aware that Italian Catholicism is not the only religious tradition to merge these attributes. William Christian's (1981) study of local religion in Spain during the early modern period, for example, suggests that Spanish saints, too, were often seen as sources of danger. Indeed, the occurrence of some natural disasters (a flood, the plague) on a particular saint's feast day was often interpreted in Spanish communities as a call from that saint for devotion and often led to that saint being adopted as the community's patron (23–69).[14] Outside the Catholic tradition, village deities in India, who are usually female, are also seen as sources of both nurturance and danger (Brubaker 1990). Nevertheless, while Italian Catholicism may not be unique in merging benevolence and malevolence within the character of an individual deity, such a merger is nevertheless central to an understanding of the cult of the saints and the Mary cult in Italy and is something very much outside the official Catholic mainstream.

5

REGIONAL DIFFERENCES

The idea that there are two distinct Italys has been around for a long time. In the early 1300s, for example, Dante Alighieri (1265–1321), in his book on Italian languages, spoke of two Italys. For Dante, the dividing line was the Apennine mountains: on the one side, he argues, are those lands that drain into the Tyrrhenian Sea, while on the other those that drain into the Adriatic (see Hay 1971). But almost all later investigators, while continuing to hold to a two-Italy schema, chose a different dividing line, preferring to contrast the North of Italy with the South.

The North is the Italy of the great city-states like Venice, Genoa, Florence, and Milan; of Rome and the papal states; of Renaissance painters like Da Vinci, Michelangelo, Raphael; of powerful leaders like Lorenzo de' Medici and Ludovico Sforza; and of political commentators like Machiavelli. More prosaically, contemporary Italian government reports define *Italia settentrionale* (northern Italy) as including Piemonte, Valle d'Agosta, Liguria, Lombardia, Trentino-Alto Adige, Veneto, Friuli-Venezia Giulia, Emilia-Romagna, Le Marche, Toscana, Umbria, and Lazio (SVIMEZ 1961).[1] The South includes those parts of continental Italy that were once part of the Regno di Napoli (the Kingdom of Naples), as well as the islands of Sicilia and Sardegna. This area is usually called the Mezzogiorno, and by modern convention is taken to include Campania, Abruzzo and Molise, Puglia, Basilicata, Calabria, Sicilia, and Sardegna.

FOREIGN SCHOLARSHIP

Most of the community studies by English-speaking scholars in Italy have been conducted in southern Italy. This scholarly bias in favor of the South

Regional Differences

seems to have been produced by two factors. First, North American scholarly interest in Italy has been structured by the fact of Italian immigration, and Italian immigrants to North America came overwhelmingly from the South. Second, most of these community studies have been carried out by anthropologists, and anthropologists have a disciplinary predilection for studying communities that are traditional, rural, and agricultural. Whether correctly or not, these attributes have been more often associated with Mezzogiorno communities than with northern communities.

Since most English-language discussions of popular religion in Italy are based upon these community studies of anthropologists, the net effect is that most descriptions of religion in Italy are really descriptions of religion in southern Italy. The overview of Italian religion by Phyllis Williams (1938), for instance, is derived mainly from information gathered from southern Italian immigrants to the eastern United States; Charlotte Gower's (1928) study of supernatural patrons deals only with communities in Sicilia; Edward Banfield (1958) studied a rural village in Basilicata; A. L. Maraspini (1968) and Carla Bianco (1974), rural villages in Puglia; Jan Brögger (1971), a rural village in Calabria; and so on. Even when English-speaking anthropologists do go beyond the bounds of the Mezzogiorno, they never go very far. Thus, Feliks Gross (1973) studied a village just to the south of Rome, and Sydel Silverman (1975), an Umbrian town that lies close to the geographical center of Italy. Given the fact that most Italo-Americans have roots in the South, and given the bias toward the South that exists in most of the English-language anthropological literature on Italy, it would be very easy for English-speaking scholars to form the impression that the South is the more populous region of Italy. One of the first things that should be established, therefore, is that the reverse is true.

Table 5.1 uses census data to indicate the regional distribution of the Italian population for selected years from 1871–1974. As is clear, the North has roughly twice the population of the South. This two-to-one ratio has

TABLE 5.1
Population of Italy, by region, selected years (%)

Region	1871 (N 27.4 million)	1891 (N 31.1 million)	1911 (N 35.4 million)	1931 (N 40.3 million)	1974 (N 55.2 million)
North	63	63	64	64	65
Mezzogiorno	37	37	36	36	35

Sources: Data for 1871, 1891, 1911, and 1931 derived from census data in SVIMEZ (1961: Table 14); data for 1974 derived from CICRED (1974).

Madonnas That Maim

maintained itself over the past century or so, despite the fact that Italy's population in this period has more than doubled and despite the massive outflow of emigrants during 1880–1920. Further, it seems likely that the ratio is long-standing. Using a variety of sources, Carlo Cipolla (1965: tables 1 and 2) estimates the population for a "standardized" Italy (that is, the regions included in the Republic of Italy since World War II) for various years going back to 1550. In every case, his estimates suggest that the North had about twice the population of the South.

ITALIAN-LANGUAGE SCHOLARSHIP

Although Italian-language scholars concerned with popular religion have also shown a bias in favor of the less populous South, this bias is not as strong as in the English-language literature. There are in fact a great many Italian-language studies of the local religion of northern communities; many are cited in this book. At this point, then, there is a large accumulation of individual studies—some in English, but most in Italian—that could be used to develop a comparative analysis of popular Catholicism in the two regions of Italy. A few investigators even call explicitly for an increased emphasis on comparative analyses of just this sort (e.g., Rosa 1976: 117–18). Unfortunately, most Italian scholars show an aversion to such analyses. It will be useful to consider this aversion to comparative analysis in detail, since the exercise will enable us to pinpoint a conceptual stumbling block that must be overcome if the study of popular religion in Italy is to progress.

ARROGANCE, *Tipicamente Britannica*

Denys Hay (1977: 1) begins *The Church in Italy in the Fifteenth Century* by noting that "in recent times church history in Italy has often been written at a very low level indeed." The remark outraged Italian scholars. It betrays, one author suggests, an "arrogance that was typically British." (Simoncelli 1979: 650). More generally, the remark was taken as being unfair and unjustified, since by the mid-1970s Italian scholars could cite any number of specialized studies dealing with the history of the Italian Church. Indeed, a specialized journal dealing with that subject, *Rivista di storia della Chiesa in Italia*, had existed since 1947. Furthermore, it can reasonably be argued that the publication of this journal, far from initiating an interest in Italian Church history, reflects a long-standing concern with such history within the Italian academic community.[2]

Regional Differences

In fairness to Hay, his larger discussion makes it clear that by "low" he does not mean slipshod or superficial, but narrow. Over and over, he returns to the same theme: Italian scholarship on Church history is far too descriptive; it is dominated by "petty local loyalties [and] *campanilismo*"; Italian scholars are often "obsessed with bibliography sometimes to the exclusion of reflection"; and so on. One consequence of the emphases identified by Hay is that Italian scholars have rarely investigated the important institutional processes associated with the Italian Church. Even Hay's critics grudgingly admit that he was the first to systematically investigate the progressive Italianization of the Curia in the fifteenth century (e.g., Simoncelli 1979: 651).

Italian scholars themselves often acknowledge this Italianate aversion to the study of institutional matters, though for them it is more likely to be a point of pride than a criticism. Gabriele De Rosa (1979: 168), for example, strongly condemns the *"mania sociologica,"* which he sees creeping into the study of the Italian Church. History, De Rosa argues, "is always made up of [subtle] distinctions, of exceptions, and diversity—all of which cannot be reduced to some monolithic scheme." Under the influence of De Rosa and others like him, it has become something of a *"mania italiana"* to argue that the study of religion in Italy must be based upon exhaustive investigation carried out at the level of the parish or, at most, the diocese.

The difference between the approaches espoused by De Rosa and Hay, respectively, is really the difference between what English-speaking philosophers of science call the idiographic and the nomothetic approaches, and it is one of the oldest debates in social science. The idiographic approach seeks to capture the richness and texture of a given situation at a given moment in history; the nomothetic approach seeks to find common patterns beneath different situations, often at different times in history, even if it means ignoring some obvious differences among the situations. In all national traditions, some scholars espouse one approach, some the other. Nevertheless, it seems fair to say that the Italian scholarly tradition, at least as it touches upon religion, is more idiographic than most.

Hay was talking about church history, but the Italianate emphasis upon the idiographic is found as well in studies of popular religion. It is routine to find Italian investigators specializing in the religious traditions of some particular locality in Italy, often the locality in which they themselves were raised. The only comparative analysis in these studies is between different communities in the same area, not between the locality being studied and some other part of Italy. Indeed, an emphasis upon the idiographic has so paralyzed Italian scholarship on religion that Italian scholars seem incapable of making analytic comparisons across regions, even when they keep stumbling upon a fairly dramatic regional difference over and over again.

Madonnas That Maim

The Step Not Taken

In 1969, a conference was held at Perugia on the *confraternite di disciplinati*. These were the confraternities established in the decades following the Flagellant Movement, which broke out in Perugia in 1260.[3] The *disciplinati* label seems to derive from the fact that public flagellations were a regular part of the ritual of the earliest of these confraternities. Very quickly, however, the flagellation element was dropped or deemphasized, although the label continued to be used. The distinguishing feature of *disciplinati* confraternities was not really flagellation but rather constitutions that encouraged members to imitate Christ and public processions in which members sang hymns in honor of Mary.[4]

One of the first presentations at the 1969 conference was Pier Melloni's (1972) summary of a "census" of these *disciplinati* confraternities in Italy, constructed from various archival documents. The first table in Melloni's report, showing the distribution of these confraternities by region, reveals a striking geographical pattern: fully 1,552 (96 percent) of the 1,615 confraternities established in Italy between the thirteenth and nineteenth centuries were established in northern Italy. The contrast is even more dramatic in the case of particular regions. While 467 and 354 *disciplinati* confraternities were established in the northern regions of Piemonte and Lombardia, respectively, only 8 were established in Campania, the region that includes Naples. The fact that the North enjoys a two-to-one advantage in overall population might account for part of this result but hardly all of it.

Surprisingly, this striking regional pattern was virtually ignored in Melloni's presentation. Another discussant (Morghen 1972: 198) has noted the pattern, but only as something that calls for future investigation. Later investigators like Mario Rosa (1976: 116–17) and Silvano Musella (1980: 343–44) make passing references to this fairly dramatic North/South difference, but it has never—as far as I know—been investigated in any depth. It would be difficult to imagine a more clear illustration of the Italian reluctance to systematically investigate regional differences in the practice of popular religion.

Stereotypical Differences

Everyone "knows" that there are global differences between the North and South of Italy. The South is economically underdeveloped; *la questione meridionale* is a problem faced by all Italian governments since Unification. The people in the two regions are different. Public opinion polls taken in Italy since the late 1950s regularly find that northerners are associated

~ 92 ~

with orderliness, rationality, hard work, and self-control. Southerners are associated with irrationality, disorder, impulsiveness, and passion. Just as important, these stereotypes are shared by both northerners and southerners, although southerners include a greater number of positive traits (generosity, a sense of humor, friendliness, etc.) in the southern stereotype.[5]

Such stereotypes are by no means restricted to the general public. Consider the following extract from a scholarly article:

> There are at least two basic "types" of Italian. First, there are those that in their personality and psychology look above all to the Mediterranean . . . and then there are those that look to the north, to the rest of Europe. . . . Those in the first category have a spirit that is more inflamed, more Mediterranean, and a religion that is more luxurious and more folkloric, while those in the second have a psychology that is substantially colder. The first have established themselves most of all in the southern part of the peninsula, the second in the *valle padana*. (Acquaviva 1975: 81–82)

The researcher who wants to understand Italy, however, must approach these stereotypes with caution. It is increasingly recognized that the traditional differences between the North and South are not all that traditional. A good case, for example, can be made for the assertion that the "underdevelopment" of the South was caused, or at least aggravated, by Unification. In connection specifically with popular religion, regional stereotypes are a particularly poor guide for predicting differences.

Consider, for instance, the matter of apparitions. If southerners *were* found to experience more apparitions, I suspect most Anglo-Saxons (and northern Italians) would see this as confirming the stereotype of the southerner as being more emotional. In fact, most apparitions have occurred in the North. Data on the regional distribution of apparitions in Italy can be extracted from Bernard Billet's (1973) study of Marian apparitions of the period 1927–71. Table 5.2 shows the regional distribution of seventy-four of the seventy-six apparitions in Billet's sample. The distribution of these apparitions matches precisely the distribution of the population in Italy (table 5.1). The North enjoys a two-to-one advantage in apparitions just as it enjoys a two-to-one advantage in population. In other words, northern Italian Catholics and southern Italian Catholics were equally likely to experience a Marian apparition during the period covered.

Now consider the matter of sanctuaries. By definition, these are churches that have become the object of pilgrimage. Acquaviva's suggestion that religion in the Mezzogiorno is more luxurious and more folkloric suggests that pilgrimages would be of more concern to southerners than to northerners. This in turn might lead to the prediction that sanctuaries would be more common in the South than in the North. Such a result, if found to be true,

Madonnas That Maim

TABLE 5.2

Marian apparitions and Marian and non-Marian sanctuaries in Italy,
by region

Region	Marian apparitions		Marian sanctuaries		Non-Marian sanctuaries	
	No.[a]	Percentage	No.	Percentage	No.	Percentage
North	48	65	1,106	72	145	65
Mezzogiorno	26	35	433	28	79	35
Total	74	100	1,539	100	224	100

Sources: Derived from Billet (1973); Marcucci (1983: 10).
[a]Does not include two of the Italian apparitions in Billet's sample, which I could not match up with a community in Italy.

would almost certainly be taken as confirming the stereotype. Table 5.2 gives the regional distribution of sanctuaries in the North and South. The regional distribution of non-Marian sanctuaries is exactly the same as the population distribution, and the small regional difference among Marian sanctuaries favors the North. If differences between northern and southern popular Catholicism exist, a reliance upon stereotypes will not get us very far in identifying and understanding them.

THE LAND WHERE TRENT NEVER ARRIVED

Gabriele De Rosa (1979: 172) suggests that the "religious history of the Mezzogiorno is the history of why the Tridentine reforms never came to be applied there in their entirety." De Rosa is fully aware that this judgment on the Tridentine reforms does not apply with equal validity to all regions of southern Italy. In particular, he acknowledges that Trent did make itself felt in the larger urban centers in the South (see Abbondanza 1987). De Rosa's point is that resistance to the Tridentine reforms was widely diffused throughout the South, a resistance much less characteristic of the North.

Certainly, the belief that religion in the South is less Tridentine than religion in the North is widely shared. What "less Tridentine" means is considered in more detail later in this chapter. For now, I will discuss the reasons commonly advanced to explain why Trent had so much less of an impact in the Mezzogiorno than in the North, as this will lead to a consideration of the one thing that, more than anything else, accounts for differences in popular Catholicism between the North and the South.

Barriers to Trent

The nature of diocesan organization in the South had much to do with the relative failure there of the Tridentine reforms. For centuries, the Mezzogiorno had far too many dioceses for its population. In the early nineteenth century, for instance, there were 131 dioceses in the Kingdom of Naples, as against 54 for all of Spain (Cestaro 1978: 103). As late as 1897, Lombardia (in the North) had 9 dioceses for a population of 3.5 million, while Puglia (in the South) had a staggering 32 dioceses for a population of only 1.5 million (ibid., 136). One result of the proliferation of dioceses in southern Italy was that any one southern diocese was generally far poorer than a northern diocese (Hay 1977: 11). This meant that southern bishops, even if they had wanted to "Tridentize" their diocese, had less income at their disposal to do it. Lack of income as much as anything else prevented the South from building and maintaining the seminaries that played such an effective role in producing a Tridentine clergy in the North.

But the relative poverty of southern dioceses was not all that worked against Trent. Pastoral visits—that is, visits by a bishop to the committees under his jurisdiction—were less common in the South. While this might be taken as an indication that southern bishops were less committed to the Tridentine ideology (which encouraged such visits as a means of control), the fact is that pastoral visits were less common in the South even in the 1400s, a century before Trent (Turchini 1977). This was partly due to the fact that, in the pre-Trent period, the South had a higher proportion of nonresident bishops than the North (De Rosa 1979: 171), partly to the fact that many episcopal sees were in areas difficult to reach and in which disease was endemic. Trent did require that bishops reside in their dioceses, but this ruling did not address the problems of rough terrain and disease. Furthermore, bishops in southern Italy were faced with a variety of local barons anxious to preserve and extend their privileges and resentful of intruders appointed by Rome. One result was that many southern bishops were "resident, but wandering," that is, resident in their diocese but unable to establish their See permanently in one place (De Rosa 1973a: 25).

Still, problems such as these should not be overemphasized. A bishop thoroughly committed to Trent could probably have overcome most of the obstacles mentioned. But there was one barrier that could not be overcome, which thwarted the implementation of Trent in the Mezzogiorno. This was the peculiar nature of parish organization in Mezzogiorno communities, especially those falling outside the ambit of the large cities like Naples.

Madonnas That Maim

Chiese Ricettizie

Based upon an analysis of reports *ad limina* made by Mezzogiorno bishops, Gabriele De Rosa suggests that, until the late 1700s, fully three-quarters of all Mezzogiorno churches, including some cathedrals, were *chiese ricettizie*.[6] A *chiesa ricettizia* was a church run collegially by a group of priests whose primary concern was the administration of the *massa commune*, the property that was collectively owned by the church. Each of these priests had a right to share in the revenues generated by that property. The number of priests participating in a given *ricettizia* could be quite large. In the seventeenth century, for example, the Cathedral at Melfi (in Basilicata) was a *chiesa ricettizia*, with forty-six participating priests (De Rosa 1979: 54). But what distinguishes the *ricettizie* most from other churches is the requirement that only priests of local origin could be "received" *(ricettizie)* into the church— that is, share in the *massa commune*.

Each participating priest was assigned a portion of the church's property, usually cultivated land, that was his to administer for a limited period of time, often three years. During this period, the priest was charged with properly maintaining his portion. The income deriving from the *massa commune* was divided among the participating priests.

These churches could be *numerate*, or *innumerate*, depending on whether the number of priests allowed to participate in the *massa commune* was fixed or open. They could also be *curate* or *semplici*, depending on whether or not they were concerned with the care of souls, that is, with the spiritual well-being of the local community. When the *ricettizia* was *curate*, the care of souls was administered collectively. This means that the tasks of saying Mass, administering the last rites, preaching, and so on, were equally the responsibility of all the priests. But it was not the income of the *massa commune* that was used to maintain the church building and the associated cults and devotions. On the contrary, such expenses were usually borne by local confraternities or families.

Having a son or sons admitted to the *ricettizia* was regarded as an important economic asset by his family. In entering a *ricettizia*, a man did not leave one world and enter another. Rather, he took on an occupation with a secure and steady income, which would maintain himself and his family. That the priests associated with the *ricettizia* were still members of their families is evident from the fact that they continued to live in their family homes. For this reason, *chiese ricettizie* were not associated with rectories of the sort typically associated with parish churches in the North.

Apart from those priests allowed to participate in the *massa commune*, a second class of clergy was associated with the *ricettizia*: those seeking participation. In the usual case, these nonparticipants had to serve an apprenticeship lasting several years. This meant performing duties, often quite menial, for no compensation whatsoever. Such duties ranged from sweeping and cleaning the church on a daily basis, to ringing the bells, to saying Mass. In a report written in 1771 on the *chiese ricettizie* in his diocese, the Bishop of Potenza notes that, after five years of service, a man could be admitted to a quarter share in the *massa commune*; after nine years, to a half share, and only after eleven years to a full share (ibid., 64). Even then, everything depended upon a secret vote of the participants, and such votes were hardly free from bias. Indeed, the nature of the *chiesa ricettizia* predisposed participants to favor relatives, which the bishop of Potenza deplored greatly. The situation for nonparticipants was worse in the churches that were *numerate*, since these men had to wait until one of the existing participants died. The Cathedral at Melfi, for instance, had been originally *innumerata*, and nonparticipants had been required to serve eight years before being admitted to the *massa commune*. In 1726, however, the number of participants was fixed at eighteen, with the result that many nonparticipants were denied access even after they had completed their eight years (ibid., 66).

As should be obvious by now, *chiese ricettizie* were not at all like parishes in the usual (read: Tridentine) sense of the term. Indeed, as De Rosa (ibid., 58) notes, "Strictly speaking, then, the *ricettizia* was not a parish but rather a private association of local priests, a closed corporation, to which no nonlocal priests could be admitted." What makes this closed corporation of local priests relevant to the failure of Tridentine reforms in the South is the fact that they were immune from the control of their bishop.

Each *chiesa ricettizia* was headed by a rector, who might also be called a vicar-curate, an abbot, or an archpriest. The rector was elected by the participating priests and usually held office for a limited term, not for life. In theory, the rector had to be certified as fit by the local bishop. But this certification was based on a fairly global assessment, and in practice it was virtually impossible for a bishop to reject the choice made by the participating priests.

But clearly the most serious handicap faced by local bishops was the requirement that priests admitted to the *chiese ricettizie*—including the rector—had to be of local origin. "A bishop who might have wanted to put forward priests who were more worthy and more prepared, priests committed to the proper doctrines, had his hands tied [by this requirement]; he could only work with those few parishes that were not *ricettizie*" (ibid., 173). In those parishes that were, he had to appoint from the local area, which severely limited the pool of available talent. The bishop's power was further weakened by the fact that the rights of the *chiese ricettizie* were enshrined in the laws of the Kingdom of Naples. Those laws dictated that disputes between *ricettizie* clergy and bishops were to be settled by civil authorities. The tendency of the state in such disputes was to side with the *ricettizie*, since by strengthening the *chiese ricettizie* state authorities not only weakened Rome's ability to interfere in the internal affairs of the kingdom but also insured that revenues that might otherwise go to Rome stayed in the local area.

THE *Ricettizie:* AN ANGLO-SAXON BLIND SPOT

Despite the centrality of the *chiese ricettizie* to an understanding of why Trent "never arrived" in the Mezzogiorno, these churches have been ignored in the English-language literature. Certainly the anthropological community studies cited earlier make no mention of the *chiese ricettizie* or of the type of priest associated with them. The oversight was likely due to the fact that these studies were conducted during the twentieth century, when the *chiese ricettizie* had passed out of existence, and the fact that anthropologists have a disciplinary predilection for assuming that societies that appear traditional are also static.

Less understandable is why the *chiese ricettizie* are ignored in a work like Denys Hay's (1977), which considers in detail the structure of parish organization in the North. Hay's only comment on parish organization in the South is to suggest, quite misleadingly, that the small size of southern dioceses allowed them to function as parishes (ibid., 24). Peter Burke's (1986) otherwise excellent account of the Italian Renaissance, which includes a section on religious organization, also ignores the *ricettizie*. The explanation for this neglect of the *ricettizie* probably lies with the fact that both these works were written in the early 1970s, when De Rosa and his colleagues were just beginning to stress the importance of the *chiese ricettizie.*[7]

A failure to take the *ricettizie* into account is not just a characteristic of the older English-language literature. Consider the following passage, which appears in a recent assessment of the effects of Vatican II on Italian Catholicism:

> For the conservative Italian church prior to [Vatican II], the priest's activity had been restricted to his sacramental role. . . . The emphasis on ministry with the community that emerged from the Council therefore represented a radical change from accepted practice. . . . *This was particularly so in the south, where the priest was traditionally a figure of authority set apart from the community* and could not achieve closer involvement without the risk of scandal. (Furlong 1988: 123; emphasis added)

Regional Differences

The reference to tradition suggests that the author is discussing a long-standing pattern, and yet—as should now be clear—this was not at all the traditional pattern. The strong tie of the *ricettizie* clergy to the local environment insured that the local population would not look upon priests as a class apart. On the contrary, local priests were men like themselves (cf. De Rosa 1979: 30–31). They rose early in the morning, dressed in normal clothes, went out into the fields and sweated under the Mezzogiorno sun, and had intercourse with women just like other men. These are the very things that led Tridentine bishops to call the southern priests corrupt; but to his neighbors such things simply meant that he was a normal male. These priests were generally popular, and complaints about them came from the bishops, not the people (De Rosa 1973b; 1977b). It was precisely because the priests of the *ricettizie* were *not* separate from the people that the Trent never arrived in the Mezzogiorno.

THE *Ricettizie* COMPARED TO NORTHERN PARISHES

In northern Italy, the structure of parish organization was quite different (Hay 1977: 20–25; Chiappa 1974; del Grosso 1983). Parish organization in the North starts with the *pieve*. This was a type of church that began to appear throughout northern Italy from the fifth century A.D. onward. Its distinctive feature is that it was a church at which baptisms could be performed, and this fact made it the administrative focus of satellite churches and chapels with no baptismal rights.

The archpriest who headed a *pieve* was quite often elected by the local laity. Denys Hay (1977: 24) notes that this pattern was already common in many areas of northern Italy by the late Middle Ages. In other areas, it was introduced in the modern period. In 1626, for example, the congregation associated with the *pieve* in the community of Pellestrina (near Venice) were granted the right to elect their archpriest indirectly, through elected representatives, and in 1776, the members in good standing of the local Eucharistic confraternity at Pellestrina were given the right to elect their archpriest directly (Gambasin 1980).

Over time, more and more of the churches dependent upon a *pieve* came to demand—and be granted—baptismal rights. Hay sees this as resulting from two things. First, there was the impracticality for those living in outlying settlements to travel to a *pieve* to baptize their children. Second, there was the matter of local pride—that is, of local communities wanting their chapel to have the same status as the more distant *pieve*. Whatever the process, the proliferation of local churches having baptismal rights did occur and did weaken the primacy of the *pieve*. It was not at all uncommon for one of these satellite churches to eventually eclipse in importance the *pieve* on which it had originally been dependent. In any event, the increasing autonomy of these churches from their *pieve* gave rise to the modern system of neighborhood parish churches.

Unlike the priests of the *chiese ricettizie*, the priests and archpriests who administered these northern churches were subject to their bishop in all things relating to the care of souls. Also unlike the *ricettizie*, northern churches typically were maintained by an endowment, which took care of the church building and various cultic activities. Even when this endowment was administered by lay members of the parish, they were held strictly accountable to the bishop for its administration (Cestaro 1978: 102f.). In the South, remember, such costs were met from contributions from local confraternities and other pious organizations, not from the revenues associated with the *massa commune*.

Local parishes in the North, then, were strictly subordinated to the local bishop, in both spiritual and financial matters, and it was this that enabled Tridentine bishops to have far more influence in the North.

THE ORIGINS OF THE *Ricettizie*

There is still a fair amount of debate over the origins of the *chiese ricettizie*. Eighteenth-century commentators favor the view that the *ricettizie* were a continuation of the communal organization that had been a part of the earliest Christian communities. However, there is no evidence of a continuous tradition of communal organization that dates from the early Christian era, and this hypothesis is now regarded as a self-justification put forward by those defending the *ricettizie*.

Another hypothesis, and the one favored by De Rosa and several others, is that the *chiesa ricettizie* is a Spanish import. Two pieces of evidence lend support to this possibility. First, *chiese ricettizie* did exist in Spain (although no one seems to be quite sure how common they were). Second, the first clear mention of the *ricettizie* in ecclesiastical regulations occurs in the records of the Twenty-fourth Session of the Council of Trent, held in November 1563. This suggests at the very least, that such churches were relatively common by then. What makes this significant, at least for those who prefer the Spanish origin hypothesis (Delle Donne 1973: 1030), is that this first reference appears in the period following the beginning of Spanish rule.[8]

Other investigators reject the Spanish origin hypothesis and argue that the *chiese ricettizie* developed autochthonously. In support of this possibility, they point to records that indicate that a few churches resembling the *chiese ricettizie* existed during the Middle Ages in southern Italy. In a variant of the autochthonous origins hypothesis, Giovanni Vitolo (1982, 1984) argues not so much that the *chiese ricettizie* existed in the Middle Ages as that they developed from other institutions that did exist then. He suggests that it was common in many areas for the laity not simply to elect their local priests but also to take an active role in administering church property. Over time, he argues, this active lay intervention became passive but gave rise to the insistence that local priests be natives of the area.

The biggest problem with the hypothesis of autochthonous development is that it does not explain the absence of the *chiese ricettizie* in the North. As Silvio Tramontin (1977) points out, most features associated with the *chiese ricettizie* in the South can also be observed in the North: some churches in the North had strong local input, if only because they elected the arch-priest; some northern churches were organized collegially; and many northern priests made a living from church land. But somehow, in the North, none of these things ever gave rise to the requirement that priests be of local origin, which is the one element that most distinguishes the *chiese ricettizie* from other types of churches and that most insured that popular Catholicism in the South would be insulated from the efforts of Tridentine reformers.

But if there is disagreement on the historical origins of the *chiese ricettizie*, there is one point upon which everyone seems to agree: the *ricettizie* were ideally suited to the closed local economies of the South.[9] If this is correct (and I suspect it is), the issue of precise origin is not important. Possibly the *chiese ricettizie* were introduced by Spain, possibly they developed autochthonously, possibly both things happened. Whatever way they were introduced into the South, the fact that they were ideally suited to a society composed of closed local economies explains why they proliferated in the South, where such economies lasted far longer than they did in the North.

THE DECLINE OF THE *Ricettizie*

The first attacks on the *chiese ricettizie* came from the southern monarchy itself.[10] In 1797, for example, Fernando IV issued new rules governing the *ricettizie*. One of his stated goals was to insure that using years of service as a criterion for achieving participation in the *massa commune* did not preclude entrance on the basis of merit. Toward this end, applicants were required to take a written test. But the concern here was only to establish minimum levels of competence, and the requirement of local origin was left intact.

A more serious assault on the *ricettizie* came during the *Decennio*, the period of French rule, which lasted from 1806 to 1815. During the *Decennio*

Madonnas That Maim

much of the property controlled by lay religious organizations was seized and put under the direct control of the state. This deprived the *ricettizie* of the contributions from local confraternities that had previously been used to defray the costs of the church building and associated cultic activities. Moreover, the strong ties of the *ricettizie* clergy to their own families, the private nature of the income they derived from the *massa commune*, and the fact that lay patrons had originally established the *ricettizie* made the *ricettizie* vulnerable under the new laws, and many of their properties were seized. The net result was that by the end of French rule the number of local churches that were *ricettizie* had been significantly reduced. By 1820, only 29 percent (1,087 of 3,734) of the parishes in the continental Mezzogiorno were *ricettizie*.

The end of French rule did not bring a reprieve for the *chiese ricettizie*. On the contrary, the Restoration brought with it a new alliance between the monarchy and Roman authorities, with the result that the state now supported (rather than hindered) attempts to reduce the autonomy of the *ricettizie*. In particular, the state supported a program of reform initially proposed by Bishop Carlo Maria Rosini of Pozzuoli. Rosini's plan aimed at reducing the number of participating priests in a *ricettizie* until it reached a number justified by the religious needs of the local population and the income associated with the church. The plan also aimed at increasing the importance of the archpriest (thus making him more like the typical pastor of a parish in the North) by requiring that his income be one-third higher than the other participants.

The final blow to the *chiese ricettizie* came in 1866–67, when the new Italian state passed a law allowing the seizure of ecclesiastical properties. Despite claims by the *ricettizia* clergy that the *massa commune* was held and administered collectively, state authorities decided (with some justification) that it was composed of a number of segments, each held individually. The result was that most of the property associated with the *chiese ricettizie* was seized and sold at auction. Those same laws left most of the property held by northern parishes intact. The net result was that the very process that undermined the *ricettizie* and insured that ecclesiastical organization in the South would come more and more to resemble the more Tridentine North also insured the impoverishment of these new southern parishes.

The era of the *ricettizie* in the South lasted something like three centuries, from the mid-1500s to the mid-1800s. The unique nature of the *ricettizie* insured that the local priest in the South was quite different from the local priest in the North. It is only to be expected that this difference would have an influence on the forms of popular Catholicism that developed in the North and South—and it did.

Regional Differences
THE EFFECTS OF THE *Ricettizie* ON POPULAR CATHOLICISM

The fact that the priests who administered the *chiese ricettizie* were only weakly controlled by their local bishop explains why they could not easily be pressured into adopting Tridentine emphases. But the structure of the *chiese ricettizie* did more than just insulate them from Trent. The insistence upon local origin, the strong ties to family, the economic importance of the *massa commune* in the local economy—all of these things worked to insure that local priests would share the same beliefs as those living in the area. Priests associated with the *chiese ricettizie* were thus naturally far more indulgent toward forms of popular piety, often involving magic, than their northern counterparts. After Trent, priests in the North were increasingly more likely to be selected on the basis of their commitment to Tridentine ideals. These North-South differences had consequences for how local populations defined Catholicism.

In both North and South, a ceremony or practice was only truly Catholic if it was legitimized by the local clergy. In the North, this meant that Catholicism, in contrast to folk beliefs, came to be permeated by Tridentine emphases. This did not happen in the South. Since the local priest was often willing to legitimate practices and devotions at variance with Trent, there was less divergence between Catholicism and folk beliefs. In the South, Catholicism was the religion practiced in the local Catholic church by local Catholics under the guidance of the local Catholic priest. If it differed from the Tridentine image, then it was the Tridentine image that was not truly Catholic.

The unique nature of the *chiese ricettizie*, then, had three important results: (1) it insulated the Mezzogiorno clergy from the influence of Tridentine bishops; (2) it insured that the local clergy would share the beliefs of the local population; and (3) it insured that southern populations would be far less likely to borrow from the Tridentine ideology in developing their variant of Catholicism.

To understand the collective impact of all this, remember that popular religion (as I define it here) is the form of local religion that crystallizes around concepts and beliefs that have been borrowed from official Catholicism. Until now, what determines the number of concepts and beliefs borrowed from official Catholicism has not been discussed. But obviously, forms of local Catholicism that borrow a lot from official Catholicism are different from forms that borrow little. The net effect of the *chiese ricettizie* was to insure that Mezzogiorno communities borrowed only a little; the nature of parish organization in the North, at least after Trent, insured that northern communities would borrow a lot. It is this that explains differences in popular religion between the North and South. The fact that the North is more Tridentine

Madonnas That Maim

than the South has little to do with cultural orientation—the "one region looks to Europe, the other to the Mediterranean" theme. Nor is this difference derived, at least proximally, from differences in climate and geography. It derives from differences in parish organization: the nature of parish organization in the North insured that northern Catholics would be far more easily pressured into accepting the emphases promulgated at Trent.

A TRIDENTINE MARKER: MARIAN CORONATIONS

The North's greater vulnerability to Trent, as well as the insulating effects of the *chiese ricettizie* in the South, can be detected in a fairly precise manner by looking at the practice of coronation. A coronation *(incoronazione)* is a solemn ceremony, attended by high Church officials, during which a crown made of precious metal, usually gold or silver, is placed upon the image of a madonna (which could be a painting, a fresco, a statue, etc.) associated with a particular sanctuary. Devotional guides relate the practice to medieval traditions about Mary being crowned Queen of Heaven and see in these coronations an expression of the great honor in which Mary is held (e.g., Medica 1965: xiv–xvi).

Although the Mary-being-crowned-Queen-of-Heaven theme was common in the high art of the Middle Ages, the actual practice of coronation was a solidly Counter-Reformation phenomenon. The first solemn coronation in Italy was the coronation of the Madonna della Steccata at Parma in May 1601, and the practice quickly spread to other Italian sanctuaries. Several things made coronation appealing to the Counter-Reformation Church. The first was the fact that a coronation was executed only upon the approval of the local bishop or the Vatican. A coronation, in other words, was a means by which the Church hierarchy could give its approval to a cult formed around some particular madonna. But this in turn meant that a successful coronation—one attended by a substantial proportion of the local community—was an implicit acknowledgment by the members of that community that approval from above was valued. Inculcating this view was a major Counter-Reformation goal. Finally, the very word *incoronazione* conjured up associations with hierarchy and hierarchial control, associations consonant with the spirit of Trent, which sought to subject local Catholic communities and local clergy to the hierarchial control of bishops and other Church officials.

The practice of coronation therefore indicates the degree to which the Counter-Reformation Church was successful in getting local populations to accept the spirit of Trent. Giacomo Medica's (1965) guide indicates that the madonnas at 272 sanctuaries (of a total of 697) were crowned, and the precise date of the coronation is given in each case. Of these 272 coronations, 193

Regional Differences

TABLE 5.3

Marian coronation in Italy, by region and time period

Period	North		Mezzogiorno	
	No.	Percentage	No.	Percentage
1600–49	19	10	0	0
1650–99	12	7	0	0
1700–49	18	9	5	6
1750–99	14	7	9	11
1800–49	14	7	3	4
1850–99	35	18	13	17
1900–65	81	42	49	62
Total	193	100	79	100

Source: Derived from Medica (1965).

were in northern Italy and 79 in southern Italy. By itself, the greater number of coronations in the North could be explained by the fact that the North had twice the population of the South and slightly more than twice the number of Marian sanctuaries.[11]

But less important than the number of coronations in each area is the historical pattern. Table 5.3 gives the frequency of these coronations in the Medica sample, by region and by period. These data indicate that in the North the practice of coronation was established in the seventeenth century and continued to be practiced at a fairly steady rate until the mid-nineteenth century. During the late nineteenth century, the pace of these coronations picked up; and during the first part of the twentieth century the number of coronations came close to equaling the number in all previous centuries together. In the South, too, there was an increase in the practice during the late nineteenth century and a veritable explosion of coronations in the twentieth century.[12]

But most notable about coronations in the South is their general absence in earlier periods. Not a single coronation is recorded in southern Italy in the entire seventeenth century, and there were only seventeen coronations in all of southern Italy prior to 1850. The Counter-Reformation Church, in other words, was able to promulgate the practice of coronation in northern Italy as soon as it first began to be practiced, but it was not able to do this in the South until the breakdown of the *chiese ricettizie* removed the barrier that insulated the South from Trent.

Madonnas That Maim

SOME FURTHER CONSEQUENCES OF THE NORTH'S
GREATER VULNERABILITY TO TRENT

The ideal priest in the eyes of Tridentine reform was separate from the laity (Zambarbieri 1983: 191–224; Montanari 1987: 105–55). This ideal could be implemented in the North, so northern priests began to give up the things of normal men: they stopped having sex with women; they began to wear clothes that set them apart; they stopped frequenting taverns and gathering in the piazzas to gossip; they gave up card playing, dancing, and other public amusements. Most of all, they set themselves apart from popular superstitions at variance with Trent. This process took a long time, and there were of course some northern priests who resisted change. Nevertheless, the northern clergy did—eventually and in general—become Tridentized. This shows up most of all in the reports of pastoral visits made in the North, where attributions of corruption to the clergy are relatively infrequent. The clergy in the South, by contrast, were insulated from Trent and so could not be forced to set themselves apart from their neighbors in this way.

But it was not just the northern clergy that was changed by the North's greater vulnerability to Trent; the shape and texture of popular Catholicism in the North was also affected. For instance, one of the most important doctrinal emphases at Trent was a renewed insistence upon the centrality of Christ as compared to the saints and Mary. The North's vulnerability to Trent meant that this renewed Christocentric emphasis would be injected into popular Catholic practice. At one level, this meant a renewed emphasis in the local community upon standard Christocentric ceremonies like the Mass, the Easter duty (the requirement that all Catholics of appropriate age receive Holy Communion at Easter), and so on.

The fact that Christocentric emphases more easily permeated popular Catholicism in the North is a likely explanation for the regional pattern mentioned earlier, namely, the fact that *disciplinati* confraternities were disproportionately a northern phenomenon. Remember that the central emphasis of these organizations was upon imitating the life of Christ. True, the *disciplinati* confraternities did predate the Counter-Reformation, but Pier Melloni's (1972: 22) census, cited earlier, indicates that it was during the Counter-Reformation that these confraternities saw their greatest growth. In particular, more *disciplinati* confraternities were established in Italy during the sixteenth century than during the previous three centuries together.

The greater Christocentrism of the Counter-Reformation in the North also shows up in connection with relics. Relics had been a part of Catholicism in the West at least since the tenth century. Most relics were associated with saints, but there had always been a few associated with Christ. Churches in both Argenteuil (France) and Trier (Prussia), for instance, claimed to have the Holy Coat of Christ; a church at Prüm (in Lorraine) had the sandals of Christ; and several churches in France claimed to have Christ's burial shroud.[13] The point is that the only Italian sanctuaries containing important relics of Christ were in northern Italy. These include the well-known Shroud of Turin and the less-known Santo Sudario at Genoa.[14] The Cathedral at Genoa also claimed to have the Holy Grail, the vessel used by Christ at the Last Supper. Pieces of the pillar on which Christ was flagellated were to be found in the church of San Marco in Venice and at the church of Santa Prassede in Rome. Thorns from the Crown of Thorns were scattered across churches throughout Christendom, but the only Italian church with a substantial piece of the Crown of Thorns was located in Pisa. One or more of the nails used to nail Christ to the cross were in the church of Santa Croce in Rome, as well as at churches in Venice and Florence.

Most of these relics predated the Counter-Reformation, certainly, but they were all given a renewed importance by Counter-Reformation leaders like Carlo Borromeo. Thus, when the Burial Shroud of Christ first came to Turin in 1578 and was exposed there for public veneration, Borromeo made a special trip to Turin from Milan to legitimize the new cult. At Rome, Borromeo helped to restore the church of Santa Prassede, which contained the Column of the Flagellation, and he regularly said morning Mass in that church when visiting Rome. Borromeo also had replicas of the Holy Nails constructed, had these replicas touched to the real Holy Nails, and then distributed the replicas to various churches (Cruz 1984: 42). Finally, Borromeo had a special devotion to the Santa Casa di Loreto (in Le Marche), which was piously believed to be the house in which Christ had lived as a boy (and which had been transported to Italy by angels).

Quite often the interaction between Trent and local conditions in the North gave rise to forms of popular Catholicism not at all like what outsiders would expect to find in northern Italy. A good example of this, which deserves wider visibility among English-speaking audiences, is to be found in Silvano Cavazza's (1981) study of the temporary resurrection of dead infants in Friuli.

TEMPORARY RESURRECTIONS

In 1686 Antonio Dall'Occhio, inquisitor general of the dioceses of Aquileia and Concordia, submitted a report on the practice of temporary resurrections in Friuli.[15] The first few sentences of that report describe what these temporary resurrections involved:

> Above the city of Tolmezo . . . there is a small church dedicated to the Madonna del Carmine, who is more commonly called the Madonna di Trava.

Madonnas That Maim

The cadavers of stillborn infants are brought continuously to this church. Here they are turned over to two women who have been delegated the task of receiving said cadavers. These women present themselves before the altar of the Madonna. There they say a brief prayer. With all the people present, and while the curate or some other priest is celebrating mass, the women suddenly begin to shout: "Grace, grace; miracle; miracle." [The reason for this is] that the dead baby has given signs of life: it has cried warm tears; opened one or both eyes; moved its hand, right or left, or moved both; opened its mouth; breathed; or passed saliva or urine. For this reason, it is capable of being baptized. Quickly the women do baptize it. The baptism completed, then they say that the infant has died again. The body is immediately buried. Then the notary of the villa, one Giovanni Lischiutta, issues a certificate saying that the infant gave signs of life and was baptized. This is given to whoever brought the dead child [to the church], so that it can be brought to the parents of the dead child. (Cavazza 1981: 112–13)

In the remainder of his report, Dall'Occhio gives his reasons for believing these temporary resurrections to be false. First, he notes, the only ones who ever actually see the signs of life are the two women, and that seems suspicious. Second, he finds it strange that although these resurrections have occurred over and over again, not a single child has lived longer than a few moments. Surely, Dall'Occhio suggests, if the Virgin can intercede to bring them back from the dead, then at least occasionally she would certainly obtain what is really a lesser miracle, namely restoring them to their families. Finally, he suggests that the whole procedure seems a bit cumbersome. The parents who brought their dead infants to the sanctuary of the Madonna di Trava would certainly have prayed to the Madonna before coming to the sanctuary. Why had not a single one of these requests been granted? Why would the Madonna insist upon having the infants brought to the sanctuary and only then revive them? But although Dall'Occhio rejected these temporary resurrections, not a single one of the principals involved in the ceremony (the two women, the notary, the priest in charge of the sanctuary) was ever brought before the Inquisition in the five years during which he was conducting his investigations.

When the temporary resurrections first came to his attention, Dall'Occhio had been in Friuli only four years and was unfamiliar with its customs. Possibly he thought that these resurrections were recent phenomenon. Certainly he seems initially to have associated the practice only with the sanctuary and the two women at Trava, and this particular sanctuary had been established only in 1659. The questionnaires he sent out to various authorities in the area, however, quickly established that he was dealing with a more far-reaching phenomenon. For one thing, these temporary resurrections had regularly occurred at another Marian sanctuary in the area prior to the establishment of the sanctuary at Trava. Furthermore, in 1663, just four years after the sanctuary at Trava had been established, a bricklayer had been sufficiently convinced of the orthodoxy of these temporary resurrections that he had denounced to the Inquisition an eminent and respected priest who had denied the miracle in private conversation.

But it was not only the public who believed in these resurrections. In 1686, the vicar-general for Friuli gave the priest at Trava a letter saying that at least for now the devotions at the sanctuary should not be hindered. It declared irregular only the practice of allowing the two women to baptize the child, given that a priest was present. From this point forward, the priest at the sanctuary performed the baptisms himself and issued certificates saying that he had been authorized to do this by the vicar-general.[16] Dall'Occhio, then, was confronting a long-standing practice, firmly rooted in the popular mind, and endorsed by most of the local clergy and some of the higher clergy. Little wonder that, having written his report, Dall'Occhio abandoned the matter.

It is now known that the temporary resurrection of unbaptized infants was not of Italian origin at all. On the contrary, the first documented reference to the practice appears in France in 1393. Throughout the course of the fifteenth and early sixteenth centuries, the practice was explicitly condemned by a number of provincial synods, almost all in west-central France.[17] The fact that it had to be condemned over and over again suggests that it continued to flourish.

During the latter part of the sixteenth century, the practice spread further afield, appearing in southern France and northern Italy. As far as I can tell, the first reference to the practice in Italy occurs in 1558. In that year a woman accused of witchcraft in the Valle d'Aosta told of having brought a dead infant to the church to be resurrected and baptized (Corrain and Zampini 1970: 35). Reports of the practice being carried out on a regular basis, however, do not appear until the seventeenth century. The *Atlas marianus*, published for the first time in 1657, notes that such resurrections occurred at two sanctuaries in the Diocese of Trent. At one of these sanctuaries alone there were twenty-five temporary resurrections between 1652 and 1655. Information relating to these resurrections had been provided to the author of the *Atlas* by the Bishop of Trent himself, which suggests that the good bishop did not disapprove of the practice.

What is most significant, given our purposes here, is that in Italy the practice remained a northern phenomenon. Silvano Cavazza (1981: 98) points out that, apart from a single temporary resurrection attributed to Santa Rosalia in Sicilia, the practice did not establish itself in the South. Cleto Corrain and Pierluigi Zampini (1966) analyzed the records of synods held all over Italy for references to various forms of popular religion condemned by these synods. Although most of the popular religious practices they

Madonnas That Maim

identify appeared in both North and South, they found references to temporary resurrection only in the synods of northern Italy. Why just the North?

The fact that temporary resurrections proliferated during the Counter-Reformation is explained by the fact that during this period the Church emphasized Baptism as the *sine qua non* of salvation (Cavazza 1981). This was by no means a new doctrine, but a number of theologians in the fifteenth and sixteenth centuries had raised the possibility that through divine intercession infants who died without Baptism might still go to Heaven (ibid., 104–6). This position was explicitly rejected at the Council of Trent.

Cavazza argues that this renewed Counter-Reformation emphasis upon Baptism as an absolute prerequisite for salvation added more pain to lives already permeated with pain. Given the high rates of infant mortality, it was inevitable that a fair number of infants would die without Baptism. To the suffering imposed by war, pestilence, and natural catastrophe was now added—for the parents of these dead infants—the probability that their children would forever suffer eternal damnation. To make matters worse, unbaptized infants had to be buried outside of consecrated ground, which usually meant that their bodies were disposed of like the carcasses of dead animals. A belief in temporary resurrection, Cavazza concludes, was a way of alleviating this added pain.

As far as it goes, Cavazza's explanation seems correct. But it does not answer the question, Why in the North and not in the South? The stereotypical distinction between the magical South and the rational North seems particularly useless, since it is difficult to imagine a ceremony more magical than one that brings the dead back to life. Furthermore, life in the South was at least as "painful" as in the North, and as far as I have been able to determine, rates of infant mortality in the South were as high, if not higher. Nor is there any reason to believe that southern parents were less saddened by the death of their children than northern parents. Finally, given the nature of the *chiese ricettizie*, a southern villager was far more likely to find his local priest willing to engage in the magical in order to make life easier for grieving parents. Why not the South, then?

The answer, I suggest, lies in the obvious: only parents who placed a high value on an otherworldly salvation and who accepted the notion that Baptism was necessary for this salvation would need to revive their dead infants long enough to be baptized. Both of these conditions were far more likely to obtain among parents in northern Italy than in southern Italy.

The reader may have missed it, but the fact is that I have nowhere suggested that salvation was important to Italian Catholics. As strange as this may seem to the modern mind, which tends to define salvation as the be-all and end-all of Christianity, I can find no evidence that it was of great importance in popular Italian Catholicism. What was important were overcoming some current infirmity or other problem and securing protection from natural and social disasters. These very this-worldly concerns were on the minds of ordinary people. Southern Italian Catholics did believe in an afterlife; such a belief is implicit in the cult of the saints. But they were far more concerned about their fate in this world than their fate in the next.

During the Counter-Reformation, the Church not only promoted a greater concern with otherworldly salvation but also—as Cavazza suggests—a greater emphasis upon Baptism as a prerequisite to this salvation. The nature of parish organization in the North insured that these Counter-Reformation values would become part of the popular consciousness, a condition under which grieving parents would find temporary resurrections appealing. The nature of parish organizations in the South, in contrast, insulated southern Italian Catholics from these values, just as it insulated them from other values of Counter-Reformation zealots. Being far less committed to the Tridentine emphasis on Baptism, they would have little interest in resurrecting their dead infants long enough to receive that sacrament.

Although an emphasis upon Baptism and salvation was consistent with the spirit of the Counter-Reformation, the magical quality of temporary resurrections was not. Thus the practice produced disagreement within the Church, with some officials supporting the practice and others (like Dall'Occhio and the members of the various synods) condemning it. Eventually, Rome itself stepped in to settle the matter: in 1755 Pope Benedict XIV prohibited the administration of Baptism to any infant that did not show signs of life. He did admit that some seemingly dead infants carried into a sanctuary might show signs of life, but this was because their death had only been apparent. In this case, the infants might be baptized, but there were to be no shouts of "resurrection!" This decision insured that local clergy in the North would turn against the practice, which in turn insured that it would eventually die out.

Nevertheless, the extinction of these temporary resurrections was by no means sudden. The last *ex voto* at the Trava sanctuary testifying to a temporary resurrection is dated 1856, which means it occurred fully one hundred years after Benedict XIV's interdiction, and a priest is clearly visible in the picture (Cavazza 1981: 110).

6

MAGIC

P art of the stereotype of southern Italy is that popular religion there is more magical than popular religion in the North.[1] By the early twentieth century, this was undoubtedly true. But if we look at popular Catholicism in Italy in earlier periods, this particular contrast between the North and the South is not so easily established. Mary Rose O'Neil (1981, 1984), for example, used the records of the Inquisition to identify a number of "popular errors" existing in the northern cities of Modena, Venice, and Bologna in the sixteenth and seventeenth centuries. Her investigation turned up a great many examples of "Catholic magic" being practiced openly. Consider the case of Fra Geremia da Udine.[2]

Fra Geremia was brought before the Inquisition at Venice in 1590 on account of a procedure he used to cure people suffering from fever. This procedure involved writing the name of a different Apostle on each of twelve different pieces of paper. The pieces were then folded and given to the sick person, who unfolded only one. If the fever abated by the end of the day, that was evidence that the Apostle whose name was on the chosen piece of paper had cured the fever. The recovered person was required to honor that Apostle on his festa—for example by presenting the Apostle with an *ex voto*. If the fever did not abate, then that first piece of paper was burned and the procedure repeated again the next day with the remaining pieces of paper. The procedure continued until the fever was cured.

That an Apostle might cure a fever is not problematic: this is the sort of power routinely attributed to the saints and the madonnas in Italy. The Church has always tolerated this view by interpreting it as falling within the limits of the "saints and madonnas as intercessors" doctrine. What made the good friar's procedure objectionable, and what the Inquisition focused on,

Magic

was the clear suggestion that the threat of burning an Apostle's name might coerce that Apostle into effecting a cure.

Readers familiar with James Frazer's *The Golden Bough* will recognize here something that regularly appears within the logic of magical thought: an effect can be worked on some being (in this case a saint) by manipulating something in intimate contact with that being. Such things can include bits of hair, nails, blood, or other body parts; an image of the being; or, as in this instance, the being's name. Indeed, Frazer (1922: 224–62) devoted an entire chapter to magical beliefs and procedures that make use of the intimate link between a name and the bearer of that name.

It is not the simple fact that Fra Geremia used a magical procedure that is of interest here; what makes the case interesting is that he was a northern Italian cleric who practiced magic openly. Indeed, the Inquisition established that Fra Geremia's willingness to dispense this cure was widely known within the city and that many people sought him out at his Franciscan convent. O'Neil does not indicate if the Inquisition was able to ascertain how long all this had been going on, but the fact that Geremia said that he had learned of the procedure while growing up at Udine (in Friuli) makes it likely that he had been openly practicing the procedure for some time (O'Neil 1981: 235). The mechanical nature of Geremia's procedure makes it unmistakably magical. Yet it also made reference to supernatural beings (the Apostles) legitimated by the Church and was practiced openly by a legitimate Catholic cleric. Using the definition being employed here, then, Fra Geremia's activity must be considered a part of popular Catholicism.

Fra Geremia was by no means a novelty among northern clerics. O'Neil also establishes that similar magical procedures were practiced openly by a fair number of other clerics and that, generally, these clerics did not believe their practices were inconsistent with Church doctrine (ibid., 224–91). Luciano Allegra (1981: 898–900) makes much the same point, contrasting the fairly casual attitude of Church authorities toward priests in Modena who openly mixed magic and religion in the early 1500s with the fairly severe attitude toward the same mix of elements in the late 1500s. Furthermore, ecclesiastical attitudes aside, we know that the general public in the North was willing to resort to magic for a long time after Trent. A variety of synods held in northern Italy during the sixteenth and seventeenth centuries make reference to a range of magical practices that were well entrenched among the laity (Corrain and Zampini 1966, 1970).

One particularly well-documented example of this continuing northern willingness to believe in magic can be found in Giovanni Levi's (1988) account of an exorcist who practiced in an area of Piemonte just to the southeast of Turin in the late 1690s. Giovan Battista Chiesa, a Catholic priest, openly preached that nine of ten people were possessed by the Devil and that such possessions accounted for most human ills. While Chiesa does not appear to have practiced very long before being brought before ecclesiastical authorities, he was immensely popular during his short career. In something less that two months, between 29 June and 15 August 1697, for example, he exorcised 539 people from a variety of different villages (ibid., 8). Although the Church hierarchy quickly put a stop to Chiesa's activities, his case lends support to the suggestion that, in the century or so after Trent, northern Catholics were just as willing as southern Catholics to turn to magic, if it was available from their local priests.

Still, as we approach the eighteenth and nineteenth centuries, the North and South did diverge with regard to the practice of magic within the context of popular Catholicism. Very simply, magical elements came more and more to be expunged from popular Catholicism in the North, but not in the South. This was due most of all to the systematic difference between North and South noted in the last chapter, namely, that the North was vulnerable to Trent in the way that the South was not.

TRENT AND MAGIC

It was only in the Twenty-fifth (and last) Session of the Council of Trent (begun in December 1563) that the assembled delegates issued their final judgments concerning the cult of the saints and the cult of Mary. After some preliminary remarks stressing the centrality of Christ and the distinction between veneration and worship, the delegates did endorse both of these metacults and specifically endorsed the use of images in churches. Having done that, however, they insisted that "in the invocation of saints, the veneration of relics, and the sacred use of images, every superstition shall be removed" (Waterworth 1848: 235).

It would not be correct to say that this injunction in itself led the Tridentine Church to set about the elimination of magic from Catholic ritual. The term *superstition* mentioned in the Tridentine pronouncement still had much of its medieval meaning, that is, it referred mainly to magical procedures that did not serve Church-approved goals (see Introduction). This meant that the Church in the post-Trent era was willing to tolerate magical procedures that did serve approved goals. We have seen in chapter 5, for instance, the initial tolerance of the practice of temporary resurrection, a practice tied very much to the Tridentine emphasis upon the sacrament of Baptism as a prerequisite of salvation. But it is surely the case of the "Scapular Promise" that provides the best example of magical practice tolerated by the Church hierarchy after Trent.

According to the traditions surrounding the Scapular Promise, anyone who died wearing the Brown Scapular of Our Lady of Mount Carmel would not go to Hell.[3] The belief that simply wearing the Brown Scapular would enable the wearer to avoid Hell and eventually get to Heaven makes the practice magical. The Church's position on this tradition was ambivalent: although high Church authorities pointedly did not endorse the Scapular Promise, they did explicitly permit Catholic preachers to disseminate the contents of the Promise.[4] This makes sense given the concerns of the Tridentine Church. However magical the scapular devotion was, it emphasized the pains of Hell, the value of Heaven, and the veneration of a universal Mary, who transcends national boundaries. Even so, cases like the Brown Scapular notwithstanding, over the long run the spirit of Trent did work against the inclusion of magical elements in northern popular Catholicism.

But the situation was quite different in the South, the land where "Trent never arrived" in its entirety. There, the nature of the terrain, but most of all the peculiar structure of the *chiese ricettizie*, insulated popular Catholicism from Trent and so from the Tridentine deemphasis of magic. One consequence was that the magic that had initially been part of Catholicism in the South remained. Just as important, being insulated from Trent, there was no bar in the South to an *increase* in the magical elements in popular Catholicism. In fact, such an increase (as we shall see) did occur. In a sense, then, the stereotype is correct: popular Catholicism in the South is more magical than popular Catholicism in the North. But this difference is the outcome of a centuries-old process following Trent.

Several southern Italian Catholic ceremonies containing magical elements have already been considered: the festa in honor of San Zopito, in which the excretions of an ox portend the future; the ritual of dancing of the *tarantata*, who is guided by her belief that the best way to obtain release from the effects of spider bite is to imitate the movements of the particular *taranta* that bit her. But we have not yet spoken of the one magical ceremony that to many outsiders epitomizes southern Italy.

THE BLOOD MIRACLE OF SAN GENNARO

The historical San Gennaro was supposedly a Christian bishop and martyr who was beheaded in A.D 305 at Pozzuoli, a community just up the coast from Naples.[5] In the Tesoro (treasury) attached to the Cathedral at Naples are two reliquaries containing relics of this saint. The first contains pieces of San Gennaro's skull. The second contains two glass vials: one vial is empty, the other contains his dried blood. Traditionally, the two reliquaries are exposed to public veneration three times during the year, in May, September, and December. The May ceremonies, which commemorate the

Madonnas That Maim

translation of the saint's relics to Naples in the fourth century, begin on the Saturday before the first Sunday of the month and continue over the next eight days. The September ceremonies begin on 19 September, which was the saint's feast day, and continue over the following seven days. The final ceremony takes place on 16 December and commemorates the saving of Naples from an eruption of Mount Vesuvius on 16 December 1631. In all, then, the reliquaries are exposed to public veneration eighteen days a year. The dried blood of San Gennaro is supposed to liquefy during each ceremony, and over the last several centuries, that usually has happened.

The first historical reference in the liquefaction of San Gennaro's blood occurs in a document dated 1389. There are about a dozen documentary accounts of the miracle from the fifteenth century and another dozen or so from the sixteenth century, many of them written by famous people who were eyewitnesses to the miracle.[6] A log detailing the events surrounding each year's liquefaction has been kept by Tesoro officials since the early 1630s. Lawrence Kehoe (1871) examined these records down to 1860; his data is summarized in table 6.1. The relic was sometimes liquid when it was removed from the Tesoro vault, but in most cases it liquefied during the ceremony. Notice too that, at least during the May and September ceremonies, there was never a clear-cut and total failure to liquefy; that is, on no occasion in the period covered by Kehoe did the relic fail to liquefy on at least one of the days of the festa.

Another pattern evident in table 6.1 is the steady increase in "uncertain" outcomes over the course of those two ceremonies (in May and September) that last several days. This pattern is strongest in connection with the May ceremony: there were no uncertain outcomes at all during the first or second day of the ceremony, but there were a number of uncertain outcomes during the last two days of the ceremony. Very likely this pattern can be explained by the way liquefaction is established to the satisfaction of the large crowd gathered in the cathedral. At the beginning of each day's ceremony, the officiating priest turns the reliquary holding the vial upside down a few times to demonstrate that the dried blood coating the bottoms of the vial is *not* liquid. This action is repeated every so often, and eventually the blood in the vial is seen to move. On each succeeding day of the ceremony, as the upper part of the vial becomes increasingly coated with the remnants of the preceding day's liquefaction, it becomes increasingly difficult to verify liquefaction based upon visual inspection alone,[7] hence the increasing number of uncertain judgments.

For the period 1920–70, Domenico Ambrasi (1970) presents data relating to the miracle for the first day of the May festa, the first day of the September festa, and for the December festa. The basic patterns are much the same as those in Kehoe's data: (1) during the May and September ceremonies, the

Magic

TABLE 6.1

The frequency of liquefaction of the blood relic of San Gennaro,
seventeenth to nineteenth centuries

| | Number of liquefaction instances | | | | |
Festa	Blood liquid when removed from vault	Blood liquefied during ceremony	Blood never liquefied	Liquefaction uncertain	Total
May festa, 1648–1860					
Saturday	23	189	1	0	213
Sunday	13	200	0	0	213
Monday	0	213	0	0	213
Tuesday	0	209	0	4	213
Wednesday	4	176	0	33	213
Thursday	3	155	0	56	214[a]
Friday	3	141	0	68	212[a]
Saturday	1	137	0	75	213
Sunday	2	136	0	73	211[a]
September festa, 1648–1860[b]					
19 September	12	200	0	0	212
20 September	21	191	0	0	212
21 September	21	190	0	1	212
22 September	20	191	0	1	212
23 September	22	188	0	2	212
24 September	18	193	0	1	212
25 September	17	194	0	1	212
26 September	14	196	0	2	212
16 December festa, 1632–1860	1	181	43	3	228

Source: Derived from Kehoe (1871: 24–25), reproduced from Carroll (1989) with permission from McGill-Queen University Press.

[a]The total should be 213; Kehoe does not explain the discrepancy.

[b]Kehoe makes it clear that the period covered is not inclusive; he does not indicate whether the data are missing for 1648 or for 1860.

relic was almost always either liquid when removed from the vault or liquefied during the ceremony, and (2) a failure to liquefy was much more common in the December ceremony, although even here liquefaction occurred more often than not.[8]

The San Gennaro miracle and its associated ceremonies has always been something of an embarrassment to Catholic intellectuals outside Italy. Herbert Thurston (1856–1939), for instance, was an English Jesuit and scholar who spent much of his life subjecting pious Catholic traditions and the life of Catholic mystics to the harsh glare of Anglo-Saxon rationalism. He published literally hundreds of articles on popular Catholicism, and even now, more than a half century after his death, his work remains a valuable source of information on the early history of many of these devotions.[9] It was inevitable that Thurston would address the blood miracle of San Gennaro, and he did, publishing something like a dozen different essays on the subject. Thurston's articles, like almost all English-language literature on this miracle, are concerned with searching for the physical or psychological processes that produce the effect of liquefaction.

What I want to emphasize here, however, is that it was not the simple suggestion that the liquefaction was a miracle that biased Thurston against accepting the event at face value. Rationalist that he was, Thurston was still a believing Catholic and a Jesuit priest. He accepted the reality of beings like Mary and the saints and the possibility that these beings might intercede with God in order to produce miracles. Rather, Father Thurston was convinced that liquefaction was the result of natural causation for two reasons. First, the miracle seemed so pointless. In his own words, "this marvel, repeated no less than eighteen times a year, seem[s] somewhat purposeless as a manifestation of Divine Omnipotence" (1927a: 48). Second, Thurston was offended by the regularity and certainty associated with the miracle. The very fact that the miracle has been repeated thousands of times over the centuries suggested that it was not miraculous (Thurston 1930). In Thurston's worldview, miracles are deviations from the natural order that God allows to happen only sparingly. A miracle that occurs regularly is, therefore, a contradiction in terms. As brilliant as Father Thurston was, objections such as these betray a misunderstanding of Catholicism in southern Italy.

As a start, the people of Naples do not view liquefaction as a manifestation of Divine Omnipotence, in Thurston's sense of the term. If any being caused the miracle, it was San Gennaro, not God. But even this is misleading. Naples has many patron saints, but San Gennaro is the most important. In other words, he is the being most responsible for the safety of the city. This is why the people of Naples say that the failure of the blood to liquefy portends danger. This, however, should not be taken too literally. Remember that failures to liquefy are quite common in December, and yet I have found no evidence that these December failures ever produce any generalized anxiety among the people of Naples. What matters, clearly, is that the relic liquefy on most of the eighteen days of the three festas, which always does happen. The people of Naples, in other words, may report to visiting scholars that a failure to liquefy portends disaster, but the fact is that failure to liquefy, in their definition, never really happens.

The most useful way to look upon the San Gennaro ceremony is as a *magical* procedure that causes San Gennaro to insure that no danger befalls the city. The veneration of the blood relic does not insure that San Gennaro might protect the city or that he will ask somebody higher up in the Catholic pantheon to protect the city. It means that he *will* protect the city. Within this logic, the certainty and regularity of the liquefaction of the blood relic is simply a visual expression of the certainty and regularity of the ceremony itself. In short, the very thing that Thurston (and likely a great many other English-speaking Catholics) found objectionable, namely, the certainty and regularity of the liquefactions is the very thing that assures the people of Naples that public veneration of San Gennaro will—with certainty—guarantee the saint's protection of their city.

OTHER BLOOD MIRACLES IN CAMPANIA

Prior to 1550, there are no reports of liquefying blood relics other than the one San Gennaro relic at the Cathedral in Naples. Subsequent to 1550, however, there was a veritable explosion of such relics, some of which were associated with San Gennaro, but most of which were not. Table 6.2 lists the most well known of these relics, their locations, and the date when they first began to liquefy. The list includes only relics that are reported to have liquefied on a regular and recurrent basis (almost always on the occasion of the festa in honor of the saint involved) and that became the focus of a ritual of a Catholic church and in which the local clergy participated. The list thus does not include those dozens of relics that liquefied once or twice, often spontaneously, and that therefore never become the focus of religious rituals.[10]

One important pattern in table 6.2 has to do with timing: these magical blood miracles began to proliferate in the late sixteenth century, just after the Council of Trent. Moreover, new blood miracles regularly appeared in the seventeenth, eighteenth, and even nineteenth centuries.[11] The pattern is thus very much the reverse of that in northern Italy, where public religious ceremonies containing magical elements became less and less common after Trent. The data therefore illustrate in a particularly succinct way the general failure of Trent's antimagical policies in the Mezzogiorno.

Most known blood miracles have occurred in and around the city of Naples. In my earlier work (Carroll 1989), I attribute this mainly to the fact that spontaneous liquefaction was most likely due to a distinctive set of physical conditions characteristic of this area and related to temperature and coastal location. Since spontaneous liquefactions were the core of popular blood miracle ceremonies, and since spontaneous liquefactions have rarely occurred outside coastal Campania, the rest of the Mezzogiorno never devel-

Madonnas That Maim

TABLE 6.2

Liquefying blood relics in Campania, location and year of
first reported liquefaction

Saint	Location	Year
Gennaro[a]	Naples	1389
Giovanni Battista	Baiano, then Naples	1554
Stefano	Naples	1561
Stefano	Naples	late 1500
Patrizia[a]	Naples	1570
Giovanni Battista	Naples	1577
Pantaleone[a]	Ravello	1591
Ursula	Amalfi	1591
Giovanni Battista	Naples	1623
Lorenzo	Naples	1623
Pantaleone	Naples	1623
Gennaro[a]	Pozzuoli	late 1600
Lorenzo	Avellino	1709
Vito	Naples	1725
L. Gonzaga	Naples	1841
A. Liguori	Naples	1851
Lorenzo	Naples	1864

Sources: Derived mainly from Alfano and Amitrano (1951); but see Thurston (1909; 1927b);
   Grant (1929); Petito (1983).
[a]These relics were still liquefying in the late 1980s. Descriptions of the San Gennaro relic in
   Naples can be found in the sources cited. For my own eyewitness account of the other three
   relics, see Carroll (1989: 189–96).

oped forms of popular Catholicism centered on blood miracles. But there
are magical procedures that are not dependent upon particular physical
conditions. One such procedure, quite common in southern Italy, is best
related by considering an aspect of the San Gennaro ceremonies that has so
far not been mentioned.

ON DISCIPLINING PATRON SAINTS

Although the San Gennaro relic at the Tesoro almost always does liquefy,
the time it takes can vary from a few minutes to several hours. Traditionally,

if the liquefaction was slow, a procedure was used to hurry it along. This procedure involved a group of older women called *le zie di San Gennaro* (the aunts of San Gennaro) or, more simply, *le parenti di San Gennaro* (the relatives of San Gennaro). Membership in this group is hereditary, and these women were given a place of honor, at the front of the crowd, during the ceremonies. During the early phases in each ceremony, the women chanted of the miracle. If liquefaction occurred quickly, they changed the chant to one of thanks—to the Trinity for making San Gennaro the patron of Naples and the saint himself for the many favors he had given the city. When the relic took a long time to liquefy, the women broke from their usual chant and hurled insults at the blood relic to shame San Gennaro into liquefying his blood.

For someone like Thurston, already ill at ease with the miracle, these insults made the ceremony even more embarrassing, and several times throughout his writing, he makes references to this unseemly behavior. The behavior is embarrassing as well to a great many Italian Catholics who otherwise accept the validity of the miracle itself. Some devotional commentaries that accept the miracle at face value simply ignore the *zie di San Gennaro* (e.g., Caserta and Lambertini 1972). In the atmosphere of renewed Christocentrism that swept over the Catholic Church following the Second Vatican Council, it was inevitable that the emotionalism associated with these women would be suppressed. In fact, beginning in 1970 they were forbidden to chant and hurl insults, although they were still allowed their place of honor during the ceremony. Luigi Petito (1983), though voicing no objection to the prohibition of these ritual insults, urges us to take a more indulgent view of past practice. The insults were not, he argues, expressions of hostility but were, rather, an expression of "familiarity." This remark merits careful consideration.

Although literally the words *zie* and *parenti* are *aunts* and *relatives*, respectively, the *zie di San Gennaro* never claimed to be literal descendants of San Gennaro. On the contrary, according to their own origin legend, they are related (whether by ties of blood or friendship is not clear) to the slave Eusebia, who was San Gennaro's wet nurse (De Simone 1974: 63). When San Gennaro was executed, it was Eusebia who supposedly collected the blood now contained in the vial at the Tesoro. Through Eusebia, then, these women are related to San Gennaro by "ties of milk," not "ties of blood." Within this mythologic, the insults they directed toward the saint were like the insults a loving mother surrogate might direct to her young charge in order to get him to do something he does not want to do. Petito is thus quite right. There was no hostility here; the insults were simply ways to coerce someone you love to do something he *should* do.

That human beings can coerce saints is of course completely at variance with official Catholic teaching, but it is very much in accord with the logic of magic. A standard principle of magic, already mentioned in connection with Geremia da Udine, is that by manipulating something in intimate contact with a being you can affect that being. In Geremia's case, the name of a saint is manipulated, the manipulation being a threat to burn the name and so harm the saint himself. In the case of San Gennaro, a blood relic was manipulated, a manipulation consisting of hurling insults at the relic.

The practice of insulting something associated with a saint (or madonna) in order to coerce that being is not limited to Italy. Patrick Geary (1983) recounts a dozen or so examples, which he calls the "humiliation of saints." All the examples given by Geary occurred during the tenth, eleventh, and twelfth centuries, and most occurred in France. About half of Geary's examples involve members of monastic communities who insulted saintly relics after the rights of the community had been violated by outsiders; the other half concern peasants who insulted such relics after being in some way oppressed by a local lord. In both situations, the underlying logic was the same: a saint had failed to protect people he was supposed to protect and was being punished in order to insure that this did not happen again. [12] The practice in France was increasingly condemned by high Church officials and was formally outlawed at the Second Council of Lyon in 1274 (ibid.). The implication is that the practice died out or, at least, became far less common. Whatever the case may have been in France, this is definitely not what happened in Italy.

In the early modern period, the humiliation of objects associated with a saint or madonna occurred in both northern and southern Italy. In the late 1500s, when the people of a community near Chiavari (in Liguria) decided that a particular madonna had not done enough to protect them from the effects of a devastating plague, a statue of that madonna was thrown into a garden plot filled with garbage. Only much later, when it was felt that the madonna had been punished enough, was her statue removed from this "place of pain" and installed in a new sanctuary (Lombardi Satriani 1978: 32). Still, as the effects of Trent came more and more to be felt in the North, the practice of humiliation came more and more to be a distinctively southern Italian phenomenon.

Emilio Sereni (1968: 196), for instance, identifies the practice of insulting saints as one of the distinctive features of Mezzogiorno religion. Salvatore Salomone-Marino (1981: 175–76) gives several examples of the practice in Sicilia. When the patron saint of Licata, the Holy Knight of Jerusalem, refused to send the needed rain, the people took his statue in procession to the sea. There, the saint was given an ultimatum: either send the rain soon or get thrown into the water. Similarly, when the community of Nissena failed to receive a request made of their patron, San Michele, they removed the fine cloak usually draped around his statue and replaced it with one that was worn and patched. The statue was then carried in silent procession (and thus one lacking the usual exuberance associated with Sicilian processions) to a nearby church, where he was to remain and do penance until the required favor was granted.

At Monterosso, it was an image of Christ that suffered: when the people prayed for rain and did not get it, an image of Christ called the Five Holy Wounds was carried to the public watering trough and thrown in, where it remained until the rains did come. Giuseppe Cocchiara (1971: 334) reports that, when Palermo was hit by a long drought in 1893, the citizens brought a statue of San Giuseppe (the same San Giuseppe whom Pitrè and Sereni judge the most beloved of Sicilian saints) to one of the gardens ravaged by the heat and left it there. The idea was that the saint would be induced to end Palermo's suffering by having to endure the savage heat himself. And so on.

It must be emphasized that the cases just described are quite unlike the instances of disrespect toward saints and madonnas by individuals—for example, the case of the boys who insulted Sant'Antonio abate or that of the woman who insulted the Madonna dell'Arco. A distinguishing feature of the magical procedures described above is that they are communal, that is, they are done in the name of the entire community and with the support of that community. Nor should these procedures be seen as expressions of hostility; they are simply technologies (magical technologies to be sure, but still only technologies) used by a community to coerce a supernatural being into fulfilling his or her obligation to protect that community from harm.

A Very Magical Procedure: Exorcism

As I noted earlier, Italian Catholics have always looked to their saints and madonnas both for protection from future danger and for relief from current suffering. The magical procedures we have so far examined in this chapter were designed to insure the first goal, protection. But when Italian Catholics turn to their deities for the relief of current suffering, they often use magic. The clearest case involves the exorcism of people possessed by spirits.

Exorcism was among the magical procedures attacked most severely by Protestant reformers. As a result, Church authorities after Trent placed a number of restrictions on exorcism. O'Neil (1981: 292–381) documents these restrictions for northern Italy: first, the procedure was taken out of the hands of lay exorcists and put exclusively in the hands of ordained priests; second, the only approved procedure came more and more to be the one laid down by Roman authorities. Levi's (1988) study of Giovan Battista Chiesa, although suggesting that northerners were receptive to magic even in the late seventeenth century, also indicates the speed with which ecclesiastical authorities in the North could and did suppress the practice of exorcism. Within a month after his activities had intensified and become widely known, Chiesa was formally enjoined to stop his activity. Shortly afterward, he was brought to trial, and his career as an exorcist, as far as Levi can determine, came to an end.

But here again things went quite differently in southern Italy. In the South, well into the nineteenth century, exorcisms could be conducted openly and with little regard for the Roman ritual, without either the exorcist or the patient becoming the object of scrutiny by Church authorities. Those who felt themselves possessed by spirits (a broad category, which includes not simply demons but also the spirits of the dead) could do two things. First, they could go to one of the *magi* (who could be male or female) in the area. *Magi* were lay persons who used magical procedures to cast out spirits. In Sicilia, for instance, the most common such procedures were (1) saying certain special prayers, (2) tying a white kerchief on the arm of the afflicted person, or (3) pulling that person's hair. Should these fail, *magi* could use more energetic procedures, such as punching the person in the stomach and repeating at each blow the name of some saint.[13] Because these *magi* were not clerics, their activities were part of popular Catholicism only to the extent that they sometimes (but not always) performed their exorcisms in a church on the occasion of some particular festa.

The second option open to the possessed was going directly to a saint or a madonna. A number of sanctuaries and churches in southern Italy were known to be particular effective in helping the possessed. I have already mentioned, for example, how San Zopito came to be regarded as particularly useful in this regard and how the possessed sought out his sanctuary in Loreto Aprutino (in Abruzzo). Pitrè identifies seven sanctuaries in Sicilia that were especially well known as places in which *spiritati* (those possessed by spirits or demons) could be exorcised. At three of these sanctuaries, a madonna cast out the spirits (the Madonna di Trapani; Santa Maria di Araceli, and an unnamed madonna), while in the other four, it was a saint (San Filippo the Black in the case of two sanctuaries, San Vito, and Santa Agrippina).[14]

The unimportance of Christ in the practice of exorcism should be stressed, since this is not what would be expected on the basis of official Catholic mythology. There is, for example, the well-known incident, reported in all three Synoptic Gospels, in which Jesus drives the demons from two people who are possessed and in which those demons then enter a nearby herd of swine (Matthew 8: 28–32; Mark 5: 1–13; Luke 8: 26–33). Christ is described as casting out demons on several other occasions as well (Mark 1: 23–26; 3: 11; Luke 4: 33–37). The New Testament tells us several times that the

Magic

power to cast out demons was one of the powers Jesus gave to his Apostles (Matthew 10: 1; Mark 3: 14–15; 6: 7; Luke 9: 1). Yet despite these prominent Christian myths explicitly associating Jesus with the power to exorcise demons, and despite the centrality of Christ in official Catholic doctrine, the possessed in southern Italy have always sought out a saint or madonna, not Christ.

That the exorcisms at these sanctuaries involved magic rather than a simple appeal to supernatural beings is made clear by the fact that simple contact with an object associated with these saints and madonnas could effect the exorcism. At the sanctuary of the Madonna di Trapani (in Sicilia), the possessed who came were liberated only on the second day of the madonna's festa, when her statue was revealed to the assembled crowds (Mondello 1882: 53–54). Similarly, at Agira (in Sicilia) the possessed would spend the night before the festa of San Filippo in the sanctuary itself, near the main altar, but the exorcisms would only occur the next morning, when the relic of this saint was brought out for public view (Pitrè 1978: 4: 49–50). At the sanctuary of Sant'Antonio at Campagna (in Campania), the person possessed was bound to a column near the altar and a priest would say a series of prescribed prayers. But it was only when the person was anointed with "the blessed oil of Sant'Antonio" that the possessing spirit was expelled amid an explosion of tears (Rossi 1969: 34). An emphasis upon contact with an object occurs in almost all accounts of important exorcism sanctuaries in the South, and it is the element that most of all allows us to argue that these ceremonies are magical.

Many of the symptoms exhibited by the *spiritati* who flocked to southern Italian sanctuaries were quite dramatic. These people often emitted loud and terrible noises, threw away their clothes without shame, ran about waving their arms, and foamed at the mouth. At other times, the possessed would speak fluently in some foreign tongue, usually Latin, Greek, or Arabic, and would reveal the innermost secrets of other people. When such behaviors were exhibited by dozens, or even hundreds, of people at once, the overall effect was quite impressive.[15]

But the possession did not always involve such high drama; it often was inferred from far more mundane feelings and behaviors. In 1626, for instance, the Archdiocese of Naples conducted an investigation into a case of exorcism involving a young painter named Giovanni Battista Marchiggione.[16] In the course of the investigation, Marchiggione described the events that had occurred over a period of years and that had led to diagnosis of possession:

I continuously experienced splitting headaches and dizziness, so much so that I was forced to put aside my paintbrush during the day. My throat became swollen . . . [and] I was not able to hold down my food. . . . When we went to hear Mass, I saw everything up until the act of consecration, but from the consecration forward I did not see anything else. I seemed to have gone mad; certainly, when the Mass finished I saw many people around me, looking at me, and I didn't know why. On the basis of all these signs, my relatives suspected that I had been possessed and caused me to be exorcised in various churches. . . . Everyone told me that I had been possessed. (Strazzullo 1963: 115–16)

Later testimony indicates that the poor man had experienced other problems as well, some of which clearly indicate the presence of a severe physical illness. When asked if he had been taking any medicines, Marchiggione replied no, but he did admit to seeing a doctor a year earlier on account of having spit up some blood.

None of the exorcisms conducted on Marchiggione did him any good, and his symptoms lasted five years. Then one night he saw Mary in a dream, and she directed him to a fresco contained in an *edicola* attached to the wall of a house that was now in ruins. Once there, she told him, he was to light the lamp in front of the fresco and await his liberation from the spirits who possessed him. Marchiggione hesitated at first, but a second visit from Mary in a dream caused him to go in search of the fresco. He found it and lit the lamp. People on the scene began to pray, and Marchiggione lost consciousness. When he came to, he was told that while the prayers were being said he had let out a great shout and had vomited up a nail. On a later visit to the site of the image, he once again passed out and once again (he was told) let out a great shout and vomited up a metal object, this time a cross made of iron. The expulsion of this cross signaled the expulsion of the last of the spirits who possessed him, and from this point forward he felt healed.

One of those present at the scene in which all this occurred was a priest, who accepted these events at face value. After an investigation, so did the Archdiocese of Naples. The cult of this madonna, called the Madonna dell'Olivo Verde, was localized in a nearby church, and the abandoned building in which her image had been found was made part of an Augustinian monastery.

Marchiggione's case is instructive for several reasons. It demonstrates that (1) a broad range of symptoms could lead to a diagnosis of possession, (2) these symptoms need not be extreme (certainly not as extreme as foaming at the mouth), and (3) they might last a long time before relief is obtained directly from a saint or madonna. This case also provides another example of the centrality of contact with a physical object. Marchiggione was not simply cured by Mary; he was cured by Mary only after he came into contact with the fresco portraying Mary.

Quite apart from the object that helps to drive out the spirit, the spirit itself often comes to be localized in some physical object. In the Marchiggione case, the spirits possessing him were localized in the iron objects that he

Magic

vomited up. In fact, the vomiting up of metal objects during exorcism is common. Presumably, the underlying logic is that metal objects are unlikely to be found inside a person in the normal course of events, the fact that they are (or were) inside that person is evidence of abnormality, and thus of possession. Spirits can be localized in less substantial substances, as well. In some cases, for example, spirits are believed to escape in a gust of hot air (Pitrè 1978: 4: 47). In many cases the departing spirits are not localized in a visible object or process, but their departure causes a visible effect. The most famous miracle of this sort occurred at the sanctuary of the Madonna di Trapani, where a lamp would spontaneously burst into flame when the possessed were liberated. At least until the seventeenth century, a similar effect seems to have occurred at the sanctuary of San Filippo in Agira, where the candles in the candelabra hanging high above the altar would burst into flames as the demons were driven out (and up).[17] As late as 1948, a bell in the sanctuary of Sant'Antonio at Campagna would ring when a spirit was expelled from someone possessed, despite the fact that the bell was several meters away from the person and despite the fact that no ropes or cables were connected to the bell (Rossi 1969: 34). The important thing is that there be some visible sign that the spirits have left the person's body. Such a sign reassures onlookers and participants that the exorcism has been successful, just as the liquefaction of San Gennaro's blood reassures onlookers and participants that the ritual has secured their protection.

The belief that departing spirits can be localized in physical substances (like hot air) provides the basis for several magical procedures. For example, such a belief obviously raises the very real danger that as a spirit is being driven out of one person it might enter someone standing nearby. Pitrè (1978: 4: 45–47) reproduces a long account written in 1557 by a man who had visited the shrine of San Filippo at Agira (Sicilia) in 1538. It seems this man had traveled to Agira in the company of a peasant who was going to the same shrine. The two eventually found themselves standing together in front of the church as the statue of the saint was being brought out. Suddenly, a woman standing nearby started shouting "The Moor [San Filippo] is after me! The Moor is after me! Help me, my colleagues, help me!" That said, she fell dead. The voice was taken to be the voice of the spirit possessing her, who was calling upon his fellow demons for aid.

In any event, just as the woman dropped dead, the spirit who had been driven from her entered the peasant. This man now began to exhibit the standard symptoms: he shouted wildly and tore his clothes, and his face became distorted. He was immediately restrained by other men nearby, and while restrained began to speak fluently in Latin and Greek. This continued well into the evening, until the time when the statue of the saint was being brought back into the church. At that point, the possessed man became violent again. At this, a friar present commanded the spirit in him to leave. The poor man's throat began to swell dramatically, and as his mouth opened wide, he expelled a great gust of very warm air. With that, he was liberated, and the spirit seems to have entered no one else.

Presumably because most physical substances that enter our body get in through our mouths, this is usually taken as the most likely entry point for a spirit who has just been driven out of someone else. Most magical procedures designed to protect those present at public exorcisms are therefore associated with the mouth. The simplest thing to do is to keep your mouth shut at the moment when the relic or image of the saint or madonna is exposed to the possessed. It is therefore not uncommon for talking to cease at this point. As an extra precaution, onlookers will hold various holy objects to their lips. At the sanctuary of the Madonna di Trapani, for example, when the image of the Madonna was revealed, the nonpossessed members of the crowd would not only stop talking but also press scapulars, rosaries, or medals to their lips (ibid., 57).

CONCLUSION

There is no particular basis for believing that the North was originally any less magical than the South at the beginning of the modern era. But over time, a difference did develop, mainly as a result of the antimagical emphasis of the Council of Trent. The peculiar nature of the *chiese ricettizie* insulated the South from Trent. The result was that existing magical elements were retained in the popular Catholicism of southern Italy. In some ways, in fact, popular Catholicism in the South became more magical.

Parish organization in the North offered no such protection from Trent. Despite evidence that the northern laity was willing to turn to magic when it was available, the greater vulnerability of the North to Trent means that magic was slowly purged from the popular Catholicism of northern Italy.[18]

Apart from the issue of magic, there is a second difference between popular Catholicism in the North and popular Catholicism in the South, a difference so far not mentioned here. It is not easily explainable in terms of difference in parish organization. This second difference has to do with violence, and violence of a special sort.

MEZZOGIORNO MASOCHISM

The first edition of Sir James Frazer's *The Golden Bough* was published in 1890 and became an instant success with the educated public in the English-speaking world. Frazer suggested in that book that ritual slaying had once been central to primitive religion. Originally, Frazer argued, ritual slaying involved a divine king who was slain and replaced, and the purpose of the rite was to renew the forces of nature with which the divine king was linked. Over time, the ritual slaying of the divine king gave rise to myths about gods who died and were reborn and to annual rituals in which the representative of a god was slain and replaced. Given the immense popularity of Frazer's theory in the 1890s, it was no wonder that, when Sir Edward Clodd gave his presidential address to the Folk-Lore Society of England in 1895, he would give examples of ritual slaying that had "survived" into the modern era.[1] In fact, he came up with three such examples.

Two of these were isolated incidents that were manifestly a response to an extreme situation. In the first case, some peasants in Russia had drugged a beggar and then torn out his heart and lungs for use in rites designed to end a famine. The second case occurred in Rumania, also during a time of famine, and involved two teenaged boys who had drowned an infant. But it is Clodd's third case that is the most interesting and that provoked controversy. This case involved an event that was repeated annually and was not, therefore, done *in extremis*. Further, it was tied to a recognized European religion, namely, Catholicism. In fact, it occurred in Italy during Holy Week. In Clodd's words:

> Mr. Grant Allen told me that when he was last in Italy, he was informed by the Rev. W. Pulling, well known as the author of *Dame Europa's School*, and

editor of Murray's *Handbook to Italy*, that "in a village in the Abruzzi the young men draw lots once a year to decide which should die for Christ. Whoever drew the fatal lot was secretly killed by another, equally drawn for the purpose, before the next Good Friday. It was accounted a great honour to die for Christ. Although these facts are known to the Government, it is unable to catch the perpetrator, because none will betray him." Mr. Allen had forgotten the name of the village, but no doubt Mr. Pulling would supply it. (Clodd 1895: 57)

Clodd expressed no doubts whatever about the veracity of the report, despite the fact that he had received it thirdhand and despite the suspicious absence of the name of the village in question.[2] Nor was the appeal of this Frazerian fancy limited to Clodd. The next year, in the postscript to an article on executed criminals and folk medicine, Mabel Peacock (1896: 282), who was at that time a regular contributor to *Folk-Lore*, repeated the "ritual slaying in the Abruzzi" story without any qualification.

English Catholic commentators saw Clodd's remarks as just one more example of the antipathy toward religion generally and Catholicism in particular that was characteristic of so many modern scientists (e.g., Britten 1898). But most of the outrage generated by Clodd's remarks were felt in Italy. An Italian anthropologist, Antonio De Nino, sent off a letter to *Folk-Lore* in which he related that he had himself inquired of Canon Pullen what the name of the mysterious village was and learned that it was Gioia del Colle (De Nino 1897).[3] This was not a village at all, De Nino noted, but rather a large market town of 20,000 people, and it was located in Puglia, not Abruzzo. More important, De Nino's inquiries had turned up no accounts at all similar to those reported by Pullen. In a longer article written for an Italian anthropological journal, De Nino (1898) printed extracts from communications received from politicians and scholars who had lived in or near Gioia del Colle for most of their lives. All denied ever hearing about anything that even smacked of ritual slaying, and all were outraged that this libel would be leveled against a civilized society like Italy. To counter the charge that there was a conspiracy of silence that the local police could not penetrate, De Nino inspected (or had inspected) the police logs for all Holy Thursdays between 1850 and 1865 and found no murder victims reported on those days.

The last word in the fiasco, so far as I can tell, came from Grant Allen (1899), who complained of having been brought into the dispute. Allen said that he had simply passed along as fact a story that he had been told as fact by Canon Pullen, an English clergyman and noted editor of English guidebooks to Italy. Allen inadvertently linked the story to Frazer by mentioning that Pullen had related the story during the course of a conversation about *The Golden Bough*. But Allen's disclaimers notwithstanding, he could not resist this closing sentence: "Until Canon Pullen gives his informant's name, and enables us to examine that informant, I shall continue to believe that the story *may* have some foundation of truth, because it is hardly likely that anyone could invent a tale so wholly in accord with the rest of our knowledge unless he were a skilled student of customs." The remark "so wholly in accord with the rest of our knowledge" meant that it was consistent with Frazer's well-known theory, and this is obviously what predisposed Allen—and Clodd—to accept it at face value. The fact that no further correspondence or articles on the subject were printed in *Folk-Lore* suggests that most investigators, unlike Allen, decided that the report was untrue.

Despite their differences, both Allen and De Nino agreed on one thing: either the report of ritual slaying was true or it was a fabrication. The obvious third possibility, which nobody seems to have explored at the time, is that the report was Canon Pullen's misinterpretation of something that actually occurred, a misinterpretation heavily influenced by Pullen's commitment to the "truth" of Frazer's general theory. If so, what was that "something"?

Bloody Rituals

Cleto Corrain and Pierluigi Zampini (1970: 187) suggest that Pullen's account was a garbled description of one of the many bloody rituals that took place in the South at the turn of the century and in which people did mutilate themselves. For example, in some communities in Calabria during Holy Week, two groups of men were to be found in the streets. The first, clothed only in loincloths, ran through the streets cutting themselves with bits of glass or with bloodletting instruments borrowed from barbers. They drew so much blood, they were "as red as shrimp" (Venturi 1901: 359). The second group, called Inchiovati, walked through the streets in silent procession with arms extended and bound to a length of wood. Their hands seemed nailed (*inchiodati*, in standard Italian) to these crosspieces, just as Christ was nailed to his cross.

But it was not just during Holy Week that such bloody rituals occurred. At Guardia Sanframondi near Benevento (in Campania), such rituals took place during the procession held on 21 August in honor of the Assunta, Mary's Assumption into heaven (see De Blasio 1903). Here the first of the two groups who walked in procession were the *disciplinanti*. These wore white chemises and carried a scourge in their right hands and either a crucifix or a human skull (often with bits of dried skin still attached) in their left. The second group were called the *battenti a sangue*. They also wore white chemises, but these were opened at the front. The *battenti a sangue* carried a piece of cork in which were embedded small metal pins, and they used this device to beat their chests until blood appeared. Bloody rituals such as these also occurred in Puglia, the location of Canon Pullen's reported ritual slaying (Corrain and Zampini 1970: 187).

Perhaps surprisingly, these rituals are still being practiced. An acquaintance in Italy, Andrew Mutter, has sent me two photographs. The first is a color photo that appeared in *Il Venerdi di Repubblica,* a Rome magazine, on 13 October 1989. It had been taken at Guardia Sanframondi during the festa of the Assunta the preceding August. The photo shows a man wearing a white hood and a white chemise and holding a cork studded with pins. The chemise is unbuttoned at the front. The man's chest clearly appears lacerated, while the lower half of the chemise seems drenched in blood. Other men, also holding studded pieces of cork and with lacerations on their chests, are standing in the background. These images match perfectly the descriptions that appear in A. De Blasio's (1903) account of the same festa at the turn of this century. The second picture was taken by an acquaintance of Mutter's during a visit to Nocera Terinese, a village in Calabria, during Holy Week in 1989. It shows a man wearing a crown of thorns, a sweater, and a loincloth. The backs of his legs are covered with blood, as are the steps on which he is standing. He seems to be lacerating himself with two hand-held devices that look like the studded pieces of cork used at Guardia Sanframondi.

In light of all this, it seems likely that Canon Pullen had stumbled across a report of one of these bloody southern Italian rituals and had "made sense of it" using Frazer's then-very-popular theory. While this reconstruction allows us to lay aside any suggestion of a true ritual slaying, we are still left with some pretty extreme and regular examples of self-punishment and self-mutilation in public rituals. This masochistic element needs to be explained.

A REGIONAL DIFFERENCE?

The first task is to decide if such rituals are distinctively southern. If we focus on flagellation alone, the answer is clearly no. After all, the medieval Flagellant Movement broke out in Perugia and from there spread to the rest of northern Italy. Furthermore, most of the *disciplinati* confraternities established in the wake of the Flagellant Movement were established in northern, not southern, Italy. Although public flagellation became less and less part of these northern *disciplinati* ceremonies, here again (as in the case of magic) this may only reflect the vulnerability of northern communities to the dictates of the Church hierarchy, whose Tridentine commitment to order and control usually predisposed them against such public displays. Similarly, the fact that flagellation continued to be practiced in the South until quite recently possibly only reflects that the *chiese ricettizie* insulated southern communities from Tridentine reformers.

But we come to a somewhat different conclusion if we consider flagellation as just one of a range of similar behaviors. Italian investigators regularly note that virtually all forms of popular Catholicism in the South are permeated by a strong penitential emphasis (e.g. Mazzacane and Lombardi Satriani 1974: 43–44). But *penitential* is far too mild a word to describe what has gone on in southern Italy over the centuries. Saying five Our Fathers and five Hail Marys is penitential; what we find in southern Italy is a extraordinarily strong masochistic emphasis, across a wide range of devotional activities. Masochism appears in the North but mainly in connection with individual mystics who mutilate themselves in private. When public rituals involving masochism do appear in the North, as in the case of the public flagellations of the early *disciplinati* confraternities, they stand out precisely because they are so dissimilar from most of the other religious rituals.

What is distinctive about popular Catholicism in southern Italy is the diversity of masochistic rituals, their widespread appeal, and the fact that they have continued until recently. While some of these masochistic practices, like flagellation, have been borrowed from other areas of Italy, other masochistic practices seem to have developed more autochthonously.

TONGUE DRAGGING

Tongue dragging is a form of religious behavior that has appeared all over southern Italy. In Sicilia, it is called "la lingua a strascinuni (Pitrè 1978: 2: 249; Candura 1971: 401), and in Basilicata, "lingere lingua terram (Cilento 1975: 247). Undoubtedly, other terms are used in other regions. Whatever the terminology, the central features of the practice are everywhere the same: a person goes down on all fours, usually at the threshold of the church, and moves forward while dragging his or her tongue along the pavement of the church. This last action is to be done with sufficient force that the tongue is lacerated and made to bleed. If a sufficiently large number of people engage in tongue dragging during a particular festa, the floor of the church will be covered with bloody stripes. A manuscript written in 1608 and preserved in the archives of the sanctuary dedicated to the Madonna dell'Arco near Naples gives a good account of the practice:

> In order to fulfil a vow or to ask for favors, several of those who come to this Holy House go down on their knees at the entrance to the church. They then move forward, on their knees and with their tongues to the ground, until they

Madonnas That Maim

reach the chapel and altar of the Madonna. At times, this tongue dragging is done with such fervor that their tongues are lacerated, and they leave the floor of the church looking like the scene of a bloody massacre. (D'Antonio 1979: 43).

Tongue dragging continued to be practiced at this particular sanctuary until the 1930s, at which time a determined effort was made to stamp it out. Nino D'Antonio (1979: 49) suggests that high Church authorities were behind the drive to eliminate the practice, but Giuseppe De Lutiis (1973: 100) is likely correct in saying that the practice was suppressed by the government because it was at odds with the image of a "virile" Italy favored by the Fascist regime. Even so, Annabella Rossi (1969: 92–93) reports that tongue dragging was practiced at a variety of Mezzogiorno sanctuaries, including that dedicated to the Madonna dell'Arco, until the 1950s, and that individual instances of the practice could still be observed at several Mezzogiorno sanctuaries in the 1960s.

The practice of tongue dragging was by no means uniform from region to region. In some Sicilian communities, those dragging their tongues proceeded forward along the floor of the church in pairs; a friend or relative stood between them and guided them with a kerchief passed under the tongue dragger's armpits. In other Sicilian communities, there was one such guide per tongue dragger (Pitrè 1896; 1978: 2: 249; Candura 1971). At the sanctuary dedicated to the Madonna Incoronata at Foggia (in Puglia), pilgrims began dragging their tongues from some point on the ground beyond the church, rather than just at the threshold (Cipriani, Rinaldi, and Sobrero 1979: 76). Giuseppe Pitrè (1896: 19) reports the case of a woman in Sicilia who dragged her tongue from the boundaries of the community up to the main altar of the local church, a distance of about one kilometer. In his study of Italian immigrants in New York City, Robert Orsi (1985: xii–xiv) reports that a tongue dragger, usually a woman, would be dragged forward in the church by the members of her family. Since most of these immigrants were originally from the Naples area, it seems likely that they were repeating a pattern common there. In the Abruzzo, devotees obtained favors from San Pantaleo by dragging their tongues along the floor of the church, making sure that the tongue became lacerated in the process (Pitrè 1883). When they reached the statue of the saint, they would kiss it, thereby marking it with the blood that flowed from their lacerated tongues. In what is likely a concession to modern notions of hygiene, tongue draggers at the sanctuary of the Madonna del Pollino in the Basilicata during the 1960s were sometimes preceded by someone who wiped the pavement with a cloth (Rossi 1969: 20).

Virtually every commentator trying to convey the essence of popular Catholicism in southern Italy mentions tongue dragging. When recalling his adolescence in the Basilicata during the 1920s, Nicola Cilento (1975: 247) writes of being unable to erase certain religious images from his mind. One of these is tongue dragging. To convey the nature of the "superstitions" associated with the practice of Catholicism in the South, L. Villari (1902: 121) names three things: the San Gennaro miracle at Naples, miraculous statues ("countless curtsying Madonnas and nodding saints"), and tongue dragging. In his account of Mezzogiorno piety during the eighteenth and nineteenth centuries, Pietro Borzomati (1973: 627) singles out the tongue dragging practiced at the sanctuary dedicated to San Michele on the Gargano peninsula (in Puglia) as a particularly clear example of the fanaticism associated with this piety. Tongue dragging is also mentioned in literary works seeking to convey a sense of southern Italian Catholicism. It is prominent among the many devotional horrors that Gabriele D'Annunzio (1956: 246) caused his protagonists to observe at a southern sanctuary, and the practice is described as well in Ignazio Silone's *Bread and Wine* (1937: 233–34).

Scholarly and literary judgments of this particular practice are invariably negative. Terms like *dehumanizing, bestial, brutal, disgusting,* and *savage* are routinely and liberally used in all commentaries. Unlike, say, the festas devoted to patron saints, tongue dragging is not romanticized by commentators. Yet surprisingly, no one has yet asked the obvious question: if tongue dragging is indeed such a bestial and brutish practice, then why has it flourished in the South, despite the near-constant opposition of high Church authorities? The obvious answer is that there is something about tongue dragging particularly appealing to southerners, something missed by the elites who sniff "bestial" and "brutish" and then look away from the event itself. Indeed, in the next chapter I argue that tongue dragging does epitomize southern Italian Catholicism, since it gratifies a psychological desire that in many ways is the motive force behind this type of Catholicism.

For the moment, I simply note that the widespread popularity of tongue dragging *is* a distinctively southern Italian phenomena. Outside the Mezzogiorno, I have found references to the practice only in a few sanctuaries in Lazio in central Italy, an area on the border of the Mezzogiorno (Rossi 1969: 254–80). There are occasional references to "kissing the ground" in the North, but the strong emphasis upon lacerating and mutilating the tongue is always absent.

A PANORAMA OF MASOCHISTIC PRACTICES

Although tongue dragging epitomizes southern Italian Catholicism for many commentators, what most of all distinguishes southern Italian festas from

Madonnas That Maim

their northern counterparts is the simultaneous presence of several different masochistic behaviors. Such simultaneity is captured in an anonymous account recorded in the eighteenth century and reproduced in the *Archivio per le tradizioni popolari* in the late nineteenth century:

> The spirit of religion [which characterizes the people of Sardegna] also gives rise to the austerity of the public penances practiced in many communities on the occasion of important festas. Some people come [to the festa] from a long way away, barefoot, and with their heads uncovered. Others appear in the habit of a confraternity, with the cowls covering their face. These slash their shoulders violently, using a razor-sharp instrument, and so mark with their blood all the spaces over which they pass. Some of the women, not wearing any veil on their head and with their hair dishevelled, go on their knees from the door of the church up to the altar. Other women do this while dragging their tongue on the ground as well. In several communities, there exist confraternities in which the prior punishes some failing on the part of a member by making him hang a large stone around his neck for the entire period of the [religious] services, and each member accepts this with humility. (Lumbroso 1886: 18)

Although the author is writing about Sardegna, the same report could equally apply to the entire Mezzogiorno. Annabella Rossi (1969) studied fifty-four "liturgical" cults that flourished in the Mezzogiorno during the 1960s. She calls them "liturgical," because each cult was organized around a madonna or saint legitimated by the Church, and each was localized in a sanctuary administered by Catholic clergy. Three of the rituals that appear with some regularity have a clear masochistic component (ibid., 254–58). These three rituals, and the number of sanctuaries at which each ritual was practiced, are (1) moving on one's knees from the threshold of the sanctuary up to the relevant altar, all the while striking oneself on the chest and asking pardon for one's sins (forty-three sanctuaries), (2) walking barefoot some portion of the journey to the sanctuary (forty-four sanctuaries), and (3) tongue dragging on the pavement in the church (eight sanctuaries). Interviews conducted by Rossi also make it clear that tongue dragging was common at these sanctuaries within living memory.

Rossi also studied ten extraliturgical cults. Half of these were organized around living seers and half around people who were dead. To say that they were extraliturgical is not to say that they were completely outside the Church. On the contrary, most of these ten cults had received legitimation from Church authorities. One of these cults, for example, was organized about Marietta D'Agostino, and we have already seen how this seer came to be legitimized. Another was organized around the body of Beato Giulio, a monk who had died in 1601 and whose body was conserved in an urn kept in the sanctuary at Montevergine (Campania). A third was organized around

Mezzogiorno Masochism

Giacomo Izzo, a seer who was in constant contact with the Madonna and who received his followers in the sanctuary of Maria Santissima della Ruota dei Monti, a sanctuary that Izzo managed by authority of the local bishop. Another cult was organized about the mummified body of a man who had been discovered beneath the pavement of a church in Bonito (Campania) and subsequently kept in an urn located in that same church. And so on. The only thing that clearly distinguishes Rossi's extraliturgical cults from her liturgical cults is that the extraliturgical cults were not organized around a madonna or saint recognized by the official Church. With this in mind, it is worth noting that the masochistic practices Rossi observed in connection with liturgical cults were not associated with any of the extraliturgical cults.

Rossi's data suggest, therefore, that the masochistic practices of southern Italian festas in honor of a madonna or saint are not simply folk elements that would find their way into any religious ceremony. On the contrary, there seems to be an affinity between these practices and the concepts of *saint* and *madonna*. There is, in other words, something in the veneration of the saints and madonnas of southern Italy that elicits masochistic behavior in a way that the veneration of seers and other beings who are not saints or madonnas does not—and this needs to be explained.

THE PSYCHOLOGY OF

ITALIAN CATHOLICISM

Several times in this book, we have encountered the suggestion that danger is a potential or actual condition of life in Italy. We have seen that the primary function of the multiplicity of saints and madonnas in Italy is to protect supplicants from danger. We have also seen how, to Italian Catholics if not to the Church, the saints and madonnas of Italy are often themselves sources of danger. This danger also has an objective source, in that the Italian environment is one of unpredictable natural forces that can overwhelm and destroy. These forces are relevant to the study of Italian Catholicism because, to most Italian scholars, it seems obvious that Italian Catholicism is an adaptation to these hostile natural forces. The following remarks are typical:

> The peasant lives in the world of nature, with its mysterious forces, both benevolent and threatening; he follows its rhythms and cycles without being able to understand or to explain them. . . . At work . . . in the woods, or in the fields, he feels undefended, faced with the unknown and the unexpected. . . . The peasant wants to protect himself from violence, to safeguard himself from dangers and risks, to overcome the unknown and the unexpected. This is the psychological context into which his religiosity has been inserted. It is a type of religiosity that looks to the "world beyond" as a world of equals and of justice and that seeks in this world to find the wonder-working objects and powers that will liberate him from every evil. (Gambasin 1973: 55)

> Religious celebrations derive from the deeply felt need to feel protected during a life that is continually exposed to a thousand dangers, the need to find a

The Psychology of Italian Catholicism

sense of security in the midst of the calamities that threaten the lives of human beings. . . . Notwithstanding simple appearances, which could mislead those observers who want to see in these celebrations only "local color," they are always functional and liberating and aid in the survival of the community. (Lombardi Satriani 1971: 77)

Presumably because it is so obvious to Italian scholars that Italians live in an environment permeated by danger and uncertainty, they almost never document this contention in any precise way. Yet that is not difficult.

GEOGRAPHICAL LOCATION AND EPIDEMIC DISEASE

Italy is a peninsula that juts out into the Mediterranean Sea. Because the Mediterranean has always served as an important conduit between Europe and Asia, it was inevitable that Italy should become an important nexus between the West and the East. Sometimes the foreign traffic that passed through Italy was concerned with trade. Indeed, it was trade that fueled the fortunes of the great maritime city-states like Genoa and Venice. Sometimes the traffic that passed through Italy had a more militaristic bent. Quite apart from the foreign armies that came to conquer Italy itself were those armies on their way to somewhere else. For instance, Italy was a major embarkation point for the armies that various European states launched against the Middle East during the Crusades.

Quite often the merchants and soldiers who came to and through Italy carried a plague. The Black Death that ravaged Europe in 1347–50 appeared first in Italy.[1] Most commentaries suggest that the first carriers were sailors from Genoa who stopped in Messina (Sicilia) after returning from the Near East. Certainly, by late 1347, the plague had broken out in both Messina and Genoa and, by early 1348, had struck Venice and Pisa as well. From these four points—Messina, Genoa, Venice, and Pisa, all located on or near the coast—the Black Death spread quickly to the rest of Italy and to the rest of Europe. Urban areas, in which the plague could spread quickly, were hardest hit. A variety of sources indicate that, overall, Italy lost about a third of its population during this period, which is about the same proportion that was likely lost by most other Western European states.[2]

Just as important, Italy was struck by twenty-seven more outbreaks of the plague between 1360 and 1657. Not all these outbreaks affected all regions of Italy: northern Italy was struck far more often than southern Italy (Del Panta 1980: 118). The very conditions that made travel in the South difficult and that would later impede the diffusion of the Tridentine reforms also impeded the spread of the plague. Still, the threat of plague spreading to any community in Italy, North or South, was ever present during these years.

Madonnas That Maim

In fact, after the 1347–50 outbreak, Italy was struck by at least six plagues that ravaged the entire peninsula (1360–63, 1422–45, 1476–79, 1493, 1522–30, and 1656–57).

While modern readers can perhaps appreciate the emotional significance of a single catastrophe, like that of 1347–50, it is more difficult to appreciate the cumulative impact of successive plagues, each reducing the population by a significant amount. Yet this is the horror with which Italians had to contend. The plague that struck northern Italy in 1575–77, for instance, reduced the population of Venice by about 30 percent and Padua by perhaps a similar percentage (Pullan 1971: 324; Del Panta 1980: 146). The proportion of the population that died from the 1630–31 plague in the North has been estimated as 46 percent for Milan, 57 percent for Verona, 24 percent for Bologna, 33 percent for Venice, and 38 percent for Lucca (Del Panta 1980: 160). The last of the great Italian plagues struck in 1652–57; it took 50 percent of the population in Naples, 8–12 percent in Rome, and 60 percent in Genoa (ibid., 168f).

As the threat of plague began to evaporate in the seventeenth century, a new horror arose to fill the void.[3] In the middle of that century, a series of agricultural crises in Italy provoked widespread famine, which in turn brought on typhoid fever. The pattern of famine followed by typhus was to repeat itself regularly, at least until the beginning of the nineteenth century.[4] Although less deadly than the plague, typhoid epidemics could elevate the death rate in a community far above normal. In the epidemic of 1764–67, for instance, an estimated 200,000 people in the Kingdom of Naples died of the combined effects of famine and typhus (ibid., 212).

Then there was smallpox. Although there had been a few smallpox epidemics in Italy during the fourteenth and fifteenth centuries, it was only in the sixteenth century (and in particular, during the latter half of the sixteenth century and thus in the period immediately following the Council of Trent) that the number of smallpox epidemics in Italy increased dramatically. Such epidemics became rare again in the seventeenth century, only to explode once more in the eighteenth and early nineteenth centuries. Between 1750 and 1850, for example, there were 265 smallpox epidemics in Italy, compared to 93 in the period 1500–1749 (ibid., 220).

The last of the really serious typhoid and smallpox epidemics in Italy occurred in the first half of the nineteenth century. But starting in the 1830s, Italy—along with most other European countries—was struck with cholera. Some idea of the effects of this disease can be gleaned from the fact that cholera struck 22 percent of the communes in Italy in 1836 and caused nearly 68,000 deaths; in 1855 it struck 37 percent of the communes and caused over 83,000 deaths; in 1867, it struck 26 percent of the communes and caused over 128,000 deaths (ibid., 228).

The Psychology of Italian Catholicism

During the modern period then, from the fifteenth century forward, Italian Catholics had to live with the threat of being struck down by epidemic diseases over which (until the late nineteenth century) they had little control. Italy was probably not unique in this regard. The Great Plague of 1347–50 struck most other nations of Europe as hard as it struck Italy. Furthermore, most of these other nations, like Italy, were struck regularly by later plagues, famine, typhoid fever, smallpox, and cholera. But in addition to these threats, Italians faced threats unique to the Italian peninsula.

CHTHONIAN DANGERS

Italy is a land of earthquakes. Although not as deadly as the great epidemic diseases of the past, earthquakes strike Italy often and cause great damage. Thus they contribute greatly to that sense of being at the mercy of hostile natural forces, which (if the commentators cited earlier are correct) is the motive force behind popular Catholicism in Italy. Although the most quake-prone region of Italy is the center spine of the peninsula from southern Umbria to Basilicata, severe quakes have been experienced both farther south and farther north.

Italian government reports indicate that between 1899 and 1960 there were 621 earthquakes in Italy with a rating of VI or more on the Mercalli scale (SVIMEZ 1961: table 11).[5] Of these, almost exactly half (311 of 621) struck northern Italy, while the other half (310 of 621) struck southern Italy. The same reports estimate that 184 "disastrous" earthquakes—that is, earthquakes with a rating of IX or more on the Mercalli scale—hit Italy in the period 1501–1960 (ibid., table 12).[6] Here again, almost exactly half (89 of 184) struck northern Italy, while the remainder (95 of 184) struck southern Italy. The number of dead in some of these quakes is truly horrendous: 30,000 dead in the quake that struck southern Italy (including parts of Molise, Campania, and Basilicata) in 1456; 60,000 dead in the quake that struck Siracusa (Sicilia) in 1693; 30,000 dead in Calabria in 1783; 80,000 dead at Reggio (Calabria) and Messina (Sicilia) in 1908.[7]

As horrible as such numbers are, they still fail to convey the devastation felt in particular local communities. Andrea De Leone (1783) provides an assessment of the effects of the earthquakes that struck Catanzaro (Calabria) in February 1783. His report makes it clear that the devastation was not uniform and that some communities suffered far more than others. Table 8.1 provides information on the number dead as a percentage of the existing population for some of those communities in Catanzaro that were particularly hard hit. Over the course of a few days, from one-fifth to one-half of the local community simply ceased to exist, and this change was sudden and

TABLE 8.1

Deaths from the earthquakes that struck the province of Catanzaro
(Calabria) in February 1783, by selected local communities

Community	Prequake population	Deaths	Percentage killed
Sinopoli and surrounding villages	8,471	2,029	24
Palmi	4,900	993	20
Sitizzano	715	221	31
Oppido	2,356	1,156	49
Terranova and surrounding villages	7,538	3,043	40
Casalnuova	5,590	2,008	36
San Giorgio	2,734	1,308	48
Cusoleto	752	174	23

Source: Derived from De Leone (1783: 19–47).

unpredictable. Furthermore, even communities that suffered less lived with
the fear of suffering such devastation in the future.

Some sense of Italy's uniqueness (at least in Europe in 1966–86) with
regard to earthquakes can be seen in table 8.2. Several patterns are evident.
First, countries bordering the Adriatic (Italy, Greece, and Yugoslavia) are
particularly prone to earthquakes. Second, in terms of number of quakes,
Italy ranks near the top of the list. Finally, and most important, Italy suffers
the most from these quakes, at least in regard to number of people killed.
The single quake that struck southern Italy in 1980, for instance, caused
3,105 deaths, whereas the quake that struck northeast Italy in 1976 caused
965 deaths. Overall, 4,359 people died as a result of the earthquakes that
struck Italy in this period. This is about 2.5 times the number who died from
earthquakes in all other European countries together.

Why Italy is struck by so many earthquakes is explainable in purely
geological terms. Why quakes cause so much more human damage in Italy
compared to other countries is usually explained in terms of the techniques
used to construct buildings in Italy and the looseness of the soil under these
buildings. My only interest here is with the net effect: Italians, more than
other Europeans, live in an environment of danger that the earth itself will
suddenly and unexpectedly cause death and destruction.

Other dangers also spring from the earth. In the North, the best example

The Psychology of Italian Catholicism

TABLE 8.2
Deaths from earthquakes in Europe with a Richter magnitude of 5.0 or greater, 1966–1986, by country

Country	Number of earthquakes	Deaths
Italy	9	4,359
Greece	10	94
Yugoslavia	5	166
Romania	1	1,500
All other Western European nations	1	1
All other Eastern European nations	4	2

Source: Derived from UNEP (1987: 306–11).

involves the Po. Although the Po makes the *valle padana* one of the most fertile regions in Italy, it also has caused great damage as a result of its periodic flooding. Southern Italy, at least on its Tyrrhenian side, is virtually the only area of Europe in which local populations live with active volcanoes, the two most well known of which are Vesuvio near Naples and Etna in Sicilia. Both of these volcanoes have erupted on a fairly regular basis since the sixteenth century. Although most of these eruptions cause no great damage, the threat of a disastrous eruption—like the eruption of Vesuvio that took place in 1631—is ever present.

ON THE OBVIOUSNESS OF OBVIOUS EXPLANATIONS

To most Italian commentators it has been obvious that, since Italian Catholics have always lived with hostile natural forces that could strike without notice, they would naturally come to believe in powerful supernatural deities who could offer protection from those dangers. At first sight, the argument here might seem to be a variant of the argument that the social anthropologist Bronislaw Malinowski offers to explain magic (1935; 1954: 17–92).

Malinowski suggests that people turn to magic when they face a dangerous and uncertain environment and lack the technology to control that environment so as to reduce the danger and uncertainty. The belief in magic in itself

~ 143 ~

reduces the anxiety that a dangerous and uncertain environment induces. Although Malinowski's argument, like all functionalist arguments, has fallen from favor among anthropologists, it receives a surprisingly warm endorsement by Keith Thomas in his *Religion and the Decline of Magic* (1973), probably the most important study of magic published since the 1920s. Although Thomas is sometimes interpreted as falsifying Malinowski (Willis 1985), in fact he only revised Malinowski's original argument. Thomas starts by noting that the pattern in medieval and early modern England very much fit the Malinowskian prediction: magic was used when English farmers were dependent upon natural processes over which they had little or no control but was not used when effective technologies did exist. Thus, for example, English farmers used magic to influence the weather and the fertility of the soil but not when they reaped corn or milked cows (Thomas 1973: 775–76).

What Malinowski's theory cannot explain, Thomas argues, is that the widespread use of magic (all forms of magic) began to decline in England in the seventeenth century, well before there were effective technological solutions to the problems previously addressed by magic. For Thomas, the weak point in Malinowski's theory is that it sees magic and effective technologies as the only ways to reduce the anxiety associated with a dangerous and uncertain environment. Thomas suggests that this anxiety can be reduced in other ways as well. In the particular case of England, Thomas maintains that one such functional alternative was provided by the increasing acceptance of the Protestant worldview.

Thomas's argument is complex, but his final conclusion is that Protestant theology led people to believe that God's will was constantly operative in the world and that, as a result, there was a link between material success and the absence of moral defects. Such a theology led, says Thomas, to the development of a philosophy of self-help when confronting danger and uncertainty. For Thomas this Protestant-derived emphasis upon self-help began the decline of magic in England. Once begun, this decline was aided by the explicitly antimagical orientation of Protestant reformers and by the fact that the rise of the mechanistic philosophy in the natural sciences increasingly brought the practice of magic into disrepute.[8]

The arguments offered by Malinowski and Thomas can easily explain why Italians have historically turned to magic. The dangers faced by Italians (plagues, earthquakes, volcanoes, the flooding of the Po, etc.) were beyond the control of human technology (many still are). Furthermore, Protestantism made little headway in Italy, and so Italians—unlike their post-Reformation counterparts in England—never developed an ideology linking self-help to material success.[9] In this situation, it is perfectly consistent with the Malinowski/Thomas argument that magic should flourish in Italy. Furthermore, a belief in supernatural beings, such as saints and madonnas, who could and did offer protection from natural danger would also (like a belief in magic) reduce the anxiety associated with these dangers. It is thus reasonable to expect that a belief in such supernatural patrons would flourish alongside the practice of magic.

The practice of magic, the Mary cult, and the cult of the saints can be seen as functionally equivalent adaptations to the same thing: the dangerous and hostile environment faced by Italians and the anxiety that such an environment produces. At this point, then, we seem to have arrived where we were at the beginning of this chapter—that is, we seem to have come to the same conclusion reached by most Italian commentators. The problem is that there is still a problem.

STILL UNEXPLAINED

I concede that Italians have historically faced a dangerous and uncertain environment and that this has generated anxiety. I further concede that the popularity of the metacults considered in this book (and of magic) derives largely from their ability to reduce this anxiety. And yet I fail to see how this argument, although correct in itself, explains any of those distinctive features of Italian Catholicism that this book has established. This argument, for instance, does not explain why the Mary cult and the cult of the saints are more popular than the Christ cult; it does not explain why the Mary cult and the cult of the saints are characterized by psychological separation; it does not explain why the popular image of Mary is splintered into a range of separate and distinct madonnas, each with a different personality and yet all related; it does not explain why Italians create more saints than other nationalities; and it certainly does not explain the masochistic emphasis that permeates Catholicism in southern Italy. In short, while some variant of the dangerous-environment/anxiety-reduction hypothesis might explain the psychological processes that maintain Italian Catholicism, we still need to explain those things that make Italian Catholicism distinctive.

At this point it seems reasonable to turn to the one theoretical perspective concerned with powerful male and female figures who are simultaneously loved and feared and who are often splintered into separate personalities. That perspective is psychoanalysis.

A PSYCHOANALYTIC APPROACH TO RELIGION

The starting point for all psychoanalytic investigations of religion is Sigmund Freud's *The Future of an Illusion* (1927). There, Freud suggests that the

Madonnas That Maim

deities who populate the religious pantheons of the world are modeled upon our infantile memories of our parents. He argues that when as adults we feel helpless in the face of a threatening environment, we are reminded of the helplessness we experienced as children when we similarly faced an environment over which we had little or no control. These infantile memories in turn predispose us as adults to believe in powerful and transcendent supernatural beings who have the power to protect us from threat, just as our parents had the power to protect us from threat when we were children. Given that Italians face an environment permeated with danger and uncertainty, it is certainly consistent with Freud's argument to find, as we have found, that Italian Catholics believe in saints and madonnas who have the power to protect them from that environment.[10]

At one level, Freud's argument adds little to the commonsense hypothesis advanced in the last section, namely, that Italian Catholicism is a response to the anxiety produced by a dangerous and uncertain environment. The one advantage of the Freudian argument is that it points the way to a theoretical perspective on the splintering process that is so distinctive a feature of Italian Catholicism. After all, if Freud is right, then what is being splintered to create the plethora of saints and madonnas in Italy are our infantile memories of our parents, and there is in fact a fairly substantial psychoanalytic literature on the splintering of parental images. Most of this literature is associated with the object-relations tradition in psychoanalysis and, in particular, with the theories developed by Melanie Klein.

Klein, far more than Freud, stresses the importance of an infant developing relationships with objects in the infant's environment.[11] Since nursing is one of the first and most important experiences for most infants, Klein argues that one of the most important relationships in the life of the young child is the early relationship established with the breast, or more precisely, with the image of the breast that forms in the infant's mind. In Klein's view, infants early on make a distinction between the "good breast" (the breast that provides warmth and nourishment) and the "bad breast" (the breast that withholds milk when the infant is hungry). Both the good breast and the bad breast are assumed to have an independent and separate existence. The separation between these two images is reinforced not only by innate tendencies (which Klein calls the life instinct and the death instinct) but also by the infant's experience of warm gratifying experiences (when being nursed) and by frustrating, unpleasant experiences (when the infant wants to be nursed but is not).

Because some readers will undoubtedly recoil at the use of terms like *good breast* and *bad breast*, it is important to emphasize that these terms refer to rough mental images in the mind of the infant. In Kleinian theory, the image of the good breast need not derive from the infant's experience with a real breast. The bottle-fed infant will also develop an image of a good breast, since the good breast is simply the object that provides food and conveys a sense of nurturance; this object can just as easily be a bottle as a breast. Once the image of the good breast has developed, from whichever experience, then the fact that feeding is always to some degree intermittent rather than continuous will give rise to the image of the bad breast.

Klein goes on to argue that the images of the good breast and the bad breast are introjected; that is, the infant comes to see them as objects in its own mind, and they become the core around which the ego develops. The good breast becomes the prototype for all satisfying experiences and objects and the bad breast for all unpleasant experiences. Very quickly, infants also develop paranoid fears about the bad breast; that is, they see the bad breast as a source of threat and danger.

Klein calls this early period, which lasts for about the first six months of life, the paranoid-schizoid position: *schizoid* because of the separation between the good breast and the bad breast, and *paranoid* because the fear of being harmed by the bad breast dominates the mental life of the infant. Klein does not argue that these fears of persecution are clearly conceptualized in the infant's mind. On the contrary, she suggests that these fears are diffuse, disordered, and unconscious. But they are nevertheless real, and the infant reacts to these very real fears by throwing up defenses, the first of the many psychological defenses we establish during the course of our lives.

The most important of these earliest defenses is the splintering of the image of the bad breast into distinct parts. This process has the effect of diminishing the threat from the bad breast. But the process does not stop there. The splintered parts of the bad breast are projected onto things in the infant's environment, and these external things are then reintrojected, that is, brought back into the child's mind. The process of splitting a single image (in this case the bad breast) into several parts, projecting those parts onto objects in the environment, and then reintrojecting them is what Klein calls "projective identification." Klein's isolation of this process is generally regarded as one of her most important psychoanalytic discoveries (Grosskurth 1986: 373–75), if only because the objects brought into the infantile mind as a result of projective identification constitute a template that largely determines the shape of the adult personality. The important thing for us to note is that each part of the splintered object acquires a unique identity.

Eventually, infants realize that the bad breast and the good breast are simply two aspects or attributes of the same person, the mother (or the person who performs the maternal role), and with that the infant passes from the paranoid-schizoid position to what Klein calls the depressive position. What happens during the depressive position is for Klein very important to later development, but at this point I refer the interested reader to Klein's own

Madonnas That Maim

work. What I want to stress here is the structural similarity between Klein's description of the infant's splintering of its image of the bad breast during the paranoid-schizoid position, and the splintering of the concepts of *madonna* and *saint* so central to popular Catholicism in Italy. This similarity is not coincidental; the same splintering process is operative in both cases. Do I really mean to imply that a defense mechanism used (if Klein is correct) during the first six months of life can affect the structure of religious belief among adults? Yes, I do. Hanna Segal (1974: 35) says: "No experience in human development is ever cast aside or obliterated; we must remember that in the most normal individual there will be some situations which will stir up the earliest anxieties and bring into operation the earliest mechanism of defence. . . . [The] achievements of the ego in the paranoid-schizoid position are indeed very important for later development, for which they lay the foundations."

We have already seen that Italy is an especially threatening environment, in which powerful natural forces—ranging from plague to earthquakes to floods—can unexpectedly destroy human beings. Italians, in other words, have historically found themselves in an environment similar to that of the infant in the paranoid-schizoid position. This, in turn, activates unconscious memories of the first defense erected to diminish such perceived dangers: splintering.

The Basic Argument

The argument draws upon both Freud and Klein. Freud suggests that when adults are faced with danger and uncertainty they activate the memory of the parents, since they are the beings who protected them from danger; and so the adult seeks protection from current danger from a god or gods modeled upon these parental memories. But parents are not just a source of protection in the infantile mind; they are a source of threat, as well. Some of these threats derive from processes described in the psychoanalytic literature. In her clinical work, Klein found evidence that the fear of the bad breast generalizes and comes to be associated with the infantile image of the father (Klein 1975: 27–30). Freud stresses the importance of the fear of castration from the father that develops in sons. Beyond all this, parents eventually put restrictions on those activities that produce pleasure in the child, like breast feeding and excretion, and seek to regulate the child's desire for immediate gratification. For a variety of reasons, then, at least from a child's point of view, parents are an external threat.

It is thus to be expected (given Freud's basic argument) that, when current anxieties activate infantile images of the father and the mother and these come to be associated with the concepts of *saint* and *madonna*, these supernatural beings, like their parental prototypes, also are seen as sources of both protection and threat. But current anxieties also reactivate infantile memories of the first defense used to ward off the paranoid fears associated with the bad breast: splintering. Through a process of projective identification, this defense is now used against the concepts of *saint* and *madonna* to minimize the dangers associated with these beings. The result is the creation of a number of saints and madonnas.

A Second Defense Mechanism

Recall from chapter 1 that madonnas, more than saints, are kept at a distance. This is reflected both in the terms of address used in connection with madonnas and saints and in the fact that madonnas are more likely to be associated with distant sanctuaries. We are now in a position to explain why Italian madonnas are more distant than saints. Remember that, although Klein found that an infant's paranoid fears do generalize to the father, these paranoid fears are attached first and foremost to the mother. This leads us to expect that those supernatural beings most modeled upon the mother should be the beings who are most feared.

Although Freud's general argument suggests that beliefs about both female saints and madonnas are shaped by infantile memories of the mother, an association with the mother is stronger in the latter case. Madonnas after all are at least vaguely associated with the Mary of the official Church, and Mary's preeminence in Catholic theology has always rested upon her being the Mother of God. But this in turn means that madonnas, more than female saints (and certainly more than male saints) are associated with the paranoid fears associated with the mother in the infantile mind. This greater fear of madonnas evokes a second mechanism of defense (apart from splintering): separation. Establishing geographical distance between the local community and some particular madonna is—like splintering—a defense mechanism, a way of establishing psychological distance from the danger that the madonna represents.

On Just-So Stories

One of the greatest barriers to a wider diffusion of psychoanalytic explanations (like the one just offered) is the sense that they are just-so stories, explanations made to fit whatever data happen to be at hand. Someone committed to the psychoanalytic perspective, so the objection goes, will be able to develop a psychoanalytic account no matter what the data. There is a large measure of truth in objections like these, and psychoanalytic investigators who ignore them will never reach the larger audience that Freud always wanted to reach. In response, let me first point out that there is not a great deal of theoretical novelty in the psychoanalytic explanation just presented. I have invented no new theoretical arguments to fit the case at hand. Rather I have made use of theoretical conclusions developed by Freud and Klein, mainly on the basis of their clinical experiences. The suggestion that religious belief can be shaped by infantile experience belongs to Freud. The description of what happens in the mind of the infant during the first few months of life derives from the work of Klein.

As N. Cheshire (1975) notes, the great appeal of psychoanalytic arguments is precisely their ability to provide "comprehensibility," that is, their ability to order a range of seemingly disparate observations into a single pattern. This is what I have tried to do here. My goal has been to demonstrate that the conclusions reached by Freud and Klein help us to make sense of some of the patterns associated with Italian Catholicism, patterns that otherwise seem puzzling. The fact that an explanation provides comprehensibility is not in itself evidence that it is correct, but it does provide a basis (as Cheshire also suggests) for the comparative evaluation of different theoretical explanations of the same phenomenon. Different theories, in other words, can be evaluated in terms of the degree to which they allow us to order disparate observations into a coherent pattern. The final worth of the argument being developed here will be established only when other investigators develop other explanations, psychoanalytic or not, of the same patterns.

WHY NO GESÙ DELLE GRAZIE
OR SALVATORE DEI MIRACOLI?

A feature of Italian Catholicism easy to overlook is that the image of Christ has not been splintered into separate personalities in the way that the image of Mary has. The reasons for this are not obvious, since the splintering of Christ would in no sense be incompatible with Catholic tradition. Catholics throughout the world worship Christ as the Infant of Prague, the Sacred Heart of Jesus, the Holy Face of Jesus, the Precious Blood of Jesus, the Holy Agony of Jesus, the Five Wounds of Jesus, and so on. There is therefore no official barrier to prevent Italian Catholics from creating a multitude of *salvatores* equal in number to their multitude of madonnas. Yet that did not happen. Why?

The argument presented in the last section suggests that Italian Catholics model their beliefs about supernatural beings upon their infantile memories of their parents. But as I indicate in the Introduction, popular Catholicism is best seen as the interaction between official Catholicism and the psychological processes that spring from the nature of the environment in Italy. Official tradition presents only three types of supernatural being sufficiently powerful to be parental surrogates and thus sources of both protection and danger. These are Mary, the saints (some male, some female), and Christ.

While memories of the mother shape beliefs about both Mary and female saints, this shaping is likely to be stronger in the case of Mary, given Mary's role as the Mother of God. The male saint, however, is the father surrogate. This image is then splintered, just as young children splinter their image of the father on account of the fears associated with that image. Why this has happened to the concept of *male saint* rather than that of *Christ* derives, I suggest, from something that has long been an important part of the cult of the saints but not the Christ cult.

Relics

Saints have been venerated in the Church since the earliest centuries of the Christian era. Early commentators often stress the continuities between the cult of the saints among Christians and the hero cults of the classical world. Modern commentators, however, tend to stress the differences between the two cults. Peter Brown (1981: 5–6), for example, points out that in the classical world dead heroes were thought of as just that—dead—and were not associated either in ritual practice or in religious thought with the gods. Saints, by contrast, are seen as active beings endowed with a supernatural power, which can influence the affairs of the world.

Very quickly, the physical remains of dead saints became a central element in the practice of saintly veneration.[12] It was common in the early Church, for example, for Christians to hold their religious services and bury their dead in or near the resting places of the early martyrs. But eventually, pressure arose to bring the physical remains of these dead saints into the community. At first this gave rise to the practice of moving (*translating* is the formal term) the remains of a saint from their burial place to a church. Soon there was pressure on Church leaders to divide up the physical body of a saint, so that bits and pieces of the same saint could be sent to different locations. Brown (ibid.: 4f) notes that to educated pagans this Christian tendency to disturb the dead and blur the separation between the space occupied by the dead and the space occupied by the living was one of the most disgusting aspects of the new religion.

Whereas the dismemberment of saintly bodies seems to have occurred early in the history of the Eastern Church, it was initially opposed by many leaders of the Western Church. When the Empress Constantina asked Pope Gregory the Great (c. A.D. 540–604) for some part of the body of Saint Paul, preferably the saint's head, Gregory refused on the grounds that

Madonnas That Maim

dismemberment was sacrilegious (Thurston 1913b: 736). Leaders of the Western Church were far more likely to meet the demands for relics with objects that had been in close physical proximity to the saint. Gregory, for instance, offered to send the Empress Constantina some filings from the chains that had bound Saint Peter. Quite often, secondary relics of this sort were simply created. Thus to supply relics for the consecration of churches, Gregory would lower into the tomb of the Apostles a box containing pieces of cloth, called *brandea*, which thereby became relics (ibid.) But this initial opposition to physical dismemberment was eventually overcome, and by the ninth century dismembering saintly bodies for relics had become common in both the Western and the Eastern Churches (Chiovaro 1967: 236).

The use of saintly relics served a number of functions. Patrick Geary (1978: 64; 1984: 266), for example, points out that they could be used to legitimate new religious organizations, to increase the prestige of a local community, and even to aid the local economy if a shrine containing the relics attracted a significant number of pilgrims. Relics were also a symbolic medium of exchange, which could build solidarity between giver and receiver. Under this interpretation, the flow of relics served to bind together disparate sections of the Church or to strengthen the ties between a bishop and the more remote settlements under his authority.

What is often noted but never satisfactorily explained is that, around the eleventh century, this emphasis on saintly relics faded rapidly in the Eastern Church, to be replaced by an emphasis on icons (Geary 1984: 265). In the Western Church, by contrast, the use of relics taken from the dismembered bodies of saints continued to be widespread. A report written in 1597, for instance, indicates that in Milan alone 124 bodies, 73 heads, and 2,600 pieces of bone were venerated (Signorotto 1985: 411–12). In the diocese as a whole, the numbers were 141 bodies, 91 heads, and 3,800 pieces of bone (ibid.). These relics were augmented by the arrival of a collection of several thousand relics at Milan in the early 1600s (ibid.).

There is nothing comparable to the bodily dismemberment of saints in connection with Christ. A central dogma of the Church, that Christ rose from the dead in possession of the same body that he had used during his earthly life and that he ascended into Heaven in that body, makes the existence of body-part relics of Christ highly unlikely. There were Christ relics, but these were usually pieces of physical objects that had been in contact with him during his life.[13]

Two collections of relics, one at the Cathedral of Ancona (Le Marche) installed in 1603 (Saracini 1675: 1490–91) and one exhibited at Santa Maria della Scala in Siena on the Feast of the Annunciation early in the 1700s (Quinza 1722: 58) follow. The relics in the Cathedral at Ancona:

~ 152 ~

— Thorn from the Crown of Thorns
— Piece of a nail used at the crucifixion
— Point of the lance used to pierce Christ
— Piece of the sponge used to give Christ a drink on the cross
— Threads from a gown of Christ, made by the Blessed Virgin
— Piece of the cloth that covered part of Christ's body on the cross
— Girdle of the Blessed Virgin
— Piece of gown belonging to S. Simeone
— Some bones of SS. Pietro and Paolo
— A half finger of S. Tommaso
— Bones from the head of S. Giacomo Minore
— Bones from the arm of S. Giacomo Maggiore
— Bones of S. Stefano, the first martyr, and one of the stones used to stone him
— A finger of S. Ciriaco
— A shinbone, along with the kneecap, of S. Alessandro
— A bone from the throat of S. Vincenzo
— Bones of S. Ignatio
— Part of the head of S. Orsola and a piece of bone of one of the 11,000 virgins and martyrs
— Bones of S. Sigismondo
— Bones from the rib of S. Margherita
— Bones of S. Romano
— Bones and burned flesh of S. Lorenzo
— The head of S. Candida
— Bones of S. Probo
— The head of S. Felicita
— Bones from the head of S. Lucia
— Relic of S. Ambrogio
— A book of writings by S. Marcellino
— The right arm and hand, with flesh, and a bone of S. Antonio abate
— The right foot, with flesh attached, of S. Anna, mother of the Virgin Mary
— Bones of S. Costanzo
— Bones of S. Cesare Seruo
— Bones of S. Eusebius
— Bones of S. Nicolò
— The shoulderblade of S. Rocco
— Bones from the head and some of the hair of S. Maria Maddalena
— Bones of S. Leone

The relics exhibited at Santa Maria della Scala:

— Part of the wood of the Holy Cross, the purple cloak, the reed and sponge, the lance and other instruments of the Passion of Our Lord
— A toe bone of S. Pietro and one of S. Paolo
— A bone of S. Bartolomeo

Madonnas That Maim

— A rib of S. Andrea
— A finger of S. Filippo
— A bone of S. Tommaso
— A bone from the arm of S. Biagio
— A bone of S. Giovanni Crisostomo
— A bone of S. Quirico
— A bone of S. Teodoro
— Part of the head of S. Antonio abate
— The head of S. Cristina
— A bone from the head of S. Stefano Juniore
— Two bones, one of S. Eusrosina and one of S. Maria Egizziaca
— A bone from the leg of S. Andromaco
— Bones of Pope S. Martino, S. Gregorio Magno, S. Giorgio, and S. Giovanni Elimosinario
— A finger of Blessed Ambrogio Sansedoni

The two collections differ in size but are much the same in structure: the bulk of each collection consists of small fragments of bone from the bodies of saints, with a smaller number of Christ relics. This pattern is typical of most relic collections in Italy (and likely most other areas of Catholic Europe as well).

The relevance of relics to the concerns of this chapter lies in the similarity between the dismemberment of saints' bodies to Klein's view of the splintering process. After all, what does splintering involve? It involves taking a whole and dividing it into parts, which are then kept separate. And what happens to the body of a saint, at least in the Western Church? It is dismembered and split into bits and pieces, and these are dispersed to different (and clearly separated) geographical areas—an arm here, a toe there, a head (or head bone) somewhere else.

I suggest there is a psychological association of saints with dismemberment, a structural similarity between dismemberment and splintering, and therefore an affinity between saints and splintering. When Italian Catholics want to defend themselves against danger by splintering the image of a dangerous father surrogate, this association makes it more likely that they will splinter the concept *male saint* rather than the concept *Christ*. Ordinary Catholics, of course, do not have custody of the physical remains of dead saints, so they cannot splinter the *saint* concept by dismemberment. But they can splinter the concept *saint* by creating a number of saints, each with its distinct and separate personality. And that is precisely what they have done.

The psychoanalytic argument developed so far provides a way of understanding most of the patterns identified in this book, including the greater popularity of the Mary cult and the cult of the saints compared to the Christ cult; the tendency to see madonnas and saints not only as sources of protection but also as sources of danger; the fact that the concepts *Mary* and *saint* are splintered into many separate and distinct personalities; and the fact that madonnas are likely to be associated with distinct sanctuaries. But one final pattern remains: the association of popular Catholicism in southern Italy with a strongly masochistic emphasis.

THE SOCIAL ORIGINS OF MEZZOGIORNO MASOCHISM

There is as yet no systematic study of masochistic religious practices in southern Italy. Indeed, at this point in time, it is entirely possible that the historical materials that would be needed to conduct such a study are simply not available. Still, as chapter 5 makes clear, anecdotal examples of masochistic practice are easy to come by, and Italian scholars investigating religion in southern Italy have often called attention to the strong penitential emphasis permeating religious practice in the South. What leads ordinary Catholics in southern Italy to subject themselves to religious practices like tongue dragging?

In the anthropological reports on southern Italy, especially as they relate to family structure and gender roles, certain themes recur (Cucchiari 1990; Giovannini 1981; 1987). First, the father-ineffective family is widely prevalent. The father-ineffective family structure is characterized by a father who is absent for long periods but who regularly returns; as a result, de facto authority within the home rests with the mother. (Why this form of family organization is widely prevalent in southern Italy is an issue that I will address momentarily.)

Southern Italy is also characterized by the machismo complex, an ideology of exaggerated masculinity, which encourages males to be hyperaggressive and to brag about their sexual conquest of women. It is fairly commonplace to suggest that the father-ineffective family and the machismo complex are linked: that a father-ineffective family produces an early maternal identification in sons, and that the machismo complex is a defensive reaction against this early maternal identification (see Saunders 1981; Paul 1989). The machismo ideology, so the argument goes, helps males raised in father-ineffective families to develop a masculine identity while simultaneously repressing their early feminine identification. On the other hand, once established, the machismo complex tends to reinforce the father-ineffective family, since it propels men to disassociate themselves as much as possible from women, which means spending as little time as possible at home (Gilmore 1990: 956–57). Finally, there is the southern Italian attitude toward female chastity, or more precisely, toward the link between female chastity and "honor." Simply put, in southern Italy the social reputation of males

Madonnas That Maim

depends upon the perceived chastity of their female relatives, notably their mothers and sisters.[14]

MASOCHISTIC MALES

This constellation of cultural traits—the father-ineffective family, the *machismo* ideology, the tie between male honor and female chastity—is responsible for the masochistic emphasis associated with popular Catholicism in southern Italy. The precise process linking these traits to masochism, however, differs by sex. In other words, although the men and women of southern Italy both mix pain with their religion, they do so for different reasons.

In my earlier work on the Mary cult, I suggest that in males a predilection toward masochism derives directly from having been raised in a father-ineffective family (Carroll 1986). The starting point here is Freud's suggestion that the strength of a son's sexual desire for his mother (by which Freud meant only the son's desire for physical contact with the mother) was a function of the son's initial cathexis with the mother.[15] In a father-ineffective family, the mother is in a position to devote herself exclusively to her child. True, this exclusive attention typically ends when the next child is born. But this early, strong cathexis with the mother affects the male child's sexual desire for his mother for life. Furthermore, the absence of her husband usually leads the mother to gratify her libidinous desires by holding and touching her child more often than would usually be the case (Freud 1910), producing that much more physical pleasure in the infant.

In the northern European middle-class family (which is what Freud was discussing), Freud argues that the son comes to see his father as someone else who wants physical closeness with the mother. The son concludes (however erroneously) that the father will retaliate against him (the son) for daring to want what the father wants and, for a variety of reasons, concludes that the most fitting retaliation will be penis detachment. Fear of penis detachment, which Freud misleadingly calls castration anxiety, leads the son to repress his desire for the mother.

In the father-ineffective family, the father does return home on a regular basis, which makes the son's castration anxiety especially intense. Not only does his especially strong desire for the mother make his "offense against the father" that much more serious, but the son is facing a father under the sway of the machismo complex, one element of which is aggressive behavior. The net effect is that the son's desire for the mother becomes even more repressed than in the situation described by Freud. It was Freud's contention, which is certainly consistent with many cases accumulated since Freud, that strong—and strongly repressed—desires give rise to a sense of guilt and a corresponding desire to be punished. One manifestation of this desire for punishment is masochism. In Carroll (1986), this line of reasoning was used to explain why Marian devotion is most associated with masochistic practices in precisely those areas of the Catholic world, like southern Italy, Spain, most parts of Latin America, where the father-ineffective family and the machismo complex are common.

THE FATHER-INEFFECTIVE FAMILY
IN SOUTHERN ITALY

Most anthropological investigators who discuss the father-ineffective family in various parts of the world see it as a result of the economic marginality of males (Lewis 1959; Gilmore and Gilmore 1979; Saunders 1981; Yorburg 1983; Gilmore 1990). The economic marginality of males has been a feature of life in southern Italy for centuries, especially in Naples and the surrounding region, long the most heavily and densely populated region of the Mezzogiorno.

In the modern era, Naples underwent what was perhaps its most consequential demographic shift during the late sixteenth century. Spain, which then controlled the Kingdom of Naples, inaugurated a number of financial policies that literally pauperized the countryside (Carroll 1989: 74–76). One result of this pauperization was a massive influx into Naples of large numbers of the rural poor. By the early seventeenth century, this influx had made Naples one of the two largest cities in Europe (the other being Paris; Mols 1974: 42), and it was during this period that the slums of Naples acquired the unsavory reputation that they still have today (Minchinton 1974: 137). We have virtually no direct information on the family structure that prevailed among the poor in Naples during this period. We do know that they were victims of economic marginality, which typically produces the father-ineffective family.

In the case of modern Naples, the work by Anne Parsons (1969) establishes that the father-ineffective family is widespread among the poor in that city. Parsons's work also provides direct evidence of the guilt produced in sons vis-à-vis their mothers as a result of this family structure. Parsons gave her respondents a version of the Thematic Apperception Test, in which one of the cards shows a son in the presence of his mother. The most common response to this card was the suggestion that the son in the picture is asking forgiveness from the mother for some wrong he has done. This response was more likely to be elicited from male respondents than from female respondents; further, the attribution of wrongdoing was not elicited in the case of the father/son card or the mother/daughter card. Although Naples is the largest city in the South and has the largest slum population, it is not unique. Slums, with the attendant economic marginality of males, exist in all the major cities in southern Italy. This is presumably why attempts to describe family structure among the poorer strata in Italian society always end up describing what is here called the father-ineffective family (e.g., Cornelisen 1976: 15–30).

What I failed to appreciate in my earlier work is that the economic marginality of males in southern Italy is by no means the only condition that breeds the father-ineffective family. Indeed, a number of Italian-language works suggest that the father-ineffective family in southern Italy has also resulted from the settlement patterns that have prevailed there. The key here is to understand what a "city" in southern Italy is, or at least was, until the relatively recent past. When most English speakers hear the word *city*, they tend to think of a settlement that has a relatively large number of people living in it and a population engaged in nonagricultural pursuits. At the very least, the Anglo-Saxon tendency is to see these two things as correlated: as the number of people living in a single settlement increases, the involvement in agriculture decreases. But in southern Italy, outside the very largest cities, no such correlation exists.

Traditionally, Italian censuses distinguish two settlement patterns: *sparsa* and *agglomerata*. Although the precise definition of these terms varies from census to census, generally, *sparsa* refers to individual family dwellings that are "dispersed" throughout the countryside, while *agglomerata* refers to family dwellings that have been "gathered together." The overwhelming majority of *sparsa* family units live on or near the land cultivated by the father. Because we tend to think of the South as a traditionally agricultural society, it would be easy to imagine that a larger proportion of the population in the South is *sparsa* than in the North. In fact, just the reverse is true.

In the census for 1871, for example, the only regions whose population was over 40 percent *sparsa* were the Veneto, Emilia, Toscana, Le Marche, and Umbria—all northern regions (Almagià 1949). In the other major regions of northern Italy—Piemonte, Liguria and Lombardia—the proportion of *sparsa* ranged from 20 to 25 percent. In the South, by contrast, the proportion of *sparsa* was 5 percent in Basilicata, 6 percent in Puglia and Sardegna, 7 percent in Sicilia, and 11 percent in Calabria and Campania.[16] This dramatic North/South difference in settlement patterns persisted at least until the 1950s (Barbagli 1984: 118–19).

In the North, then, agriculturalists tend to live on or near the land they work. In the South, by contrast, agriculturalists tend to congregate in large settlements. In terms of sheer numbers, these settlements might seem like cities, but the fact that the population is so overwhelmingly involved in agriculture and related occupations gives them more the appearance of "overgrown villages" (Almagià 1949). The historical reasons for this difference in settlement are complex. Perhaps there exists some overview of this complexity in the Italian-language literature, but if so, I am not aware of

The Psychology of Italian Catholicism

it.[17] In any case, my only concern here is with the effect of this difference in settlement patterns on family dynamics.

When a man lives on or near the land he works, he is in the home almost every night and likely returns to the house during the day for meals and rest. This schedule allows him more contact, including physical contact, with his wife and children. Furthermore, the proximity of the home to the fields means that it is easier for his wife and children to work in the fields.

The situation is quite different in the overgrown villages of the South. Here agricultural workers travel a relatively great distance to reach the land they work. The result is that, in the southern countryside, a farmer or agricultural worker is less likely to return home during the day and more likely to be absent from the home for longer periods of time. Similarly, their wives are less able to travel to the fields to work with their husbands. Marzio Barbagli (1984: 119) provides a good description of what is involved:

> The peasants would leave these [large villages of the South] every morning in order to reach the fields, which were several kilometers distant. Often they returned home in the evening. But sometimes, when the distance to the land that needed to be cultivated was especially great, they would leave Monday morning and return Saturday evening. In these cases, they lived on food they brought from home and slept in small shelters or in the open, far from their wives and children. Regardless of whether the men returned every evening or only on Saturday, the wives remained at home. The distance between the place of residence and the place of work prevented them from following their husbands and, thus, of alternating and combining domestic work with agricultural work.

It seems, then, that *both* the economic marginality of males and the prevailing settlement pattern among agriculturalists have worked to promote in southern Italy a form of family organization (the father-ineffective family) that engenders in sons a strong but strongly repressed desire for the mother. This produces a strong sense of guilt and a resultant desire for self-punishment in those sons. It is this process, I am arguing, that has engendered in the southern Italian males a predilection for mixing religious ritual with masochistic practice.

MASOCHISM IN FEMALES

Freud devotes a fair amount of attention to female masochism, work that has provoked strong criticism among feminist authors. They especially object to Freud's suggestion that women are constitutionally prone to masochism as a result of genital structure; that is, that their having a vagina, which "receives" a penis, predisposes them to passivity and thus to masochism.[18] However,

~ 159 ~

at least one feminist commentator notes that Freud relies very little on the genital structure argument and more on the fact that females were surrounded by a greater number of social restrictions than males (Young-Bruehl 1990: 283; Freud 1924; 1933).

Freud argues that all human beings possess a death instinct, by which he means a tendency to regress to earlier stages of psychological development. For development to occur, the death instinct must be subverted, and this is done by channeling it into aggression. In the first instance, the objects of this aggression will be other people. But the social restrictions surrounding women inhibit them from expressing their aggression in this way, so they turn their aggression against themselves. The result is masochism.

The specifics of Freud's argument must be rejected on empirical grounds: there is simply too much evidence that the "passivity" of women, upon which Freud relies so heavily for both arguments regarding female masochism, is culturally conditioned and context-specific. In the case of southern Italy, for example, Salvatore Cucchiari (1990: 687) points out that women are commonly—and legitimately—assertive within the family environment, even if they defer to their husbands in public.[19] Indeed, one of the defining characteristics of the father-ineffective family is that de facto authority is concentrated in the hands of the mother. And Cornelisen's (1976) account, in particular, provides any number of examples of how this authority can be actively used and also demonstrates that in certain contexts the women of southern Italy can be just as aggressive as the men.

On the other hand, although Freud may have gotten the precise mechanism wrong, his suggestion that there is a link between female masochism and the social restrictions placed on women is likely correct. Both Bruce Malina (1990) and Nawal El Saadawi (1980) point to the restrictions on female sexuality as inducing masochistic behavior in Mediterranean women. These restrictions derive from the final element in the constellation of cultural traits that characterizes southern Italy, namely, that a man's honor depends upon the chastity of his mother and sisters.

There are several ways to explain why males in southern Italy (or anywhere else in the Mediterranean) place a high value on the chastity of female relatives. Jane Schneider (1971), for example, suggests that such an emphasis helps maintain family solidarity in the face of ecological pressures that would weaken that solidarity. David Gilmore (1987) suggests that under conditions of economic scarcity female chastity functions as a family asset that can be used to attract affines useful in the struggle for survival. Whatever the cause, this emphasis on female chastity in southern Italy has proven surprisingly resistant to change (Cucchiari 1990). Moreover, it has had profound consequences for the life experience of women both before and after marriage.

The Psychology of Italian Catholicism

Driven by a concern with female chastity, men are led to surround their female relatives with a multitude of restrictions designed to preserve that chastity. The underlying rationale for these restrictions seems to be, as Malina (1990: 59) suggests, the belief that both males and females have a strong and indiscriminate sex drive and that only strong social norms can prevent violations of chastity. This view of male/female sexuality is almost certainly a fantasy generated in males by the machismo complex and then projected onto both themselves and females. Support for this interpretation is provided by the observation that, while females in southern Italy are aware that men see them to be under the sway of indiscriminate sexual urges, they do not see themselves in this way (Cornelisen 1976: 20).

The emphasis on female chastity means, first of all, that women are under great pressure to remain virgins until marriage. But marriage and an end to physical virginity does not release women from social restrictions. On the contrary, once a woman can no longer rely upon an intact hymen as a certain sign of chastity, other criteria become more important. This means, as Maureen Giovannini (1981: 416) notes, that "married women are admonished to be more modest and chaste in dress and demeanor than unmarried females." But perhaps the most serious restriction is the fact that married women are expected to demonstrate their chastity by remaining secluded in the domestic sphere and away from the more public world of men.

Wrapping the women of southern Italy in so many restrictions throughout their lives has a consequence: it means that deviance, or at least perceived deviance, is inevitable. In a small community where everyone is scrutinizing women for the slightest signs of a failure of chastity, and where even something as simple as talking to another woman's husband in public or wearing bright-colored clothing is seen as indicative of such a failure, it is inevitable that some women will do something, however unintentionally, that will be seen as unchaste (see Cornelisen 1976: 61–63). This is especially true since, by calling attention to the "unchaste" behavior of other women, a woman can demonstrate her own chastity (Giovannini 1987: 67–69).

Because there are so many restrictions, and because an apparent if inadvertent violation of these restrictions is so likely, the gap between what psychoanalysts would call a woman's ego ideal and her perception of herself will be large. In simpler terms, the number of restrictions placed upon female chastity create an impossible standard, one that many women simply cannot meet at every moment in their lives. But a gap between what we see ourselves to be and what we want to be produces guilt, and guilt—as in the case of males—generates a desire for self-punishment. This, I suggest, is why southern Italian females, like their male relatives, engage in the masochistic activities so typical of the region.[20]

~ 161 ~

EPILOGUE

G alileo Galilei holds a special fascination for academics. The reason is
not hard to fathom, since the popular imagery associated with Galileo's
life is an academic fantasy come true. He was, after all, the devoted man of
science who sought the truth using only observation as his guide, and his
observations told him that the astronomer Copernicus had been right, that
the earth does revolve around the sun. Yet for championing the Copernican
cause, he was arrested and imprisoned by the Church, which saw the
Copernican theory as a threat to the authority of the Bible. A story like this
would have to be invented if it did not already exist, and a facile identification
with Galileo has undoubtedly provided immense comfort for untold numbers
of academics who have felt that their work is underappreciated.

But Pietro Redondi (1983) suggests that most modern commentators have
misunderstood completely what happened in the Galileo case, because they
fail to understand the mind-set of the Counter-Reformation leaders who
proceeded against Galileo. Redondi's central point is that it was not Galileo's
Copernicanism that got him into trouble. True, his defense of the Copernican
system was the reason that he was first brought before the Inquisition in
1615–16. But this first brush with the Inquisition was a very low-key affair.
After all, while this first tribunal condemned the Copernican theory, it did
not condemn Galileo directly. In the next decade or so, Galileo went on to
become one of the most eminent scientists in Europe and a personal favorite
of the reigning pope. He was even given unofficial encouragement, Redondi
argues, to pursue the officially banned Copernican theory.

Galileo became a threat to the Church not because of his Copernicanism
but because of his attack on Aristotelian physics. Redondi's argument is
complex and depends upon philosophical arguments having to do with atoms,
appearances, accidents, quantum realities, and a variety of other intellectual
ghosts, but the bottom line is this: by the early seventeenth century, the
intellectual leaders of the Counter-Reformation, notably the Jesuits, were
absolutely and resolutely convinced (1) that the Eucharistic doctrine of
transubstantiation was the bedrock of Catholicism and (2) that Aristotelian
physics was the only physics that was compatible with a doctrinal belief in
transubstantiation. In attacking Aristotle, Galileo was implicitly attacking

Epilogue

Eucharistic doctrine, and that was heresy. This was why Galileo was brought before the Inquisition again in the 1630s.

But by the time of this second trial, Galileo was widely respected, even by many of those who felt compelled to proceed against him. Furthermore, he was not concerned with theological matters. Whatever theological implications the Jesuits might derive from his attack on Aristotle, the fact is that Galileo himself never wrote on the Eucharistic consequences of his new physics. As a result of these mitigating conditions, the Inquisition was willing to arrive at a relatively benign compromise: Galileo would be condemned, but only on account of his Copernicanism, a belief that did not threaten any central Catholic doctrines. This would allow the Inquisition to suppress Galileo without giving him a severe sentence, which would have to be imposed if he were condemned directly on the antitransubstantiation implications of his work.

Certainly, Galileo was treated lightly by the Inquisition. During the course of the 1633 proceedings against him, he was lodged in a suite in the palace of the Holy Office, not a jail cell. His ultimate sentence was imprisonment spent at his own estate and the estates of friends. When you remember that only a few decades earlier (in 1600) Giordano Bruno had been burned alive at Rome by the Inquisition after having been left to languish in prison, a real prison, for years, the lightness of Galileo's sentence is evident.

The credibility of Redondi's argument depends upon our willingness to concede that the men who acted against Galileo could honestly be so concerned about a matter that strikes the modern mind as so esoteric, namely, the theological implications of a new system of physics. Yet, Redondi argues, men of precisely this sort did exist in the early seventeenth century, and we cannot understand the events of the period without taking that into account. Galileo's opponents were not intolerant Biblical fundamentalists but highly intelligent scientists, mainly Jesuits, who took their religion seriously and who firmly believed that it was necessary to harmonize religion and science at all costs. These men honestly did feel that to criticize Aristotle was to cast doubt on the miracle of transubstantiation and so was as heretical as anything Luther or Calvin had said.

Redondi's work brings home two lessons that must guide anyone who studies Catholicism in Italy. The first is that, in previous centuries, religion was taken seriously in a way not experienced by most academic writers who now study religion. The second lesson is that distinctions and subtleties that strike us as unimportant, hardly worth mentioning, could easily have been central to the devout of previous centuries and, for that reason, might provide the key to understanding the very thing we are studying. These lessons are as important in the study of popular religion as they are in the study of the religion of the Counter-Reformation elites considered by Redondi, and this book has been written with these lessons in mind. I have focused on those things usually mentioned only in passing in most modern commentaries: on the distinction between saints and madonnas, on madonnas and saints that kill, on festas and *ex voto*, on apparitions and mountaintop sanctuaries, on relics, on earthquakes, plagues, and floods. These were important to Italian Catholics, and we must investigate them carefully if we want to understand popular Catholicism in Italy.

But there is something else that has guided the writing of this book, and I hope it has shown through: an affection for the subject matter. Just as Giordano Bruno could criticize the devotions of his time oriented around saints and madonnas and yet be proud of his roots in Nola, a town known even then for its elaborate festa in honor of San Paulinus, I have an affection for Italian Catholicism even while seeking to explain it in terms that most Italian Catholics would likely reject. I do not regard a belief in an apparition of the Madonna delle Grazie or in the liquefaction of San Gennaro's blood as simple superstitions, quaint customs, or as evidence of mental deficiency. These things simply exist. They are (or at least were) a part of Italian culture in much the same way that television, cars, and specious statements of concern for human rights violations around the world are a part of our culture. Forced to make a choice, I might opt for the security of being a tenured professor in a modern university, but I find the Italy in which ordinary people responded to very real dangers over which they had no control by constructing an intricate tapestry of religious ritual and belief to be a far more human and far more interesting society than my own.

Ciao.

NOTES

INTRODUCTION

1. For the exact number and proportion of Italian cardinals in each of the papal conclaves held between 1431 and 1590, see Carroll (1989: 169).

2. A list of English-language anthropological studies located in southern Italy can be found in chapter 5.

3. In some ways I am moving counter to academic trends within Italy itself, where in the past two decades scholars interested in religion have increasingly shifted away from a focus on Catholicism and toward the study of religiosity in general; see the overview of recent Italian language research provided by Cipriani (1990).

4. For a concise overview of the anthropological literature on the distinction between magic and religion, see Tambiah (1990: 1–83).

5. These examples appear in Bronzini (1982: 161, 163). In this context, a *furtecille* is a circular piece of wood used as a charm against the evil eye.

6. These examples and others are discussed in more detail later in this book. Note that the magical practices considered in this book always include a reference to supernatural beings. This is in contrast to Frazer, whose definition of magic led him to focus upon instances of magical practice in which there were no references to supernatural beings.

7. Mullett (1984) presents a concise overview of this revised view of the Counter-Reformation. For an overview of the individuals most concerned with religious reform during the fifteenth century, see Penco (1977: 483–579).

1. THE THREE METACULTS

1. The survey was conducted in the wake of the Second Vatican Council, a period of great change in the Catholic Church. One of the consistent emphases apparent in the resolutions passed by this council was a strong Christocentrism, and one effect of this renewed Christocentrism was an official deemphasis of the cult of the saints. This was the period, for instance, when Church officials finally decided that saints like Santa Filomena (discussed in the next chapter) and San Cristoforo (Saint Christopher) never existed. It was also the period in which popular Italian saints like San Gennaro were diminished by dropping their feasts from among those celebrated in the Universal Church. Indeed, a second Italian survey conducted by the same investigator (Burgalassi: 1976) just a few years later, and asking much the same

questions, found that there had been a marked increase in support for Christ and a corresponding decrease in support for the saints.

2. The importance of these processions has been noted by Naselli (1962: 326); Mazzacane and Lombardi Satriani (1974). In the typical case, these processions involve the carrying of several different statues, or groups of statues, through the community. These statues are often highly prized works of art and have usually been in use for centuries. Individually, each statue or group of statues is called a *mystery*, since it represents some scene associated with the Passion of Christ (the Flagellation, the Crowning with Thorns, etc.). Each mystery sits on a platform, which is carried aloft by a different confraternity, and each of these confraternities usually has a distinctive set of vestments. For a book with some excellent color photos of a very elaborate Holy Week procession in modern Italy, see De Marco (1975).

3. In the Forty Hours devotion, often called by the Italian *Quarant'Ore* even in English publications, a consecrated host is exposed to public view for a long period of time, which may or may not be exactly forty hours. A requirement of the devotion is that there be several people present during the entire period, watching the Eucharist. On the history of this devotion, see Carroll (1989: 104–13).

4. *Mezzogiorno* is the term routinely used to designate southern Italy. For a list of the regions that form part the Mezzogiorno, see chapter 5.

5. A pastoral visit is a visit made by a bishop (or his delegate) to communities under his jurisdiction in order to conduct a formal examination of the churches, the clergy, and the laity in those communities. At least in Italy, the exact questions asked during these visits varied over time. Burke's (1979) analysis of the changing content of the episcopal questionnaires used between the fifteenth and the nineteenth centuries, for instance, suggests that it was not until after the Council of Trent that bishops began gathering precise information on the religious beliefs of the laity.

6. My concern in this section is with northern Italy. Nevertheless, data relating to church and altar dedications in southern Italy, like the data on patron saints in the South, gives this same rank ordering: saints, then Mary, then Christ. See Russo (1984: 415–17).

7. For example, the data presented by Donvito and Pellegrino (1973: 61–106) show that most communities with confraternities in Abruzzo, Molise, and Basilicata during the sixteenth and seventeenth centuries either had a single confraternity, which was dedicated to the Blessed Sacrament, or had just two confraternities, one dedicated to the Blessed Sacrament and one dedicated to the Rosary.

8. On the history of this cult, see del Grosso (1983); Cardini (1983).

9. Medica (1965). Based upon Marcucci's (1983: 10) assertion that there are 1,539 Marian sanctuaries in Italy, Medica's sample of 697 sanctuaries constitutes less than half of the total. The terms used in the second part of Marian titles are discussed in chapter 3.

10. In fact, the figure is probably a bit less. In order to make the categories in table 1.6 mutually exclusive, I counted as *Vergine* any title that contained the word *Vergine* and as *Madre* any title that contained the word *Madre*. Thus for example, Maria Santissima Vergine was counted as Vergine, not Maria Santissima.

11. For a definition of the regions constituting southern Italy, see chapter 5.

2. THE CULT OF THE SAINTS

1. For Weinstein and Bell, a supernatural sign was a sign of divine origin that marked the saint as special during the course of that saint's life. Such signs include stigmata or the emission of fragrant odors or light.

2. Italian notions of sanctity are discussed in, for example, Galasso (1982: 64–120).

3. For a devotional account of this saint's life, which draws heavily upon even earlier hagiographies, see Pastrovicchi (1918).

4. I discuss community patrons in this chapter only because the majority of such patrons in Italy are saints. Madonnas, however, can also be chosen as the protector of a community, and the remarks that follow are equally true for patron saints and patron madonnas.

5. The Tesoro contains nineteen bronze statues and fifty-one silver busts, all of which are images of saints who are copatrons of Naples (Missano 1990: 70).

6. This report is reproduced in Strazzullo (1959: 137–209). In addition to San Gennaro, the patrons of Naples identified in this report were: Sant'Agnello abate, Sant'Aspremo, Sant'Agrippino, Sant'Eusebio, San Severo, Sant'Attanasio, San Tommaso d'Aquino, Santa Patrizia, Sant'Andrea Avellino, San Francesco di Paola, San Domenico, San Giacomo della Marca, San Francesco Saverio, Santa Teresa, Sant'Antonio di Padua, San Filippo Neri, San Gaetano Tieneo, San Nicola di Mira, San Gregorio Armeno, San Chiara, San Giuseppe Patriarca, San Pietro Martire, San Biase, San Francesco d'Assisi, Santa Maria Maddalena de'Pazzi, San Giovanni Battista, San Francesco Borgia, San Candida Juniore, Santa Maria Egizziaca, Sant'-Antonio abate, and San Michele Arcangelo.

7. It would be interesting to know how particular communities come to decide upon particular saints as patrons. Christian (1981: 23–69) identifies some of the processes at work in selecting community patrons in the case of Spain. As far as I can tell, however, no one has done a similar study in connection with the selection of community patrons in Italy.

8. See for instance Crimi-Lo Giudice's (1894) account of the festa of San Cono at Naso (Sicilia).

9. The suggestion that the city is a unified whole and that the major buildings "touched" by a procession stand for that whole is used by Trexler (1987) to shed light on the meaning of processions in Renaissance Florence. Trexler also suggests that nunneries were an exception to the general pattern, in that nunneries were a type of space set apart from all other space in the city. If he is right, this suggests that accounts of what went on in these nunneries tells us little about popular religion in general. See Introduction to this book.

10. Pitrè (1900), for example, collected thirty-eight well-known accounts written by thirty-one authors dealing either with the festa in honor of Santa Rosalia in Palermo or the festa of the Assunta (Mary's Assumption into Heaven) at Messina. Of the authors, fourteen were French, eleven were Italian, five were English, and one was German.

11. The best description of Santa Rosalia's festa at Palermo is given in G. Pitrè (1899: 1–48).

12. A few pictures of the Nola festa appear in Posen and Sciorra (1983), but their article is mainly concerned with a variant of the festa, involving only a single tower, that is celebrated by Italians in Brooklyn, N.Y. A full account of the Nola festa is given in Manganelli (1973).

13. The similarity between *Lucia* and *luce* has been noted several times; see for example Vecchi (1968: 85).

14. For a summary of the early traditions about Sant'Antonio abate, see Attwater (1965: 49–50); Butler (1913).

15. For a commentary on this line from the *Paradiso*, see Singleton (1975: 484–85).

16. The account of the San Zopito cult that follows relies mainly on Di Nola (1976: 269–94) and Cianfarani (1952).

17. The following account of the circumstances surrounding the development of the Santa Filomena cult in Italy is based primarily on La Salvia (1984); but see also Kirsch (1913); Rossi (1969: 36–43).

18. An imprimatur in the Catholic Church indicates that a bishop has read the book, has concluded that it contains nothing dangerous to Catholic faith or morals, and has given permission for it to be printed. For a discussion of this procedure and some account of how it has been applied in Italy and elsewhere, see Hilgers (1913).

19. This posed a delicate problem for the intellectual theologians of the Church: how to explain the many miracles attributed to this saint if in fact she never existed? The solution was to suggest that, although people had been directing their prayers to Santa Filomena, the prayers had in fact gone "directly to God"; see La Salvia (1984: 914).

3. The Mary Cult

1. I am considering apparitions in this chapter because most apparitions involve the Virgin Mary. Most of what follows, however, could just as easily apply to apparitions involving a saint or Christ.

2. An illusion is the misperception of a physical stimulus whose existence can be established by independent observers. A hallucination usually refers to a situation in which (1) a subject perceives a stimulus and believes it to be real (and thus not purely imaginary) and (2) independent observers present at the time cannot detect that stimulus. Thus if someone reported seeing the Virgin Mary hovering above a hill, and independent observers did not see Mary but did see, say, a diffuse light, then this would be an illusion. If those observers saw nothing at all, then the event would be classed as a hallucination. For a fuller discussion of these two terms, and some examples of famous Marian apparitions that fall into one or the other of these two categories, see Carroll (1986: 117–24).

3. This fact alone likely explains why the Church has not given official approval to the apparitions at Medjugorje in Yugoslavia, where a group of children have been experiencing apparitions of Mary on a near-daily basis since the early 1980s. For more on the Medjugorje apparitions, see ibid.

4. My account of Marietta's experiences and cult are derived from Rossi (1969: 70–75); Castiglione (1981: 131–43).

5. The Madonna di Altomare was a popular madonna who had been venerated in a sanctuary at Andria, near Bari, since the seventeenth century.

6. My account of this seer and his cult is based upon Cipriani (1976); Barbati, Mingozzi, and Rossi (1978: 81–97); Castiglione (1981: 122–31).

7. On the special appeal of this saint to Mezzogiorno Catholics see De Rosa (1979: 80–101).

8. The wounds of the stigmata are supposed to correspond to the wounds that Christ received in his hands, feet, and side during the crucifixion. Hundreds of Roman Catholics over the centuries have displayed such wounds; on the likely psychological processes that give rise to stigmatization, see Carroll (1989: 79–103).

9. From this point forward, I will be using the term *madonna* to refer to the various Marys venerated or worshipped in Italy, even though *madonna* is only one of the terms of address commonly used in Marian titles (see table 1.6).

10. The term *edicola*, which is encountered over and over again in the literature on Italian Catholicism, has no precise English translation, although *outdoor shrine* comes close. Basically, *edicola* is applied to any structure—a niche in a wall of a building, a pedestal, an enclosed space, a small chapel—that holds or contains a holy image, usually of a saint or madonna. Ferrari and Lanzi (1985: 136) point out that other terms used to designate various types of *edicole* include *pilastrino, cellettina, sacello, tabernacolo, romitorio,* and *santella*. They also note regional variation in usage; thus, the preferred term for these structures in Toscana is *maesta*, while in the Veneto it is *capitelli*.

11. Because Mary is so often portrayed as a modern reincarnation of Mediterranean agricultural goddesses like Demeter or Ceres, it is worth pointing out that very few Marian titles fall into categories that have any connection with agriculture. By my count, less than 1 percent of all the titles in Medica's sample associate Mary with cultivated land.

12. See Kaftal (1952, 1965, 1978, 1985). Occasionally, investigators have looked at the iconographies associated with the popular images of a single madonna over time; see Vecchi (1968: 52–53); Beffa, Gaggioni, and Snider (1980). My concern here, however, is with the comparative study of the iconographies associated with different madonnas.

13. The apparition of the Madonna della Guardia on Monte Figogna is discussed in detail in chapter 4.

14. A painted *ex voto* is a painting brought to a church in recognition of the donor's having received a favor from the saint or madonna associated with that church. This sort of *ex voto* is discussed more fully in chapter 4.

15. My account of the origin legends surrounding this sanctuary is based upon Casini's (1981) devotional account of the Montallegro apparitions.

16. These contrasts were established on the basis of my own visual inspection of the various portrayals of these three madonnas in their sanctuaries and in other churches I have visited in coastal Liguria.

17. This incident was one of the many examples of popular religious practice

uncovered by Corrain and Zampini (1970: 149–50) in their analysis of synodal records.

4. THE DARK SIDE OF HOLINESS

1. The two names of this central character are certainly not randomly chosen. San Pietro and San Paolo are quite routinely twinned in Italy; their festas are usually celebrated jointly. Furthermore, within the logic of official Catholic mythology, San Paolo was the early Christian leader most associated with bringing Christianity to a wider Mediterranean audience, just as Spina/Spada's escape to the countryside will (however unintentionally) allow him to bring his ideas to a wider audience than would otherwise have been possible. Finally, *spina* in Italian means thorn, and *spada* means sword, thus underlining Silone's implicit suggestion that his central character will be far more effective in his disguise than he would have been had he been able to pursue his original objectives as an urban revolutionary.

2. An English-language account of the modern festival dedicated to this madonna can be found in Tentori (1982).

3. This legend and the one that follows are condensed and paraphrased from the accounts that appear in D'Antonio (1979: 7–11); but see also Tentori (1982).

4. *Palla e maglio* is a game in which a wooden ball is hit with a wooden mallet. The *edicola* associated with the Madonna dell'Arco seems to have been a specially constructed small wall. This part of the countryside outside Naples was called dell'Arco on account of the nearby remains of a Roman aqueduct, and the term came to be applied to the madonna whose image was contained in the *edicola*.

5. Whether Aurelia had bought this pig at the fair that accompanied the festa of the Madonna dell'Arco or whether she intended to sell it at the fair is unclear.

6. De Lutiis (1973: 102) presents a variant version of the Aurelia del Prete legend, in which the vengeful Madonna also emerges quite clearly. In this version, Aurelia (not her husband) had received a favor and had promised to bring two "silver feet" to the sanctuary as an *ex voto*. She showed up empty-handed, however, and it was for this reason that the Madonna detached Aurelia's feet. Whichever legend is preferred, the devout who visit the sanctuary can still view two mummified feet. These are supposedly the feet detached from the unfortunate Aurelia del Prete.

7. Although Sandys reports hearing of *Tarantismo* in Calabria, he also says that the spiders involved are called tarantulas on account of their association with the city of Tarentum (= Taranto), in Puglia.

8. While traveling through Puglia in the late eighteenth century, the Englishman Henry Swinburne (1790: 304–10) prevailed upon a woman who had once been bitten by a *taranta* to replicate the dance that had released her. She began dancing with quick steps, emitting loud shrieks. The effect was sufficiently at odds with Swinburne's Anglo-Saxon sensibilities that he put an end to the dance before it was finished.

9. On the other hand, reports suggesting the demise of *tarantismo* should be considered with skepticism. Writing in the early nineteenth century, Hecker (1838:

81–82) reports that the heyday of *tarantismo* was over and that the phenomenon was being extinguished. Yet *tarantismo* was still very much alive over a century later, when De Martino and his team studied it.

10. One of the Sacred Heart traditions that gave rise to the use of heart *ex voto* was the experience of heart exchanges reported by Catholic mystics. These mystics reported an encounter with Jesus in which Jesus removed the mystic's physical heart and replaced it with his (Jesus') own heart. For a fuller discussion of these heart exchange traditions see Carroll (1989: 141–43).

11. A particularly good selection of these modern *ex voto* can be seen in Cazzoli (1968).

12. These inscriptions are discussed in greater detail by Turchini (1980: 86f); Cambiè (1971); Tempèra (1977: 61–62). I have given only Italian abbreviations. In earlier *ex voto*, it seems clear that many inscriptions were abbreviations of Latin. Given the similarity between Latin and Italian, however, there is often little difference in the initials on the *ex voto*. Thus V. F. G. R. could mean either Voto Fatto Grazia Ricevuta or Votum Fecit Gratiam Accepit.

13. On the history of painted *ex voto*, see Ciarrocchi and Mori (1960); Vecchi (1968: 97–98); Tempèra (1977: 39–40).

14. It would be interesting to know if patron saints were chosen in the same way in Italy. Unfortunately, this issue—how patron saints were chosen by local communities—has generally been ignored by Italian scholars, except for those relatively few cases in which patron saints were imposed by aristocratic decree.

5. Regional Differences

1. In these reports, and in this book, northern Italy thus includes those regions—like Lazio, Le Marche, and Umbria—that in some discussions are called central Italy.

2. The events leading up to the founding of the *Rivista di storia della Chiesa in Italia* are described in Maccarrone (1987).

3. The exact nature of the link between the Flagellant Movement and the *disciplinati* confraternities is still a matter of some debate. While the confraternities did, at least initially, practice flagellation, they were not associated with the apocalyptic emphasis that was part of the Flagellant Movement. For a discussion of the Flagellant Movement, see Henderson (1978).

4. Flagellation was indeed one way to imitate Christ, since Christian tradition holds that Christ was whipped just prior to his crucifixion. But many of these confraternities interpreted the imitation of Christ as implying good works, which led them to establish hospitals and other charitable organizations.

5. For a summary of some of this research on regional stereotypes, see Battacchi (1972); Galasso (1982: 186).

6. Reports *ad limina* were those reports local bishops carried with them to Rome on the occasion of their periodic visits to that city. The practice of making a visit to "the tomb of the Apostles" (*ad limina Apostolorum*) and consulting with the pope

dates from the earliest days of the Church. In 1585, Sixtus V made these visits and the associated reports a requirement: Italian bishops were required to make their reports every three years; bishops outside of Italy, less frequently. Like the reports of the pastoral visits made by bishops to the communities in their dioceses, reports *ad limina* are a valuable source of information on the Church in Italy.

For *chiese ricettizie*, see De Rosa (1973a; 1975; 1976). These last two essays are reprinted in De Rosa (1979), which includes an additional essay on the *chiese ricettizie* (21–46). Robertazzi (1977), D'Andrea (1977), and Greco (1986) also provide some useful material on the *ricettizie*. Unless otherwise noted, the description of the *chiese ricettizie* that follows is based on these works. The statement that three-quarters of the churches in the South were *ricettizie* appears often in De Rosa's essays, although he only occasionally makes it clear that this estimate is derived from his analysis of reports *ad limina* (De Rosa 1977a: 174).

7. Hay's 1977 book was originally delivered as a series of lectures in 1971; Burke's 1986 book is an updated version of a book he published in 1972; the only new reference work on the Italian Church that he cites is Hay (1977).

8. Spain gained control of the continental Mezzogiorno in 1504.

9. The suggestion that there is a fit between the *chiesa ricettizia* and a closed local economy appears often in the literature on the *ricettizie*. Unfortunately, presumably because such a linkage seems obvious, no study has justified it in any detail. Some brief comments on the affinity between the *chiese ricettizie* and closed local economies can be found in Cestaro (1978: 149f); De Rosa (1977a).

10. The conditions that led to the decline of the *chiese ricettizie* need to be investigated in greater detail. The best available discussion is in Cestaro (1978), and I have relied heavily upon that account here.

11. Table 5.2 indicates that there are 1,106 Marian sanctuaries in northern Italy and 433 in southern Italy. The ratio of northern to southern sanctuaries is thus 2.6:1, while the ratio of northern coronations to southern coronations in the Medica sample is 193:79, or 2.4:1.

12. The fact that coronations were especially prominent in both North and South during the late nineteenth and early twentieth centuries suggests that they were part of the romanization campaign launched by the Vatican during this period. *Romanization* is the term used by historians to describe the Church's attempt to centralize ecclesiastical authority in Rome and to promote a standardized variant of Catholicism. This would certainly make sense given the interpretation of the coronation procedure being offered here. For more on the Romanization campaign, see Holmes (1978); Aubert et al. (1981); Taves (1986).

13. A succinct discussion of relics associated with Christ can be found in Cruz (1984); Thurston (1913a, 1913b, 1913c, 1913d).

14. The Santo Sudario is a picture of Christ's face kept in the church of San Bartolomeo degli Armeni in Genoa and only occasionally exposed for public veneration. Like the Shroud of Turin, it belongs to a class of pictures traditionally believed to have been made without hands. The most common of the legends surrounding the Santo Sudario suggests that, when Jesus was alive, his reputation as a wonder-worker reached Abgar, king of Edessa. Abgar, who was suffering from leprosy, sent a

legation to Jesus with instructions to ask that Jesus return with them and cure the king. Foreseeing the possibility that Jesus might not come, Abgar sent an artist along with the delegation and instructed the artist to at least bring back Jesus' picture. The artist, however, was unable to get the picture just right. During the visit, Jesus washed his face and dried it with a piece of linen. Miraculously, an image of his face was imprinted on the linen. That linen was brought back to Abgar. The history of what (supposedly) happened next is long and complicated; suffice it to say that the image now at San Bartolomeo degli Armeni is supposed to have arrived in Genoa in the late fourteenth century.

Whatever it may have been originally, the image is now a painting on a wooden tablet enclosed in a gilt sheath. An investigation conducted in 1968 suggests that the painting might initially have been done on fabric, which was then glued to the wood. I myself saw it on the occasion of an exposition in May 1989, and it is somewhat smaller than would be expected of a life-size image of a human being. For more on the Santo Sudario, see Ciliberti (1988); Leclercq (1913).

15. The following discussion of temporary resurrections in Friuli relies almost entirely upon Cavazza (1981). Cavazza's article is a good example of an informative Italian language work that should be translated and made available to English-speaking audiences. A somewhat shorter account of these resurrections can also found in De Biasio (1980).

16. For the text of one such certificate, see ibid., 52–53.

17. Cavazza (1981: 95–96) gives a useful overview of the practice of temporary resurrections in France and provides references to more detailed studies on this subject.

6. MAGIC

1. For a general definition of what constitutes magic in Italy, and a consideration of the general criteria used in this book to decide if a magical practice is part of popular Catholicism, see the Introduction.

2. All the details reported here concerning Fra Geremia's case are taken from O'Neil's account (1981: 228–36; 1984: 57–60), and it is to her that all credit is due for retrieving this case from the files of the Inquisition.

3. A scapular consists of two small pieces of material (usually wool and usually rectangular) held together by strings, such that when placed around your neck, one piece hangs on your chest and the other on your back. The Brown Scapular was made from brown wool.

4. The history of the Church's view on the Scapular Promise and the related tradition of the Sabbatine Privilege, are discussed in Carroll (1989: 114–31). The Sabbatine Privilege is defined by the belief that, if someone wearing the Brown Scapular dies and goes to Purgatory, Mary will descend into Purgatory on the following Saturday and bring the person to Heaven.

5. This discussion of blood miracles is derived from ibid. 57–78.

6. Extracts from the texts of these early accounts can be found in Caserta and Lambertini (1972: 22–24); Petito (1983: 163–86).

7. The vial is never opened, so visual inspection is the only way to verify liquefaction. And since the vial is never opened, there is of course no way to establish with certainty that the substance in the vial really is blood.

8. The fact that the relic has always liquefied less often in December, a much cooler month in Naples, suggests that ambient temperature is one of the physical variables implicated in liquefaction. For some speculation on what other physical factors might be responsible for liquefaction, see Carroll (1989: 182–87).

9. A bibliography of Thurston's writings can be found in Crehan (1952).

10. For a list of relics of this sort, see Alfano and Amitrano (1951).

11. Four blood relics are still liquefying. One of these is the relic at the Tesoro in Naples. The second is located at a parish church in Pozzuoli, which contains the stone on which San Gennaro was supposedly beheaded; the blood stains on this stone are thought to liquefy on the same occasions as the blood in the vial at the Tesoro. The third is the blood relic of Santa Patrizia, which is kept in the convent church of San Gregorio Armeno in Naples; this relic liquefies every Tuesday, as well as on the saint's festa. Finally, there is the blood relic of San Pantaleone at Ravello (down the coast from Naples), which liquefies on 26 July of each year and remains liquid until 11 September. The Tesoro relic is well described in the sources already cited. For my own eyewitness account of the last three relics, as well as for my own speculations as to what is producing the illusion of liquefaction in each of these cases, see appendix B in Carroll (1989).

12. In the case of monks who insult relics, Geary argues that there was a second process at work as well: the humiliation of the relics symbolized the humiliation suffered by the monastery.

13. A fuller account of these procedures appears in Pitrè (1978: 4: 44).

14. For the precise locations of these sanctuaries, see ibid., 45.

15. For a more detailed discussion of the extreme behaviors exhibited by the *spiritati*, see Pitrè (1978: 4: 54f).

16. This case is reported in Strazzullo (1963), and I have relied entirely upon Strazzullo's account for the details of the case.

17. On the lamp at Trapani, see Mondello (1882: 54); Pitrè (1978: 4: 57). On the lamp at Agira, see ibid., 50–51.

18. My argument does not address the general issue of magic in either the North or the South. My concern is only with the degree to which magical elements permeate popular Catholicism, not with the general practice of magic in either region. The ethnographic literature on communities in southern Italy does suggest that magic was widely practiced in such communities, even outside the context of Catholic ritual.

7. Mezzogiorno Masochism

1. The idea of "survivals" was a central concept in almost all social evolutionary theories of the nineteenth and early twentieth centuries. A survival is a practice

that had developed at an earlier evolutionary stage and had persisted into a later evolutionary stage.

2. This was not the first time that an English author had leveled the charge of human sacrifice at Italian Catholics. M. Pitrè (1900: 150–51) reproduces an Italian translation of a passage from a book published in London in 1859 by an anonymous English author and entitled *Unprotected Females in Sicily, Calabria and on the Top of Mount Etna*. The passage describes the Vara used at Messina during the festa of the Assunta (see chapter 4). According to the author, it had been routine for some of the children who were suspended from the Vara for long periods of time to die as a result of their experience. But this was considered acceptable by the children's parents, the author suggested, since the children were considered human sacrifices. What distinguished Clodd's charge of ritual sacrifice from this earlier charge were Clodd's position as head of the Folk-Lore Society and his suggestion that the ritual killings were an intentional part of the Abruzzo ceremony.

3. Clodd had incorrectly reported the canon's name as Pulling.

8. THE PSYCHOLOGY OF ITALIAN CATHOLICISM

1. The Black Death was really a cluster of three interrelated diseases: bubonic plague, pneumonic plague, and septicaemic plague. Ziegler (1969: 26–29) presents a concise discussion of the distinctions and relations among these three variants of plague. It is worth noting that pneumonic plague was deadlier than bubonic plague and that—contrary to what many people seem to think—could be spread directly from one person to the next, without aid of rat or flea intermediaries.

2. Estimates of population loss during the Black Death are shaky, of course. Nevertheless, the one-third figure for Italy and Europe is based on data that converge to a common conclusion. For a review of these data, see ibid.

3. The following discussion on famine, typhus, and smallpox is based on Del Panta (1980), unless otherwise noted.

4. The link between famine and typhoid fever is explained partly by the fact that malnutrition makes people more susceptible to—and less able to overcome—typhoid fever. But as Del Panta (1980: 55) points out, even more important is the fact that famine promotes the movement of people and food supplies, which spread the disease.

5. The Richter scale, more familiar to English-speaking readers, is a measure of the amplitude of the seismic wave associated with an earthquake, as measured by a seismograph. It is so constructed that an increase of one unit on the scale represents a tenfold increase in magnitude. By contrast, the Mercalli scale, developed by Giuseppe Mercalli (1850–1914), uses more subjective criteria to determine earthquake intensity. The first six levels are based mainly on the degree to which the earthquake is "felt" by the human population. Subsequent levels are based upon an assessment of the amount of damage done to buildings. There were originally ten levels to the Mercalli scale, but the quake that struck Calabria in 1908 forced Mercalli to add an eleventh level, namely "total destruction. Every work of man is destroyed. Enormous topographical transformations: rivers deviate from their course,

and lakes disappear" (Iaccarino 1973: 5). Despite its subjectivity, the Mercalli scale is probably better suited to our purposes because it provides information about the damage to human populations. This is not true of the Richter scale, since earthquakes of a given Richter magnitude typically cause a great deal more damage in Italy than they do in other European countries.

6. A rating of IX on the Mercalli scale indicates that approximately 50 percent of all the buildings in the area struck were destroyed or suffered grave damage (ibid.). The Mercalli scale can be used to estimate the intensity of past earthquakes precisely because contemporary accounts of a given earthquake usually provide information on property damage and the number of deaths caused.

7. The number of deaths from these particular earthquakes are given in Alfano (1950: 642); Baratta (1950: 722).

8. Thomas's argument here obviously has affinities with Weber's (1930) well-known argument, part of which suggests (1) that Protestants, at least Calvinists, view material success as a visible sign from God that the successful individual was among the elect—that is, destined for heaven, and (2) that as a consequence, they would strive for such material success as a way of convincing themselves that they were indeed among the elect. For a comparison of Thomas and Weber, see Tambiah (1990: 12–24).

9. Why Protestantism made so little headway in Italy is an important question and one that still awaits a convincing answer. The fact that non-Catholic religious movements, to the extent that they took root at all in Italy, took root mainly in northern Italy (see Carroll 1986: 10–16) suggests that part of the answer to this question will eventually be discovered by considering the lack of "fit" between the social institutions of southern Italy, notably the *chiese ricettizie*, and Protestantism.

10. Freud also proposes a second approach to religion, mainly in his *Totem and Taboo* (1913) and *Moses and Monotheism* (1939). In both of these works, he argues that at the dawn of human history a "band of bachelor brothers" rose up and killed their father in order to obtain sexual access to the females monopolized by the father. Overcome by guilt, these brothers repressed the memory of their patricide and sought to atone for their deed by venerating a father surrogate, the totem. For Freud, the unconscious memory of this primal patricide was passed along from generation to generation. Over the course of human history, this repressed memory came closer and closer to the conscious mind, with the result that religious belief came more and more to reflect this memory in a fairly obvious way.

This process reached its apogee in Pauline Christianity, which suggests that there had been an original sin against the God the Father (which for Freud represents an only barely disguised acknowledgment of the original father-killing) and that only the death of the Son of God could atone for this original sin (which made sense, for Freud, given that the "sons" had been guilty of the original crime). The psycho-Lamarckian nature of Freud's account—that is, the suggestion that unconscious memories can be inherited—has caused it to be generally rejected, even by those who generally favor psychoanalytic arguments in most other regards. For a fuller discussion of this "second theory of religion" and for some suggestions as to why Freud clung to it even in the face of opposition from colleagues, see Carroll (1987).

11. This discussion of Kleinian theory is reproduced with minor revisions from Carroll (1989: 156–58), with the permission of McGill-Queen's University Press, and is for the most part based upon the essays collected in Klein (1975; 1980). For an extended discussion of Kleinian theory, see Segal (1974).

12. The role of relics in the history of the cult of the saints is discussed in a number of places; see Thurston (1913b); MacCulloch (1922); Geary (1978); P. Brown (1981); Strong (1987).

13. Only body parts that Christ shed during his earthly life were possible as relics, including baby teeth, blood, and foreskin. In fact, relics of this sort did exist, in both Italy and other areas of Europe, but they were relatively rare. Physical objects he came in contact with are discussed in chapter 5.

14. There is a fairly large body of literature in anthropology suggesting that the traits listed here—the father-ineffective family, the machismo complex, the strong link between male honor and female chastity—are characteristic of Mediterranean societies, generally. For a useful overview of this position, which I tend to share, and a discussion of how such values may have shaped Mediterranean religious systems, see Malina (1990). On the other hand, the Mediterranean culture concept has recently come under attack by scholars who argue that (1) these traits are not found in many Mediterranean societies, (2) there is at least as much heterogeneity as homogeneity among Mediterranean societies, and (3) the culture of the Christian societies bordering the Mediterranean is far more similar to that of northern Europe than to that of the Muslim societies bordering the Mediterranean. For this position, see De Pina-Cabral (1989). Whatever the merits of the general argument in either case, no one has challenged the view that these traits are characteristic of southern Italy, which is the only Mediterranean society I am concerned with here.

15. *Cathexis* is a neologism invented by Freud's English translators. What it refers to (though many psychoanalysts will probably balk at my simplification here) is the degree to which young children associate something (a parent, an object, a body part) with activities that produce diffuse physical pleasure.

16. Only Abruzzo and Molise, with a *sparsa* population of 23 percent, did not fit the southern pattern.

17. Studies detailing the development of particular forms of settlement in particular areas do, of course, exist. Silverman (1975), for instance, discusses the history and development of the *mezzadria* system in central Italy. The *mezzadria* system is a sharecropping arrangement in which an entire family, as a unit, contracts to live and work on a parcel of land belonging to someone else. By its very nature, then, *mezzadria* sharecropping increases the proportion of the *sparsa* population.

18. For a feminist critique of Freud's remarks on masochism, see Caplan (1985).

19. Gilmore (1990) makes the same point with regard to female behavior within the father-ineffective family in southern Spain.

20. The one instance of masochistic activity in the South in which there appears to be a difference by sex is public flagellation, which is definitely a male activity. The likely reason is pragmatic: flagellation involves stripping to the waist, or something quite close to this, and such an activity would in the case of women be a clear violation of the prevailing chastity codes.

REFERENCES

Abbondanza, Rocchina M. 1987. "Il Concilio di Trento nella vita spirituale e culturale del Mezzogiorno tra XVI e XVII secolo." *Ricerche di storia sociale e religiosa* 16: 225–32.

Acquaviva, Sabino S. 1975. "Società religiosa e sociologia delle religioni in Italia." *Rivista di studi sociali* 9: 71–85.

Alfano, Giovanni Battista. 1950. "Terremoto." In *Enciclopedia italiana di scienze, lettere ed arti* 33: 639–44. Roma: Enciclopedia italiana.

Alfano, G. B., and A. Amitrano. 1951. *Notizie storiche ed osservazioni sulle reliquie di sangue*. Napoli: Arti Grafiche "Adriana."

Allegra, Luciano. 1981. "Il parroco: un mediatore fra alta e bassa cultura." In *Storia d'Italia, Annali 4: Intellettuali e potere*, edited by C. Vivanti, 895–947. Torino: Giulio Einaudi.

Allen, Grant. 1899. "Holy Week Observance in the Abruzzi." *Folk-Lore* 10: 111.

Almagià, Roberto. 1949. "Italia—popolazione." In *Enciclopedia italiana di scienze, lettere ed arti* 19: 740–44. Roma: Enciclopedia italiana.

Ambrasi, Domenico. 1970. "Il 'Miracolo di San Gennaro' nell'ultimo cinquantennio." In *Campania sacra: Studi e documenti*, edited by D. Ambrasi, 187–92. Napoli: M. D'Auria.

Attwater, Donald. 1965. *Dictionary of Saints*. Harmondsworth, Eng.: Penguin.

Aubert, R., J. Beckmann, P. J. Corish, and R. Lill. 1981. *The Church in the Age of Liberalism*. New York: Crossroad.

Banfield, Edward C. 1958. *The Moral Basis of a Backward Society*. Glencoe, Ill.: Free Press.

Baratta, Mario. 1950. "Italia—terremoti." In *Enciclopedia italiana di scienze, lettere ed arti* 19: 718–23. Roma: Enciclopedia italiana.

Barbagli, Marzio. 1984. *Sotto lo stesso tetto*. Bologna: Il Mulino.

Barbati, C., G. Mingozzi, and A. Rossi. 1978. *Profondo Sud*. Milano: Giangiacomo Feltrinelli.

Barbero, A., F. Ramella, and A. Torre. 1981. *Materiali sulla religiosità dei laici: Alba 1698—Asti 1742*. Cuneo: Regione Piemonte.

Battacchi, Marco Walter. 1972. *Meridionali e settentrionali nella struttura del pregiudizio etnico in Italia*. Bologna: Il Mulino.

Beffa, Bruno, Augusto Gaggioni, and Saverio Snider. 1980. "Pietà cristiana e umano dolore negli ex voto del Sasso." In *La Madonna del Sasso Fra Storia e Leggenda*, edited by G. Pozzi, 141–203. Locarno: Armando Dadò.

Bell, Rudolph M. 1985. *Holy Anorexia*. Chicago: University of Chicago Press.

References

Beringer, R. P. 1925. *Les Indulgences: leur nature et leur usage*, vol. 2. Paris: P. Lethielleux.

Bianco, Carla. 1974. *The Two Rosetos*. Bloomington: Indiana University Press.

Bigoni, Angelo. 1816. *Il forestiere istruito delle meraviglie e delle cose più belle che si ammirano internamente ed esternamente nella basilica del gran taumaturgo S. Antonio di Padova*. Padova: Nella stamperia del seminario.

Billet, Bernard. 1973. "Le fait des apparitions non reconnues par l'Église." In *Vraies et Fausses Apparitions dans l'Église*, 5–54. Paris: Editions P. Lethielleux.

Bisi, Franco. 1966. "Osservazioni sugli ex voto conservati in alcune chiese rustiche del modenese." In *La religiosità popolare nella valle padana*, edited by P. Toschi, 61–73. Firenze: Leo S. Olschki.

Black, Christopher. 1989. *Italian Confraternities in the Sixteenth Century*. Cambridge: Cambridge University Press.

Boccaccio, Giovanni. 1980 (1350?) *Decameron*, vol. 2. Roma: Editori Riuniti.

Boglioni, Pierre. 1984. "Pèlerinages et religion populaire au Moyen Âge." In *Wallfahrt kennt keine Grenzen*, edited by L. Kriss-Rettenbeck and G. Möhler, 66–75. München: Schnell and Steiner.

Borelli, Giorgio. 1981. *Chiese e monasteri nel territorio veronese*. Verona: Banco Popolare di Verona.

Borzomati, Pietro. 1973. "Per una storia della pietà nel Mezzogiorno d'Italia tra ottocento e novecento." In *La Società religiosa nell'età moderna*, 613–632. Atti del Convegno studi di Storia sociale e religiosa: Capaccio-Paestrum, 18–21 maggio 1972. Napoli: Guida.

Bottiglioni, Gino. 1922. *Leggende e tradizioni di Sardegna*. Genève: Leo S. Olschki.

Britten, James. 1898. "The Alleged Human Sacrifices in Italy." *Month* 92: 390–96.

Brögger, Jan. 1971. *Montevarese: A Study of Peasant Society and Culture in Southern Italy*. Bergen: Universitetsforlaget.

Bronzini, Giovanni. 1974. *Lineamenti di storia e analisi della cultura tradizionale*. 2d ed. Roma: Edizioni dell'Ateneo.

———. 1982. *Cultura contadina e idea meridionalistica*. Bari: Edizioni Dedalo.

———. 1985. "Cultura popolare ed ex voto." *Rivista di storia e letteratura religiosa* 21: 419–29.

Brown, Judith C. 1986. *Immodest Acts: The Life of a Lesbian Nun in Renaissance Italy*. New York: Oxford University Press.

Brown, Peter. 1981. *The Cult of the Saints: Its Rise and Function in Latin Christianity*. Chicago: University of Chicago Press.

Brubaker, Richard L. 1990. "The Untamed Goddesses of Village India." In *The Book of the Goddess: Past and Present*, edited by Carl Olson, 145–60. New York: Crossroad.

Burgalassi, Silvano. 1970. *Le cristianità nascoste*. Bologna: Edizioni Dehoniane.

———. 1976. "Santità e culto dei santi in un mondo secolarizzato." *Il santo* 16: 397–419.

Burke, Peter. 1979. "Le domande del vescovo e la religione del popolo." *Quaderni storici* 41: 540–54.

References

——. 1986. *The Italian Renaissance: Culture and Society in Italy*. Princeton: Princeton University Press.

Butler, E. C. 1913. "Anthony, Saint." In *The Catholic Encyclopedia* 1: 553–55. New York: Encyclopedia Press.

Bynum, Caroline Walker. 1987. *Holy Feast and Holy Fast*. Berkeley: University of California Press.

Cambiaso, Domenico. 1933. *Nostra Signora della Guardia e Il Suo Santuario in Val Polcevera*. Genova: Buona Stampa.

Cambiè, G. M. 1971. "Mestieri e vita populare nelle figurazioni delle tavolette votive." *Economia e storia* 18: 439–56.

Candura, Giuseppe. 1971. "Agrigento e Porto Empedocle." In *Santi, streghe e diavoli*, edited by L. M. Lombardi Satriani, 401–2. Firenze: Sansoni.

Cantarutti, Novella. 1966. "San Valentino in Friuli." In *La religiosità populare nella valle padana*, edited by Paolo Toschi, 125–40. Firenze: Leo S. Olschki.

Capaccio, Giulio Cesare. 1723. *Antiquitates et historiae Campaniae Felicis*. Lugduni Batavorum.

Caplan, Paula. 1985. *The Myth of Women's Masochism*. New York: Dutton.

Cardini, Franco. 1983. "Nostra Signora dell'Impruneta: l'immagine, il culto, la leggenda." In *Impruneta: una pieve, un paese*, 79–88. Atti del Convegno "Impruneta: una pieve, un paese. Cultura, parrocchia e società nella campagna toscana." Firenze: Libreria Salimbeni.

Carroll. Michael P. 1986. *The Cult of the Virgin Mary*. Princeton: Princeton University Press.

——. 1987. "*Moses and Monotheism* Revisited: Freud's Personal Myth?" *American Imago* 44: 15–35.

——. 1989. *Catholic Cults and Devotions*. Montreal: McGill-Queen's University Press.

Carty, Charles M. 1953. *Padre Pio: The Stigmatist*. St. Paul, Minn.: Radio Replies Press.

Caserta, Aldo, and Gastone Lambertini. 1972. *Storia e scienza di fronte al "Miracolo di S. Gennaro."* Napoli: M. D'Auria.

Casini, Alfonso. 1981. *"Nessuno osi trasferirmi da qui": storia di Montallegro*. Rapallo: Ipotesi.

Casotti, Giovambattista. 1714. *Memorie istoriche della Miracolosa Immagine di Maria Vergine dell'Impruneta*. Firenze.

Castiglione, Miriam. 1981. *I professionisti dei sogni: visioni e devozioni popolari nella cultura contadina meridionale*. Napoli: Liguori.

Castiglione, Miriam, and Luciana Stocchi. 1978. "Il tarantismo oggi: proposte per una verifica." In *Questione meridionale religione e classi subalterne*, edited by Francesco Saija, 159–84. Napoli: Guida.

Cavazza, Silvano. 1981. "Tra Teologia e pietà popolare: le false resurrezioni di Trava e la tradizione de miracoli nell'Europa de Seicento." In *Aspetti di Religiosità Popolare in Friuli*, edited by L. Ciceri et al., 79–122. Pordenone: Edizioni Concordia Sette.

References

Cazzoli, Guido, ed. 1968. *Ex voto alla Madonna della Libertà*. Bologna: Piccola Libreria dell'Antoniano.

Cestaro, Antonio. 1978. *Strutture ecclesiastiche e società nel Mezzogiorno*. Napoli: Editrice Ferraro.

Chapman, Charlotte G. 1971 (1935). *Milocca: A Sicilian Village*. Cambridge, Mass.: Schenkman.

Cheshire, N. 1975. *The Nature of Psychodynamic Interpretation*. London: John Wiley.

Chiappa, Franco. 1974. "La 'Plebs Pallazoli.' " In *Studi in onore di Luigi Fossati*, 45–70. Società per la storia della Chiesa a Brescia. Brescia: Fratelli Geroldi.

Chiovaro, F. 1967. "Relics." *New Catholic Encyclopedia* 12: 234–40. New York: McGraw-Hill.

Christian, William A., Jr. 1981. *Local Religion in Sixteenth-Century Spain*. Princeton: Princeton University Press.

———. 1984. "Religious Apparitions and the Cold War in Southern Europe." In *Religion, Power and Protest in Local Communities: The Northern Shore of the Mediterranean*, edited by E. R. Wolf, 239–66. Berlin: Mouton.

Cianfarani, Valerio. 1952. "La processione di S. Zopito a Loreto Aprutino." *Lares* 18: 88–99.

Ciarrocchi, Arnoldo, and Ermanno Mori. 1960. *Italian Votive Tablets*. Udine: Doretti.

CICRED (Comité International de Coordination des Recherches Nationales en Démographie). 1974. *La Population de l'Italie*. Roma: Viminalgrafica.

Cilento, Nicola. 1975. "Luoghi di culto, iconografia e forme della religiosità popolare nella società lucana fra Medioevo ed Età moderna." *Ricerche di storia sociale e religiosa* 4: 247–67.

Ciliberti, Giuseppe M. 1988. *Il Santo Sudario e la chiesa di S. Bartolomeo degli Armeni*. Genova: B. N. Marconi.

Cipolla, Carlo M. 1965. "Four Centuries of Italian Demographic Development." In *Population in History*, edited by D. Glass and D. Eversley, 570–87. London: Edward Arnold.

Cipriani, Roberto. 1976. "La religiosità popolare in Italia: due ricerche su magia e politica nel Mezzogiorno." In *Religione e politica: il caso italiano*, edited by A. Carbonaro et al., 61–78. Roma: Coines Edizioni.

———. 1979. "Sud e religiosità popolare." In *Sociologia della cultura popolare in Italia*, edited by R. Cipriani, 228–40. Napoli: Liguori.

———. 1990. "The Sociology of Religion in Italy." *Sociological Analysis* 51 (supplement): S43–S52.

Cipriani, Roberto, Giovanni Rinaldi, and Paola Sobrero. 1979. *Il Simbolo Conteso*. Roma: Editrice Ianua.

Clodd, Edward, 1895. "Presidential Address." *Folk-Lore* 6: 54–81.

Cocchiara, Giuseppe. 1971. "Caratteri generali." In *Santi, streghe e diavoli*, edited by L. M. Lombardi Satriani, 331–37. Firenze: Sansoni Editore.

Comandini, Romolo. 1966. "Impiego delle campane a fini sacri e profani in Val

References

Rubicone." In *La religiosità popolare nella valle padana*, edited by P. Toschi, 141–78. Firenze: Leo S. Olschki.

Cornelisen, Ann. 1976. *Women of the Shadows*. Boston: Little, Brown.

Corrain, Cleto, and Pierluigi Zampini. 1966. "Riti e credenze popolari nei sinodi diocesani dell'Alta Italia." In *La religiosità popolare nella valle padana*, edited by P. Toschi, 179–90. Firenze: Leo S. Olschki.

————. 1970. *Documenti etnografici e folkloristici nei sinodi diocesani italiani*. Bologna: Forni.

Crehan, Joseph. 1952. *Father Thurston: A Memoir with a Bibliography of His Writings*. London: Sheed and Ward.

Crimi-Lo Giudice, G. 1894. "La festa di S. Cono in Naso." *Archivio per le tradizioni popolari* 13: 379–86.

Cruz, Joan Carroll. 1984. *Relics*. Huntington, Ind.: Our Sunday Visitor.

Cucchiari, Salvatore. 1990. "Between Shame and Sanctification: Patriarchy and Its Transformation in Sicilian Pentecostalism." *American Ethnologist* 17: 687–707.

D'Andrea, Giampaolo. 1977. "La struttura sociale della parrocchia nelle diocesi lucane tra XVIII e XIX secolo." In *Società e religione in Basilicata nell'età moderna: II Comunicazioni*, 263–86. Atti del Convegno di Potenza-Matera, 25–28 settembre 1975. Salerno: D'Elia.

D'Annunzio, Gabriele. 1956 (1894). *Trionfo della morte*. Verona: Arnoldo Mondadori.

D'Antonio, Nino. 1979. *Gli ex voto dipinti e il rituale dei fujenti a Madonna dell'Arco*. Cava dei Tirreni: Di Mauro.

Davis, Natalie Zemon. 1974. "Some Tasks and Themes in the Study of Popular Religion." In *The Pursuit of Holiness in Late Medieval and Renaissance Religion*, edited by C. Trinkaus and H. A. Oberman, 307–36. Leiden: E. J. Brill.

De Antoni, Dino. 1980. "Segni della pietà, devozioni e fede del popolo chioggiotto nell'ottocento e nel primo novecento." In *Studi di storia sociale e religiosa*, edited by A. Cestaro, 829–91. Napoli: Editrice Ferraro.

De Biasio, Luigi. 1980. "Credenze ed atteggiamenti religiosi del mondo contadino friulano nel Seicento." In *Religiosità popolare in Friuli*, edited by Luigi Ciceri, 39–53. Udine: Edizioni Concordia.

De Blasio, A. 1903. "I disciplinanti in Guardia Sanframondi (Benevento)." *Archivio per lo studio delle tradizioni popolari* 22: 362–64.

De Leone, Andrea. 1783. *Giornale, e notizie de'tremuoti accaduti l'Anno 1783 nelle provincia di Catanzaro. Parte Seconda*. Napoli: Fratelli Raimondi.

del Grosso, Franco. 1983. "Origine del culto all Madonna d'Impruneta e suoi rapporti con la città di Firenze." In *Impruneta: una pieve, un paese*, 33–77. Atti del Convegno "Impruneta: una pieve, un paese. Cultura, parrocchia e società nella campagna toscana." Firenze: Libreria Salimbeni.

Delle Donne, Enrica Robertazzi. 1973. "Le chiese ricettizie nella legislazione borbonica." In *La società religiosa nell'età moderna*, 1027–48. Atti del Con-

References

vegno studi di Storia sociale e religiosa, Capaccio-Paestrum, 18–21 maggio 1972. Napoli: Guida.

Delooz, Pierre. 1969. *Sociologie et Canonisations*. La Haye: Martinus Nijhoff.

Del Panta, Lorenzo. 1980. *Le epidemie nella storia demografica italiana (secoli XIV–XIX)*. Torino: Loescher.

De Lutiis, Giuseppe. 1973. *L'industria del santino*. Rimini: Guaraldi.

De Maio, Romeo. 1973. *Riforme e miti nella Chiesa del Cinquecento*. Napoli: Guida.

De Marco, Gerardo. 1975. *Dalle Ceneri alla Settimana Santa*. Molfetta: Mezzina.

De Martino, Ernesto. 1968. *La Terra del Rimorso*. 2d ed. Milano: Alberto Mondadori.

De Nino, Antonio. 1897. "Holy Week Observance in the Abruzzi." *Folk-Lore* 8: 374.

————. 1898. "I pretesi sacrifici umani nella settimana santa in Italia." *Nuovo antologia* 33: 500–506.

De Pina-Cabral, Joào. 1989. "The Mediterranean as a Category of Regional Comparison: A Critical View." *Current Anthropology* 30: 399–406.

De Rosa, Gabriele. 1973a. "Organizzazione del territorio e vita religiosa nel Sud tra XVI e XIX secolo." In *La Società religiosa nell'età moderna*, 11–29. Atti del Convegno studi di Storia sociale e religiosa, Capaccio-Paestrum, 18–21 maggio 1972. Napoli: Guida.

————. 1973b. "Repliche dei Relatori." In *La Società religiosa nell'età moderna*, 126–29. Atti del Convegno studi di Storia sociale e religiosa, Capaccio-Paestrum, 18–21 maggio 1972. Napoli: Guida.

————. 1975. "Pertinenze ecclesiastiche e santità nella storia sociale e religiosa della Basilicata dal XVIII al XIV secolo." *Ricerche di storia sociale e religiosa* 4: 7–68.

————. 1976. "La pastoralità nella storia sociale e religiosa del Mezzogiorno." *Studium* 3: 329–45.

————. 1977a. "Dibattito sulle relazioni De Rosa, De Maio, Guarnieri, Aymard." In *Società e religione in Basilicata nell'età moderna: I Relazioni e dibattito*, 174–77. Atti del Convegno di Potenza-Matera, 25–28 settembre 1975. Salerno: D'Elia.

————. 1977b. "Dibattito sulle relazioni Cestaro e Placanica." In *Società e religione in Basilicata nell'età moderna: I Relazioni e dibattito*, 321–34. Atti del Convegno di Potenza-Matera, 25–28 settembre 1975. Salerno: D'Elia.

————. 1979. *Chiesa e religione popolare nel Mezzogiorno*. Roma: Laterza.

De Simone, Roberto. 1974. *Chi è devoto: feste popolari in Campania*. Napoli: Edizioni Scientifiche Italiane.

Di Nola, Alfonso M. 1976. *Gli aspetti magico-religiosi di una cultura subalterna italiana*. Torino: Boringhieri.

Donvito, Luigi, and Bruno Pellegrino. 1973. *L'organizzazione ecclesiastica degli Abruzzi e Molise e della Basilicata nell'età postridentina*. Firenze: Sansoni.

El Saadawi, Nawal. 1980. *The Hidden Face of Eve*. London: Zed.

Ferrari, Daniela, and Gioia Lanzi. 1985. "Pellegrinaggio bolognese." *Il santo* 25: 135–72.

Frazer, James G. 1922 (1890). *The Golden Bough*. London: Macmillan.

References

Freud, Sigmund, 1953–74. *The Standard Edition of the Complete Psychological Works of Sigmund Freud*. Edited and translated by James Strachey. 24 vols. London: Hogarth Press. The following works are found in these volumes.
———. 1910. "Leonardo da Vinci." *S. E.* 11: 57–137.
———. 1913. "Totem and Taboo." *S. E.* 15: 1–161.
———. 1924. "The Economic Problem of Masochism." *S. E.* 19: 157–72.
———. 1927. "The Future of an Illusion." *S. E.* 21: 1–56.
———. 1930. "Civilization and Its Discontents." *S. E.* 21: 57–145.
———. 1933. "Femininity." *S. E.* 22: 112–35.
———. 1939. "Moses and Monotheism." *S. E.* 23: 1–137.
Furlong, Paul F. 1988. "Authority, Change and Conflict in Italian Catholicism." In *World Catholicism in Transition*, edited by Thomas M. Gannon, 116–32. New York: Macmillan.
Galasso, Giuseppe. 1982. *L'altra Europa*. Milano: Arnoldo Mondadori.
Gambasin, Angelo. 1973. *Parroci e contadini nel Veneto all fine dell'ottocento*. Roma: Edizioni di storia e letteratura.
———. 1980. "Il giuspatronato del popolo a Pellestrina tra il 600 e il 700." In *Studi di storia sociale e religiosa*, edited by A. Cestaro, 985–1056. Napoli: Editrice Ferraro.
Geary, Patrick J. 1978. *Furta Sacra: Thefts of Relics in the Central Middle Ages*. Princeton: Princeton University Press.
———. 1983. "Humiliation of Saints." In *Saints and Their Cults*, edited by Stephen Wilson, 123–40. Cambridge: Cambridge University Press.
———. 1984. "The Saint and the Shrine." In *Wallfahrt kennt keine Grenzen*, edited by L. Kriss-Rettenbeck and G. Möhler, 264–73. München: Schnell and Steiner.
Gilmore, David D. 1987. "Introduction: The Shame of Dishonor." In *Honor and Shame and the Unity of the Mediterranean*, edited by D. Gilmore, 2–21. Washington, D.C.: American Anthropological Association.
———. 1990. "Men and Women in Southern Spain: 'Domestic Power' Revisited." *American Anthropologist* 92: 953–70.
Gilmore, M. M., and David Gilmore. 1979. "Machismo: A Psychodynamic Approach (Spain)." *Journal of Psychological Anthropology* 2: 281–300.
Ginzburg, Carlo. 1976. *Il formaggio e i vermi*. Torino: Giulio Einaudi Editore. Published in English as *The Cheese and the Worms*, translated by John and Anne Tedeschi. Baltimore: Johns Hopkins University Press, 1980.
Gios, Pierantonio. 1976. "Altari e santi nelle visite pastorali padovane all fine del XV secolo e agli inizi del XVI." *Ricerche di storia sociale e religiosa* 5: 297–315.
Giovannini, Maureen J. 1981. "Women: A Dominant Symbol within the Cultural System of a Sicilian Town." *Man* 16: 408–26.
———. 1987. "Female Chastity Codes in the Circum-Mediterranean." In *Honor and Shame and the Unity of the Mediterranean*, edited by David Gilmore, 61–74. Washington, D.C.: American Anthropological Association.
Gower, Charlotte Day. 1928. *The Supernatural Patron in Sicilian Life*. Ph.D. diss., University of Chicago.
Grant, Ian. 1929. *Testimony of Blood*. London: Burns, Oates, and Washbourne.

References

Greco, Gaetano. 1986. "I giuspatronati laicali nell'età moderna." In *Storia d'Italia, Annali 9: La Chiesa e il potere politico dal Medioevo all'età contemporanea*, edited by G. Chittolino and G. Miccoli, 531–72. Torino: Giulio Einaudi.

Grendi, Edoardo. 1976. "Le confraternite come fenomeno associativo e religioso." In *Società Chiesa e vita religiosa nell'Ancien Régime*, edited by C. Russo, 113–85. Napoli: Guida.

Grigioni, Elisabetta G. 1975. "L'empio giocatore nelle leggende dell'*Atlante mariano.*" *Il santo* 15: 345–51.

———. 1976. "Ex-voto e simbologia del cuore." *Il santo* 16: 291–300.

———. 1983. "Significato cultura tipologia dell'ex voto a forma di cuore." *Il santo* 23: 555–74.

Gross, Feliks. 1973. *Il Paese: Values and Change in an Italian Village*. New York: New York University Press.

Grosskurth, Phyllis. 1986. *Melanie Klein: Her World and Her Work*. Toronto: McClelland and Stewart.

Hay, Denys. 1971. "The Italian View of Renaissance Italy." In *Renaissance Essays*, edited by D. Hay, 375–88. London: Hambledon.

———. 1977. *The Church in Italy in the Fifteenth Century*. Cambridge: Cambridge University Press.

Hecker, G. 1838. *La danzimania*. Firenze: Ricordi e Compagno.

Henderson, John. 1978. "The Flagellant Movement and Flagellant Confraternities in Central Italy, 1260–1400." In *Religious Motivation: Biographical and Sociological Problems for the Church Historian*, edited by D. Baker, 147–60. Oxford: Basil Blackwell.

Hilgers, Joseph. 1913. "Censorship of Books." In *The Catholic Encyclopedia* 3: 519. New York: Encyclopedia Press.

Holmes, J. Derek. 1978. *The Triumph of the Holy See*. London: Burns and Oates.

Iaccarino, E. 1973. *Sismicità dell'Italia nei secoli scorsi*. Roma: Comitato Nazionale per l'Energia Nucleare.

Kaftal, George. 1952. *Iconography of the Saints in Tuscan Painting*. Florence: Sansoni.

———. 1965. *Iconography of the Saints in Central and South Italian Schools of Painting*. Florence: Sansoni.

———. 1978. *Iconography of the Saints in the Painting of North East Italy*. Florence: Sansoni.

———. 1985. *Iconography of the Saints in the Painting of North West Italy*. Florence: Casse Editrice Le Lettere.

Kehoe, Lawrence. 1871. *The Liquefaction of the Blood of St. Januarius at Naples: An Historical and Critical Examination of the Miracle*. New York: Catholic Publication Society.

Kirsch, J. P. 1913. "Philomena, Saint." In *The Catholic Encyclopedia* 12: 25. New York: Encyclopedia Press.

Klein, Melanie. 1975. *Love, Guilt and Reparation and Other Works, 1921–1945*. Introduction by R. E. Money-Kyrle. New York: Delta.

References

————. 1980. *Envy and Gratitude and Other Works, 1946–1963*. London: Hogarth.

La Salvia, Sergio. 1984. "L'invenzione di un culto: Santa Filomena da taumaturga a guerriera della fede." In *Culto dei santi, istituzioni e classi sociali in età preindustriale*, edited by S. B. Gajano and L. Sebastiani, 871–956. Roma: L. U. Japadre.

La Sorsa, Saverio. 1962. "Religiosità popolare pugliese." *Lares* 28: 134–42.

Leach, Edmund. 1976. *Culture and Communication*. Cambridge: Cambridge University Press.

Leclercq, H. 1913. "The Legend of Abgar." In *The Catholic Encyclopedia* 1: 42–43. New York: Encyclopedia Press.

Levi, Carlo. 1963 (1947). *Christ Stopped at Eboli*. New York: Farrar, Straus.

Levi, Giovanni. 1988. *Inheriting Power: The Story of an Exorcist*, translated by Lydia G. Cochrane. Chicago: University of Chicago Press.

Lewis, Oscar. 1959. *Five Families: Mexican Case Studies in the Culture of Poverty*. New York: Basic Books.

Lima, Antonietta I. 1984. *La dimensione sacrale del paesaggio*. Palermo: S. F. Flaccovio.

Lombardi Satriani, Luigi M. 1971 . "Il tesoro sepolto." In *Santi, streghe e diavoli*, edited by L. M. Lombardi Satriani, 9–92. Firenze: Sansoni.

————. 1978. "Attuale problematica della religione popolare." In *Questione meridionale religione e classi subalterne*, edited by Francesco Saija, 8–33. Napoli: Guida.

Lumbroso, Giacomo. 1886. "Usi, costumi, e dialetti sardi." *Archivio per le tradizioni popolari* 5: 17–31.

Maccarrone, Michele. 1987. "La nascita della 'Rivista di storia della Chiesa in Italia.' " *Rivista di storia della Chiesa in Italia* 41: 345–60.

MacCulloch, J. A. 1922. "Relics (Primitive and Western)." *Encyclopedia of Religion and Ethics* 10: 650–58.

McGrath, William G. 1961. "The Lady of the Rosary." In *A Woman Clothed with the Sun*, edited by J. Delaney, 175–212. Garden City, N.Y.: Doubleday.

Malina, Bruce J. 1990. "Mother and Son." *Biblical Theology Bulletin* 20: 54–64.

Malinowski, Bronislaw. 1935. *Coral Gardens and Their Magic*. 2 vols. London: Allen and Unwin.

————. 1954. *Magic, Science and Religion and Other Essays*. Garden City, N.Y.: Doubleday.

Manganelli, Franco. 1973. *La festa infelice*. Napoli: Instituto Anselmi.

Maraspini, A. L. 1968. *The Study of an Italian Village*. Paris: Mouton.

Marcucci, Domenico. 1983. *Santuari mariani d'Italia*. Roma: Edizioni Paoline.

Martin, Gregory. 1969 (1581). *Roma Sancta*, edited by George Bruner Parks. Roma: Edizioni di Storia e Letteratura.

Mazzacane, Lello, and Luigi M. Lombardi Satriani. 1974. *Perché le feste*. Roma: G. Savelli.

Medica, Giacomo M. 1965. *I santuari mariani d'Italia*. Torino: Leumann.

Melloni, Pier L. 1972. "Topografia, diffusione e aspetti delle confraternite dei

References

disciplinati." In Centro di Documentazione sul Movimento dei Disciplinati, *Resultati e prospettive della ricerca sul movimento dei disciplinati*, 15–98. Perugia: Arti Grafiche Città di Castello.

Minchinton, Walter. 1974. "Patterns and Structure of Demand: 1500–1700." In *The Fontana History of Europe: The Sixteenth and Seventeenth Centuries*, edited by C. M. Cipolla, Glasgow: Collins/Fontana.

Missano, Antonella Ferri. 1990. "Il Tesora di San Gennaro in mostra: considerazioni in margine." *Arte Cristiana* 78: 69–74.

Misson, François. 1739. *A New Voyage to Italy*. 2 vols. 5th ed.

Mols, Roger. 1974. "Population in Europe: 1500–1700." In *The Fontana History of Europe: The Sixteenth and Seventeenth Centuries*, edited by C. M. Cipolla, 15–78. Glasgow: Collins/Fontana.

Mondello, C. P. F. 1882. *Spettacoli e feste popolari in Trapani*. Trapani: Stamperia Economica Trapanese.

Montanari, Daniele. 1987. *Disciplinamento in terra veneta: La diocesi di Brescia nella seconda metà del XVI secolo*. Bologna: Il Mulino.

Morghen, Raffaello. 1972. "Discussione." In Centro di Documentazione sul Movimento dei Disciplinati, *Resultati e prospettive della ricerca sul movimento dei disciplinati*, 198, 289. Perugia: Arti Grafiche Città di Castello.

Mullett, Michael. 1984. *The Counter-Reformation*. London: Methuen.

Musella. Silvano. 1980. "Dimensione sociale e prassi associativa di una confraternita napoletana nell'età della controriforma." In *Per la storia sociale e religiosa del Mezzogiorno d'Italia, vol. I*, edited by G. Galasso and C. Russo, 339–438. Napoli: Guida.

Naselli, Carmelina. 1962. "Notizie sui Disciplinati in Sicilia." In *Il Movimento dei Disciplinati nel settimo centenario dal suo inizio*, 317–27. Convegno internazionale, Perugia, 25–28 Settembre 1960. Spoleto: Arti Grafiche Panetto and Petrelli.

Nessi, Silvestro. 1988. "Il culto antoniano a Montefalco in Umbria: aspetti iconografici." *Il santo* 28: 207–28.

Nolan, Mary Lee, and Sidney Nolan. 1989. *Christian Pilgrimage in Modern Western Europe*. Chapel Hill: University of North Carolina Press.

O'Neil, Mary Rose. 1981. "Discerning Superstition: Popular Errors and Orthodox Response in Late Sixteenth Century Italy." Ph.D. diss., Stanford University.

———. 1984. "Sacerdote ovvero strione: Ecclesiastical and Superstitious Remedies in Sixteenth-Century Italy." In *Understanding Popular Culture*, edited by Steven L. Kaplan, 53–83. Berlin: Mouton.

Orsi, Robert. 1985. *The Madonna of 115th Street*. New Haven: Yale University Press.

Pace, E. A. 1913. "Dulia." In *Catholic Encyclopedia* 5: 188. New York: Encyclopedia Press.

Parsons, Anne. 1969. *Belief, Magic and Anomie: Essays in Psychological Anthropology*. New York: Free Press.

Pastrovicchi, Angelo. 1918 (1773). *St. Joseph of Copertino*. Rockford, Ill.: TAN Books.

References

Paul, Robert A. 1989. "Psychoanalytic Anthropology." *Annual Review of Anthropology* 18: 177–202.

Peacock, Mabel. 1896. "Executed Criminals and Folk-Medicine." *Folk-Lore* 7: 268–83.

Pellegrini, Camillo. 1771. *Apparato alle antichità di Capua o vero discorsi della Campania Felice*. Napoli: Giovanni Gravier.

Penco, Gregorio. 1977. *Storia della Chiesa in Italia*, vol. 1. Milano: Cooperativa Edizioni Jaca Book.

Pesce, Luigi. 1987. *La Chiesa di Treviso nel primo Quattrocentro*, vol. 1. Roma: Herder.

Petito, Luigi. 1983. *San Gennaro: storia, folclore, culto*. Napoli: LER.

Pitrè, Giuseppe. 1883. "Il voto: uso popolare abruzzese." *Archivio per le tradizioni popolari* 2: 310.

——. 1896. *Tre feste popolari di Sicilia*. Palermo: Giornale di Sicilia.

——. 1899. *Feste patronali in Sicilia*. Torino-Palermo: C. Clausen.

——. 1978 (1870–1913). *Usi e costumi, credenze e pregiudizi del popolo siciliano*, vols. 2 and 4. Palermo: Edizioni "Il Vespro."

Pitrè, Maria. 1900. *Le feste di Santa Rosalia in Palermo e della Assunta in Messina descritte dai viaggiatori italiani e stranieri*. Palermo: Alberto Reber.

Porri, Alessio. 1601. *Antidotario contro li demonij*. Venetia: appresso R. Megietti.

Posen, I. Sheldon, and Joseph Sciorra. 1983. "Brooklyn's Dancing Tower." *Natural History* 92: 30–37.

Prosperi, Adriano. 1984. "Madonne di città e Madonne di campagna." In *Culto dei santi, istituzioni e classi sociali in età preindustriale*, edited by S. B. Gajano and L. Sebastiani, 615–47. Roma: L. U. Japadre.

Provenzal, Dino. 1912. *Usanze e feste del popolo italiano*. Bologna: Nicola Zanichelli.

Provitera, Gino. 1978. "L'edicola votiva e le sue funzioni." In *Questione meridionale, religione, e classi subalterne*, edited by F. Saija, 337–45. Napoli: Guida.

Pulci, F. 1894. "La festa di S. Rocco." *Archivio per le tradizioni popolari* 13: 60–61.

Pullan, Brian. 1971. *Rich and Poor in Renaissance Venice*. Oxford: Basil Blackwell.

Quinza, Francesco. 1722. *Diario sanese*. Siena: F. Quinza.

Ramella, F., and A. Torre. 1981. "Le associazioni devozionali." In *Materiali sulla religiosità dei laici: Alba 1698–Asti 1742*, edited by G. Romano, 41–138. Cuneo: L'Arciere.

Redondi, Pietro. 1983. *Galileo eretico*. Torino: Giulio Einaudi. Published in English as *Galileo Heretic*, translated by Raymond Rosenthal. Princeton: Princeton University Press.

Repetti, Emanuele. 1843. *Dizionario geografico, fisico, storico della Toscana*, vol. 5. Firenze: E. Repetti.

Robertazzi, Enrica. 1977. "Attività religiosa ed economica del clero ricettizio nel settecento napoletano." In *Società e religione in Basilicata nell'età moderna: II Communicazioni*, 653–79. Atti del Convegno di Potenza-Matera, 25–28 settembre 1975. Salerno: D'Elia.

Rondinelli, Francesco. 1634. *Relazione del contagio stato in Firenze L'Anno 1630*

References

e 1633 con un breve ragguaglio della Miracolosa Immagine della Madonna dell'Impruneta. Fioréza: Gio: Batista Landini.

Rosa, Mario. 1976. *Religione e società nel Mezzogiorno tra cinque e seicento*. Bari: De Donato.

Rossi, Annabella. 1969. *Le feste dei poveri*. Bari: Editori Laterza.

Rossi, Filippo de. 1689. *Ritratto di Roma moderna*. Roma: M. A. Rossi.

Rumor, Sebastiano. 1911. *Storia documentata del santuario di Monte Berico*. Vicenza: Officina Grafica Pontificia.

Russo, Carla. 1984. *Chiesa e comunità nella diocesi di Napoli tra cinque e settecento*. Napoli: Guida.

Salomone-Marino, Salvatore. 1981 (1897). *Customs and Habits of the Sicilian Peasants*, edited and translated by R. N. Norris. London: Associated University Presses.

Sandys, George. 1615. *A Relation of a Journey begun An: Dom: 1610*. London: W. Barrett.

Saracini, Giuliano. 1675. *Notitie historiche della città d'Ancona*. Roma: N. A. Tinassi.

Sarnelli, Pompeo. 1692. *Guida di forestieri curiosi di vedere, e d'intendere le cose più notabili della Regal Città di Napoli*, edited by Antonio Bulifon. Napoli: Antonio Bulifon.

Saunders, George R. 1981. "Men and Women in Southern Europe: A Review of Some Aspects of Cultural Complexity." *Journal of Psychoanalytic Anthropology* 4: 435–66.

Scherer, Heinrich. 1703. *Geographica Hierarchica*. Monachii: Typis Marie Magdalenae Rauchin.

Schneider, Jane. 1971. "Of Vigilance and Virgins: Honor: Shame and Access to Resources in Mediterranean Societies." *Ethnology* 10: 1–24.

Schotti, Francesco. 1700. *Il nuovo itinerario d'Italia*. Roma: Michel'Angelo e Pier Vincenzo Rossi.

Segal, Hanna. 1974. *An Introduction to the Work of Melanie Klein*. London: Hogarth.

Sereni, Emilio. 1968 (1947). *Il capitalismo nelle campagne (1860–1900)*. Torino: Giulio Einaudi.

Signorotto, Gianvittorio. 1985. "Cercatori di reliquie." *Rivista di storia e letteratura religiosa* 21: 283–418.

Silone, Ignazio. 1937. *Pane e vino*. Lugano: Nuove Edizioni di Capolago. Translated into English as *Bread and Wine*. New York: Harper Brothers, 1937.

Silverman, Sydel. 1975. *Three Bells of Civilization*. New York: Columbia University Press.

Simoncelli, Paolo. 1979. Review of *La Chiesa nell'Italia rinascimentale*. *Critica storica* 16: 650–53.

Singleton, Charles S. 1975. *Paradiso: Commentary*. Princeton: Princeton University Press.

Smythe, William H. 1824. *Memoir Descriptive of the Resources, Inhabitants, and Hydrography of Sicily and Its Islands*. London: John Murray.

Stella, Piero. 1967. "L'Eucaristia nella spiritualità italiana da metà Seicento ai

References

prodromi del movimento liturgico." *Rivista liturgica* 7: 141–82.

―――. 1976. "Devozioni e religiosità popolare in Italia (sec. XVI–XX)." *Rivista liturgica* 63: 155–73.

Strazzullo, Franco. 1959. *Saggi storici sul Duomo di Napoli*. Napoli: Istituto Editoriale del Mezzogiorno.

―――. 1963. "Miracoli e miracolati nella Napoli del '600." *Rivista di etnografia* 17: 114–26.

Strong, John S. 1987. "Relics." In *The Encyclopedia of Religion* 12: 275–82. New York: Macmillan.

SVIMEZ (Associazione per lo sviluppo dell'industria nel Mezzogiorno). 1961. *Un secolo di statistiche italiane nord e sud*. Roma: SVIMEZ.

Swinburne, Henry. 1790. *Travels in the Two Sicilies*, vol. 2. London: J. Nichols.

Tambiah, Stanley J. 1990. *Magic, Science, Religion, and the Scope of Rationality*. Cambridge: Cambridge University Press.

Tassoni, Giovanni. 1966. "Forme di culto popolare nel Mantovano-Sant'Antonio abate." In *La religiosità popolare nella valle padana*, edited by P. Toschi, 367–81. Firenze: Leo S. Olschki.

Taves, Ann. 1986. *The Household of Faith*. Notre Dame: University of Notre Dame Press.

Tempèra, Antonio. 1977. *Il linguaggio della pietà mariana negli ex-voto*. Roma: Pontificia Facoltà Teologica "Marianum."

Tentori, Tulio. 1982. "An Italian Religious Feast: The *fujenti* Rites of the Madonna dell'Arco, Naples." In *Mother Worship*, edited by J. J. Preston, 95–122. Chapel Hill: University of North Carolina Press.

Thomas, Keith. 1973. *Religion and the Decline of Magic*. Harmondsworth: Penguin.

Thurston, Herbert. 1909. "The Miracle of St. Januarius." *The Tablet*, 22 May, 803–5.

―――. 1913a. "Holy Nails." In *Catholic Encyclopedia* 10: 672. New York: Encyclopedia Press.

―――. 1913b. "Relics." In *Catholic Encyclopedia* 12: 734–38. New York: Encyclopedia Press.

―――. 1913c. "Santa Casa di Loreto." In *Catholic Encyclopedia* 13: 454–56. New York: Encyclopedia Press.

―――. 1913d. "The Holy Shroud." In *Catholic Encyclopedia* 13: 762–63. New York: Encyclopedia Press.

―――. 1927a. "The Blood Miracles of Naples I." *Month* 149: 44–55.

―――. 1927b. "The Blood Miracles of Naples II." *Month* 149: 123–35.

―――. 1930. "The 'Miracle' of St. Januarius." *Month* 155: 119–29.

Tittarelli, Luigi. 1979. "Alcune caratteristiche strutturali della popolazione perugina nel 1782—le famiglie." *Genus* 35: 155–95.

Tomasi, Silvano M., and Edward C. Stibili. 1978. *Italian-Americans and Religion: An Annotated Bibliography*. New York: Center for Migration Studies.

Toscani, Xenio. 1969. *Aspetti di vita religiosa a Pavia nel secolo XV*. Milano: Dott. A. Giuffrè.

Tramontin, Silvio. 1977. "Dibattito sulle relazioni De Rosa, De Maio, Guarnieri,

References

Aymard." In *Società e religione in Basilicata nell'età moderna: I Relazioni e dibattito*, 151–53. Atti del Convegno di Potenza-Matera, 25–28 settembre 1975. Salerno: D'Elia.

Trexler, Richard C. 1980. *Public Life in Renaissance Florence*. New York: Academic Press.

———. 1987. "Ritual Behavior in Renaissance Florence." In *Church and Community: 1200–1600*, edited by R. C. Trexler, 11–36. Roma: Edizioni di Storia e Letteratura.

Triputti, Anna Maria. 1978. "Le tavolette votive del santuario della Madonna del Pozzo a Capurso." *Lares* 44: 183–214.

Turchini, Angelo. 1977. "Per la storia religiosa del '400 italiano: visite pastorali e questionari di visita nell'Italia centro-settentrionale." *Rivista di storia e letteratura religiosa* 13: 265–90.

———. 1980. "Lo straordinario e il quotidiano negli ex voto bresciani." In *Lo straordinario e il quotidiano*, edited by A. Turchini, 9–106. Brescia: Grafo.

Turner, Victor, and Edith Turner. 1982. "Postindustrial Marian Pilgrimage." In *Mother Worship*, edited by James Preston, 145–73. Chapel Hill: University of North Carolina Press.

UNEP (United Nations Environment Programme). 1987. *Environmental Data Report*. Oxford: Basil Blackwell.

Vecchi, Alberto. 1968. *Il culto della immagini nelle stampe popolari*. Firenze: Leo S. Olschki.

Venturi, Silvio. 1901. "La settimana santa in Calabria." *Archivio per lo studio della tradizioni popolari* 20: 358–64.

Villari, L. 1902. *Italian Life in Town and Country*. London: George Newnes.

Vitolo, Giovanni. 1982. "Dalla pieve rurale alla chiesa ricettizia." *Storia del Valle di Diano* 2: 127–58.

———. 1984. "Pievi, parrocchie e chiese ricettizie in Campania." In *Pievi e parrocchie in Italia nel basso Medioevo*, 1095–107. Atti del vi Convegno di Storia della Chiesa in Italia. Roma: Herder Editrice e Libreria.

Waterworth, J. 1848. *The Canons and Decrees of the Council of Trent*. London: C. Dolman.

Weber, Max. 1930. *The Protestant Ethic and the Spirit of Capitalism*. New York: Scribner's.

Weinstein, Donald, and Rudolph Bell. 1982. *Saints and Society*. Chicago: University of Chicago Press.

Weissman, Ronald. 1982. *Ritual Brotherhood in Renaissance Florence*. New York: Academic Press.

Williams, Phyllis H. 1938. *South Italian Folkways in Europe and America*. New York: Russell and Russell.

Willis, Roy. 1985. "Magic." In *The Social Science Encyclopedia*, edited by A. Kuper and J. Kuper, 478–79. London: Routledge and Kegan Paul.

Yorburg, Betty. 1983. *Families and Societies*. New York: Columbia University Press.

Young-Bruehl, Elisabeth, ed. 1990. *Freud on Women: A Reader*. New York: Norton.

References

Zambarbieri, Annibale. 1983. *Terra uomini religione nella pianura lombarda*. Roma: Istituto per le ricerche di storia sociale e di storia religiosa.

Zannini, Antonio M. 1974. "La visita pastorale di mons. Annibale Grisonio alle parrocchie della pianura occidentale bresciana." In *Studi in onore di Luigi Fossati*. Società per la storia della Chiesa a Brescia, 123–38. Brescia: Fratelli Geroldi.

Ziegler, Philip. 1969. *The Black Death*. London: Penguin.

INDEX

Index

Index

Index

Index

Index

Index

Index